JEREMIAH AND LAMENTATIONS

VICTORIOUS SERVICE IN BARREN TIMES

Light to My Path Series
Old Testament

Ezra, Nehemiah, and Esther

Job

Isaiah

Jeremiah and Lamentations

Ezekiel

Amos, Obadiah, and Jonah

Micah, Nahum, Habakkuk, and Zephaniah

Haggai, Zechariah, and Malachi

New Testament

John

Acts

Romans

1 Corinthians

2 Corinthians

Philippians and Colossians

James and 1 & 2 Peter

The Epistles of John and Jude

Jeremiah and Lamentations

Victorious Service in Barren Times

F. Wayne Mac Leod

Authentic

Authentic
We welcome your comments and questions.
129 Mobilization Drive, Waynesboro, GA 30830 USA authentic@stl.org
and 9 Holdom Avenue, Bletchley, Milton Keynes, Bucks, MK1 1QR, UK
www.authenticbooks.com
If you would like a copy of our current catalog, contact us at:
1-8MORE-BOOKS
ordersusa@stl.org

Jeremiah and Lamentations
ISBN: 1-932805-46-X

09 08 07 06 / 6 5 4 3 2 1

Published in 2006 by Authentic

Cover design: Paul Lewis
Interior design: Angela Duerksen
Editorial team: Bette Smyth, Carol Johnson, K.J. Larson

Printed in the United States of America

Contents

Preface   ix

Jeremiah

1. Jeremiah's Call   1
   Read Jeremiah 1
2. Why Go to Egypt?   6
   Read Jeremiah 2:1–19
3. The Broken Yoke   11
   Read Jeremiah 2:20–37
4. Return, Faithless People   16
   Read Jeremiah 3
5. A Ruined Land   22
   Read Jeremiah 4
6. Backsliding Israel   28
   Read Jeremiah 5
7. Disaster from the North   34
   Read Jeremiah 6
8. Temple Sermon   40
   Read Jeremiah 7
9. Why Is There No Healing?   45
   Read Jeremiah 8
10. Tears for God's People   51
    Read Jeremiah 9
11. God and the Idols   55
    Read Jeremiah 10:1–16
12. Distress in the Land   60
    Read Jeremiah 10:17–25
13. The Broken Covenant   64
    Read Jeremiah 11
14. Why?   69
    Read Jeremiah 12

15. Jeremiah's Linen Belt   75
    Read Jeremiah 13:1–11
16. Pictures of Judgment   79
    Read Jeremiah 13:12–27
17. Drought in the Land   83
    Read Jeremiah 14
18. Difficult Words   88
    Read Jeremiah 15
19. The Life of the Prophet   94
    Read Jeremiah 16
20. The Evil Heart   99
    Read Jeremiah 17:1–13
21. Broken Sabbath   104
    Read Jeremiah 17:14–27
22. At the Potter's House   108
    Read Jeremiah 18
23. The Valley of Ben Hinnon   113
    Read Jeremiah 19
24. Jeremiah in Stocks   117
    Read Jeremiah 20
25. Zedekiah's Inquiry   123
    Read Jeremiah 21
26. A Word to the King   127
    Read Jeremiah 22
27. Careless Shepherds and Lying Prophets   132
    Read Jeremiah 23
28. A Basket of Figs   138
    Read Jeremiah 24
29. The Cup of the Lord's Wrath   141
    Read Jeremiah 25
30. Jeremiah's Life Is Threatened   145
    Read Jeremiah 26
31. Nebuchadnezzar's Time   150
    Read Jeremiah 27
32. Hananiah the Prophet   155
    Read Jeremiah 28

33. Jeremiah's Letter   159
   Read Jeremiah 29:1–14
34. A Word to the Exiled Prophets   163
   Read Jeremiah 29:15–32
35. Israel and Judah Restored   167
   Read Jeremiah 30
36. Renewed Promises for Israel   172
   Read Jeremiah 31:1–17
37. A Renewed Covenant   177
   Read Jeremiah 31:18–40
38. Jeremiah Buys a Property   183
   Read Jeremiah 32
39. God's Promise of Restoration   188
   Read Jeremiah 33
40. Zedekiah and the Slaves   193
   Read Jeremiah 34
41. The Recabites   197
   Read Jeremiah 35
42. Jeremiah's Scroll   200
   Read Jeremiah 36
43. Jeremiah and Zedekiah   205
   Read Jeremiah 37
44. Cast into a Cistern   210
   Read Jeremiah 38
45. Jerusalem Conquered   215
   Read Jeremiah 39
46. Governor Gedaliah   219
   Read Jeremiah 40:1–41:3
47. Fear in the Camp   222
   Read Jeremiah 41:4–42:22
48. In the Land of Egypt   227
   Read Jeremiah 43–44
49. A Brief Word to Baruch   232
   Read Jeremiah 45
50. A Word to Egypt   236
   Read Jeremiah 46

51. A Word to the Philistines   241
    Read Jeremiah 47
52. A Word to Moab   244
    Read Jeremiah 48
53. A Word to Ammon and Edom   251
    Read Jeremiah 49:1–22
54. A Word to Damascus, Kedar, Hazor, and Elam   256
    Read Jeremiah 49:23–39
55. A First Word to Babylon   260
    Read Jeremiah 50:1–16
56. God's Vigorous Defense of His People   264
    Read Jeremiah 50:17–46
57. Babylon's Incurable Wound   269
    Read Jeremiah 51:1–12
58. The Prosperity of the Wicked   273
    Jeremiah 51:13–40
59. Remember Jerusalem   278
    Read Jeremiah 51:41–64
60. The Conquest of Jerusalem   282
    Read Jeremiah 52

Lamentations

61. Self-Made Yokes   289
    Read Lamentations 1
62. The Lives of the Children   294
    Read Lamentations 2
63. It Is Good to Wait Quietly   299
    Read Lamentations 3:1–27
64. The Justice of God   303
    Read Lamentations 3:28–66
65. Your Punishment Will End   308
    Read Lamentations 4
66. Remember Us   313
    Read Lamentations 5

Preface

In this book you will meet the prophet Jeremiah. He is sometimes called the "weeping prophet." This is not without reason. Jeremiah had a tremendous burden to bear. Chosen as a young man, Jeremiah felt unworthy of the task to which God had called him. He had to discover that his ability was not in himself but in obedience to his enabling Lord.

Jeremiah's ministry was not an easy one. God required him to live a lifestyle that reflected the ministry to which he had been called. He was not to marry and have children. He was not to attend the joyous festivals of the nation. There were times when this was a tremendous burden for the prophet, but God would not release him from his calling. His ministry brought him into conflict with religious and prophetic figures of his day. The people of his own hometown wanted to kill him. His message was not appreciated, yet for forty years he faithfully proclaimed the word of the Lord.

Jeremiah's ministry was an international one. He spoke to kings and political rulers of many nations, challenging them with the word of the Lord. He was thrown into prison, left to die in a cistern, put in stocks, and insulted and mocked by those who were closest to him; but he did not give up. That is not to say that he did not feel like giving up. There were times when Jeremiah was brutally honest with God. In those times he questioned why God's call on his life was so difficult.

I am struck with the devotion of Jeremiah. The hand of the Lord was on his life even before he was born. God preserved, strengthened, and protected him until he had completed his divine task. Jeremiah was a man powerfully used of God, but he saw very little fruit in his ministry. What he did see, however, was the wonderful presence of God with him every step of the way.

Through the ministry of Light To My Path Book Distribution, this book will work its way into the hands of pastors in Africa, Asia, and Latin America. It will also work its way into the hands of Christian works and ordinary believers in North America and Europe. My prayer is that the Spirit of God would be pleased to use it to encourage and bless you in your personal walk and ministry for the Lord.

This commentary is not to be read in a single sitting. Please read the Bible passage listed at the beginning of each chapter. This commentary is merely a tool. It is not intended to replace the Bible, and it will not have any particular value without the ministry of the Holy Spirit applying the truth it contains to individual lives.

I encourage you to use it in your personal devotions. I will consider this project a success if it draws you as a reader just a little closer to the Lord God and his purpose for your life. May God richly bless you as you read and study this important prophecy of Jeremiah.

F. Wayne Mac Leod

Jeremiah

1

Jeremiah's Call

Read Jeremiah 1

These are the words of Jeremiah the prophet. He was the son of Hilkiah the priest. He came from the town of Anathoth, which was located about 3 miles (5 kilometers) northeast of the city of Jerusalem. Jeremiah grew up in the home of a priest with a good understanding of the temple and its rituals.

In verse 2 we read that the word of the Lord came to Jeremiah from the thirteenth year of King Josiah (627 BC), through the reign of King Jehoiakim, and to the fifth month of the eleventh year of King Zedekiah when the people went into exile (586 BC). He ministered for approximately thirty years. During this time he received words from the Lord for his people.

The Lord called Jeremiah to the ministry of prophet. The Lord told him in verse 5 that he had a plan for his life from the beginning of time. God knew Jeremiah before he formed him in the womb. Even before Jeremiah was born, God had set him apart and appointed him a prophet to the nations.

The Lord knows the plans he has for our lives even before we are born. It would even be safe to say that we are born with a purpose. From the time of our birth, the Lord God allows circumstances to come our way to challenge and shape us for the purpose he has for our life. Even before a child is shaped in the womb of a mother, God has a sovereign purpose in mind for that child.

Notice in verse 5 that Jeremiah was appointed to be a prophet to the nations. His ministry would not be limited to his own people. Jeremiah would share the word of the Lord to the surrounding nations as well.

Notice in verse 6 the response of Jeremiah to the call of the Lord God on his life: Jeremiah felt unworthy. "I am only a child," he said to God. From this we understand that Jeremiah was young and inexperienced in ministry and life. In particular, Jeremiah struggled with the fact that God was calling him to speak. God had spoken to this young and inexperienced youth, telling him that he would have an international ministry of speaking his word to the nations. Jeremiah felt inadequate for the task.

God challenged him about his attitude in verse 7. God told him that he was not to say that he was only a child. This was a command from God. Instead, he was to go out and say what the Lord told him to say and go wherever the Lord told him to go.

While Jeremiah might have feelings of inadequacy, he was not to let those feelings keep him from being obedient to the call of God. He was commanded to move beyond his emotions to be obedient to the will of the Lord. How Satan loves to keep us inactive under feelings of inadequacy. How he loves to keep our attention away from the fact that the Lord is an awesome and all-powerful God. It is true that we are not able, in ourselves, to do anything of eternal significance, but with God all things are possible. How we need to be individuals who are willing to take God at his word and move forward in faith. Jeremiah was challenged to obey in faith despite his personal inadequacies.

The Lord also told Jeremiah in verse 8 that he was not to be afraid of his audience. God promised to be with him and to rescue him from all enemies. The prophet was to prophesy in the boldness and strength of the Lord, trusting in his protection.

Having challenged the prophet to go, the Lord then empowered him. Verse 9 tells us that the Lord reached out and touched Jeremiah's mouth. In so doing, the Lord symbolized putting his words in the prophet's mouth. We are not told how the Lord did this. The act of touching the mouth of Jeremiah, however, was an act of consecration and empowering. His mouth was to be given completely over to the Lord. Jeremiah's mouth would communicate God's heart to God's people.

That day, God set Jeremiah over nations to uproot and to overthrow (verse 10). He was called to build and to plant. Jeremiah was called to announce God's will for the nations. Because God spoke through Jeremiah, his prophetic words had divine authority. God's word is so true and powerful that his word and his deed are the same to him. What Jeremiah spoke from the Lord would surely come to pass. God would give Jeremiah messages of both comfort and destruction.

In the verses that follow, the Lord burdened Jeremiah's heart with a message to deliver. The Lord also placed a strong sense of urgency in the prophet to proclaim his word. To accomplish this, God gave Jeremiah two visions. These visions were very important, as they formed the basis for Jeremiah's ministry.

The first of these visions was of an almond branch (verses 11–12). What is the significance of the almond branch? There may be a play on words here. The Hebrew word for "almond" is *shaqed*, which also means "awake." The Hebrew word for "watching" is *shoqed*. In verse 12 God reminded Jeremiah that he was "watching" to see that his word was fulfilled. Every time the prophet saw an almond branch, he would be reminded of this play on words and be reassured that God was awake and watching over his word to bring it to pass. Jeremiah could prophesy with a deep assurance that God would accomplish all he had spoken. Nothing would stand in the way of the fulfillment of God's plan for the nations.

There is something else about the almond tree that we should note. The almond tree was the first tree to blossom in Israel, producing blooms in January. It was a reminder that spring was soon coming. God would fulfill his word and bring the judgment he promised on the land as surely as the blossoming almond tree announced its fruit to come.

The second vision Jeremiah saw was that of a boiling pot (verses 13–14). The boiling pot was tilted away from the north.

This particular pot would overflow and pour out its boiling contents toward the south. That is to say, an enemy would attack God's people from the north. The day was coming when God would summon a people from the north to invade Judah. They would overflow in a judgment on God's people like the contents of that boiling pot.

These enemies from the north would set up their thrones in the entrance of Jerusalem. They would destroy the walls of that great city (verse 15). They would invade the towns of Judah because God was angry with his people. Judgment would fall on God's own people (verse 16).

Why was God angry with his people? Verse 16 tells us that it was because they were wicked. They had forsaken God and burned incense to other gods. They made idols and worshiped them.

God warned Jeremiah that speaking out against this wickedness would not be easy. God promised, however, to make him like a fortified city, an iron pillar, and a wall of bronze (verse 18). God would put a defense around his prophet that no one could penetrate.

The word Jeremiah was called to speak would not always be accepted. Jeremiah would have to stand against kings, officials, priests, and all the other inhabitants of Judah (verse 18). They would fight against him, but they would never be able to overcome him.

It is important for us to see the various aspects of Jeremiah's call to ministry. Jeremiah was called (verses 4–5). In that call Jeremiah would find his purpose in life. Second, Jeremiah was empowered (verses 6–9). God particularly gifted him to do the work that he was called to do. These gifts were spiritual gifts and not natural abilities. Jeremiah knew his weaknesses but was to step out boldly in God's strength and gifting. Third, Jeremiah also received the authority of God to go out in his name (verse 10). Finally, Jeremiah was given a very particular burden (verses 11–16). That burden came to him in the form of two visions. God showed in those visions that judgment was coming on Judah.

As a young man, Jeremiah was called of God to move forward in faith. He did not feel adequate for the task, but he dared not doubt the call and enabling of God for the task. Jeremiah was promised a difficult ministry, but he was also promised God's presence. And that was all that Jeremiah really needed.

For Consideration:

- What has God called you to do?

- What particular burden has the Lord placed on your heart?

- Do you feel inadequate in ministry? What is the challenge of the Lord to you here in this passage?

For Prayer:

- Thank the Lord that he has a particular purpose for you and your life.

- Ask the Lord to give you a particular burden for the ministry he has called you to do.

- Ask him to enable you to be sensitive to the way he is leading you and to what he is calling you to do.

- Thank the Lord that you can be assured of his provision and protection as you act in faith to do his will.

2

Why Go to Egypt?

Read Jeremiah 2:1–19

In chapter 2 the word of the Lord came to the prophet Jeremiah. He was to go to the city of Jerusalem with a particular word from the Lord. Judah was guilty of great sin against her tender and loving God.

God told Jeremiah to remind his people of the relationship they enjoyed in days gone by. He was to remind them of the devotion of their youth (verse 2). Like a bride, Israel had loved her Lord with all her heart and followed him through the desert to a land not sown. The picture here is of a bride willing to suffer hardships and trials to be with the one she loves. It is true that the children of Israel did their share of grumbling and complaining in the wilderness. This must be put aside for a moment, however, for the sake of the illustration. Here Israel is presented as a loving wife, enduring all things for the sake of her husband.

Israel had once been holy to the Lord (verse 3). She had separated herself from all others for him. Israel was described here as the firstfruits of the harvest. The firstfruits were the first crops of the harvest brought to the Lord. The people did not eat these but gave them to God as a token of thanksgiving. Israel was once committed and devoted to God, like those firstfruits. She was the first nation to worship the true God, and God jealously kept her as his own.

Anyone who tried to hurt Israel ("devoured her") would answer to God. There was a close relationship between God and his people. It was an intimate and loving relationship, compared here to the relationship between a husband and his loving and devoted wife.

Jeremiah told his people in Jerusalem that the Lord had a question to ask them: "What fault did your fathers find in me that they strayed so far from me?" (verse 5). Why did the children of Israel choose to follow worthless idols instead of their own God who had brought them out of the bondage and slavery? In their rebellious and adulterous state, they were of no value to the Lord.

Their unfaithfulness to God resulted in his presence departing from them. No longer did they experience his blessing. Though they wasted away, they did not even ask about God (verse 6). They did not remember God, their loving husband, who took them through the desert and brought them to a land filled with rich fruit and produce.

They defiled the land the Lord their God had given them (verse 7). Even the priests did not ask, "Where is the Lord?" (verse 8). They were unconcerned about the lack of spiritual blessing in the land. The people who administered the law of the Lord did not know the Lord (verse 8). The leaders had rebelled against God. Even the prophets prophesied by Baal and served worthless idols. The whole land was polluted and defiled with sin and rebellion against God.

God's people had enjoyed a wonderful relationship with their Creator and God. But the rebellion of the leaders, priests, and prophets had driven him from their midst, and they had no regret about this. They were so steeped in sin and rebellion that they cared nothing for their loss of intimacy with the Lord God.

Jeremiah reminded Judah that the Lord was going to judge her because she had defiled the land with her idolatry (verses 7–8). Her loving husband was about to uncover her unfaithfulness and bring charges against her.

God challenged his people to look at their neighbors and see that no other nation had forsaken their gods, even though these gods were worthless (verse 11). Yet God's people had turned their backs on the one true glorious God to serve useless idols. The Lord called the heavens to shudder at this great horror (verse 12). How could a people who had such an all-powerful and glorious God turn their backs on him to serve a piece of wood? The very thought of this was absurd.

In verse 13 God charged his people with two evils. The first was that they had forsaken him who was the spring of water. The second was that they had replaced him with broken cisterns that could not hold water. In God, their loving husband, there was joy and blessing. God's people had everything they needed or could ever want. Yet they gave it all up for a lifestyle that could never satisfy.

Jeremiah asked rhetorically in verse 14 if Israel was a servant or slave. God had set his people free. They were no longer slaves but children of the King of Kings. They enjoyed the blessing of Almighty God. Why then were they plundered? Why were they living as slaves when they were children of the King? Lions had come to devour them (verse 15). Their land was a wasteland with their towns burned and deserted. Yet they were children of Almighty God. Why were these things happening?

The men of Memphis and Tahpanhes had shaved Israel's head (verse 16). God's people were humiliated before these Egyptian cities. There was something desperately wrong with this picture.

In verse 17 God told his people that they had brought this evil and shame on themselves. By forsaking the Lord their God, they had lost much. By turning their backs on their Creator, they turned their backs on life and blessing.

God asked his people a very striking question in verse 18: "Why go to Egypt to drink water from the Shihor? And why go to Assyria to drink water from the River?" The word *shihor* means "darkness" or "blackness." This may be a reference to the Nile River in Egypt. The Assyrian River could very likely be the Euphrates. What God asked his people was something like this: Why should you go and drink from the river of darkness when your God is the "spring of living water"? Why would God's people turn to false gods when their God was the source of life?

They were a people who had turned their backs on the source of living water and had drunk from the river of darkness. There could be no blessing in drinking from these foreign streams. The Nile River and the Euphrates River were very large and wonderful rivers to look at. They brought productivity and fruitfulness to their respective lands. Spiritually, however, Egypt and Assyria brought death. They represented this world and its influences. This world will never give us life and blessing. It is filled with death and destruction. There are believers who are still drawing from these wells and wonder why there is no victory and blessing in their lives.

"Your wickedness will punish you," God told his people in verse 19. Their own deeds would destroy them. They were filling themselves with the waters of death by their rebellion. Their backsliding would rebuke them. One day they would realize how evil and bitter their life was.

How many people have discovered the truth of these verses? How many have suffered the bitterness and fruitlessness that come when we turn from God and from the spring of his living waters. The broken cisterns of this world have nothing of any value to offer us. May God enable us to drink deeply from the spring of living water.

For Consideration:

• Have you remained true to your first love?

• What does this passage teach us about the futility of seeking the things of this world?

• Is there any way that you have been guilty of drinking from the river of darkness? Explain.

For Prayer:

• Thank the Lord for the blessings you have experienced in him.

- Ask the Lord to show you if there is any way that you have been drawing from the wells of this world.

- Do you know someone who has backslidden in his or her faith? Ask the Lord to cause this person to return to him.

3

The Broken Yoke

Read Jeremiah 2:20–37

"Long ago you broke off your yoke and tore off your bonds," God told his people in verse 20. The yoke represented the commitment they had to their God. In the beginning of this chapter, the Lord compared the relationship he had with his people to a marriage. He reminded them of how they had been devoted to him in love. Once they had been holy to the Lord (set apart for him and his glory). But that relationship had changed. God's people had turned their backs on him and broken their covenant commitment to him. They told him that they did not want to serve him any longer. They went up to the high hills of the land and offered sacrifices to other gods. Under spreading trees they were unfaithful to God. Like a prostitute, they offered themselves and their love to others but abandoned their own God.

God had planted them like a choice vine (verse 21). They were from a reliable stock. He expected much fruit, but they did not produce that fruit. Instead, they turned against him and became a wild and corrupt vine. God's disappointment was obvious. The stain of their sin was such that even though they washed themselves with soda and an abundance of soap, they could not remove their guilt before God (verse 22). But God's people did not even realize their condition. In verse 23 they said, "I am not defiled; I have not run after the Baals." They were blinded to their own sins.

Our enemy does not advertise his presence—he sneaks up on us. He slowly acclimatizes us to sin. Little by little, he stretches us and moves the moral boundary. We do not even realize that our boundaries have changed. Gradually, we become accustomed to our sin and rebellion. This seems to have been the condition of God's people at this time. They had lost all discernment of their immoral condition.

Israel and Judah had gone so far in this sin and rebellion that God compared them to a she-camel and a wild donkey sniffing the wind in her craving (verse 24). The image here is of a female animal in heat looking for a mate. In the time of her heat, she is unrestrained. Any male can find her. This is how God's people were when it came to their sin. They intensely sought after it. Their hearts were sold out to it. There was no stopping them in their pursuit of moral defilement.

In verse 25 Jeremiah described God's people as chasing after sin until their feet were bare and their throats were dry. The prophet told his people that their lust for sin and rebellion was unrestrained. Like the wild donkey in heat, they chased after sin and rebellion until they were exhausted.

"It is no use trying to resist!" God's people said. "I love foreign gods, and I must go after them" (verse 25). They could not see a way of escape. Their sin had captured their hearts. They loved it too much to leave it.

Jeremiah reminded his people that the day was coming when they would be ashamed of their sin. As a thief caught in the act is ashamed of his deeds, so it would be for Israel and Judah (verse 26). From their kings and officials to their priests and prophets, they would all come to recognize their sin and rebellion against God and be ashamed. God would not let them continue in rebellion.

Notice what Jeremiah said in verse 27: "They say to wood, 'You are my father,' and to stone, 'You gave me birth.' They have turned their backs to me and not their faces." Israel and Judah turned their backs on God. They did not confess him any longer to be their Creator.

While God's people wanted nothing to do with him in the good times, when things got bad, they would come running to him, asking him to save them. Listen to God's response to his rebellious people in verse 28: "Where then are the gods you made for yourselves? Let them come if they can save you when you are in trouble! For you have as many gods as you have towns, O Judah."

Despite all that God had done for them, his people constantly complained against him (verse 29). In reality they were the ones who were guilty before him. They had devoured the prophets that God had sent to them. God had disciplined them, but they would not respond to his correction (verse 30).

In verse 31 God called his people to consider the foolishness of what they were doing. He did this by a series of questions. In the first of these questions, God asked his people: "Have I been a desert to Israel or a land of great darkness?" Why had his people turned from him? Was it because he had refused to bless them? Obviously, this was not the case. Despite what God had done for his people, they said, "We are free to roam; we will come to you no more." In saying this, they turned their backs on the source of all their blessing. This was foolish indeed.

The second question God asked his people is in verse 32. "Does a maiden forget her jewelry, a bride her wedding ornaments?" These are not things young women easily forget. If a young bride remembers her jewelry, how could God's people forget their glorious God who is of far greater value? What these people did made no sense.

God's people were skilled at pursuing love (verse 33). Jeremiah told them that even the worst of women could take lessons from them. Like the wild donkey spoken of earlier, their lust was unrestrained.

The lifeblood of the innocent poor could be seen on their clothes (verse 34). Injustice prevailed in Israel, and innocent people were condemned to death on false charges. Despite their sin, God's people claimed to be innocent (verse 35). They believed the lie that God would not judge them. They somehow believed that they could be unfaithful and still experience all of God's love and blessing. How confused they were. It was precisely because they said, "I have not sinned," that God would judge them. In saying this, they rejected the Lord's forgiveness that follows true repentance. Imagine a wife being regularly unfaithful to her husband and seeing nothing wrong with it. Imagine that she felt no shame. This is what was happening to God's people. This is why God would punish them severely.

Jeremiah prophesied that God's people would turn to Egypt for help in their time of trouble, but they would be disappointed (verse 36). Egypt would let them down as Assyria had done. We are not clearly told when Assyria let God's people down, but we read of a time under King Ahaz when this was the case. Tiglath-Pileser, king of Assyria, came to Ahaz but gave him trouble instead of help (2 Chronicles 28:20).

Jeremiah told his people that the day was coming when they would be forced to leave their land with their hands on their heads (verse 37). This would be in submission to a conquering enemy. God would judge them for their evil. This would clearly take place when God's people were taken into exile.

It is easy to see how confused the people of God had become. They turned their hearts from the one true God who loved them. They lusted after other gods but believed that God would not punish them for this. They had become trapped in a lifestyle of sin and rebellion. Jeremiah warned them that God was not blind to this evil.

For Consideration:

• How does the description of the people in Jeremiah's day compare to our own day?

• Have we too lost all concept of what sin is?

• How does a society get to the point of losing all sense of righteousness?

For Prayer:

• Ask God to help us to recognize our sin as a society.

- Ask God to move in our midst and make his righteous and holy presence known to us again.

- Ask God to help you to see sin in your life as he sees it.

4

Return, Faithless People

Read Jeremiah 3

The relationship that God had with his people is here compared to a marriage. Israel, however, had not been faithful to her marriage vows. She had turned her back on her husband and been disloyal to him.

Jeremiah began chapter 3 with a question: "If a man divorces his wife and she leaves him and marries another man, should he return to her again?" The law of Moses was quite clear on this matter in Deuteronomy 24:1–4:

> If a man marries a woman who becomes displeasing to him because he finds something indecent about her, and he writes her a certificate of divorce, gives it to her and sends her from his house, and if after she leaves his house she becomes the wife of another man, and her second husband dislikes her and writes her a certificate of divorce, gives it to her and sends her from his house, or if he dies, then her first husband, who divorced her, is not allowed to marry her again after she has been defiled. That would be detestable in the eyes of the LORD. Do not

bring sin upon the land the LORD your God is giving you as an inheritance.

When a man and woman married, they were to take their vows seriously. They could not come and go as they pleased. In marriage the man and woman entered a covenant relationship for life.

Jeremiah related this law to illustrate Israel's relationship with the Lord. Not only had Israel been unfaithful, she had lived as a prostitute with many lovers (the false gods of other nations). Israel had rejected her husband, the Lord God, many times. After all this unfaithfulness, why should the Lord take her back? She had broken her covenant with him and polluted the Promised Land.

The Lord had withheld rain from the land as a consequence (verse 3). This should have indicated to the people that their fertility rites with their idols were in vain. The Lord controlled the rain, not the false gods that his people had turned to.

This unfaithfulness to God was evident everywhere. On the barren heights, by the roadside, and in the desert there were evidences of unfaithful and sinful practices. Like a brazen prostitute, Israel had no shame. She openly and publicly rebelled against God. Israel was so insensitive to spiritual things that she could not blush any more. Israel no longer recognized or felt ashamed of her sin and rebellion.

In verses 4–5 God reminded his people how they had talked about him. They were guilty of breaking their covenant with him but still called him their Father and friend from youth. They could not understand why God would be angry with them since he had been their provider and companion from their beginning.

God's people recognized that God was their Father and friend, but they had no sense of obligation to him. They abused his kindness. They felt that he should forgive and forget all their sin. They believed that a loving father and friend would not even consider their sin. They believed that they could do whatever they wanted, and God would be obligated to love and forgive them. But even a loving father must discipline his children. God's people did not see things this way. They were self-centered and proud.

"I thought that after she had done all this she would return to me but she did not," the Lord said in verse 7. Though she saw the results of her rebellion, Israel did not learn her lesson. Instead, she continued in her sin and grew harder.

What a surprise it was when Israel received a certificate of divorce from God (verse 8). God sent the northern kingdom of Israel into captivity in Assyria in 722 BC because of her unfaithfulness and rebellion. God removed his presence and his blessing from her.

Despite this terrible consequence, Israel's sister, the southern kingdom of Judah, fell into the same trap. She too had no fear of God and followed the evil example of her sister Israel who committed spiritual adultery with idols of stones and wood (verse 9). Israel worshiped false gods and turned her back on the one true God. Judah repeated the same treachery as Israel. According to verse 10, Judah made a pretense of repentance and returning to the Lord, but she did not return with all her heart. Judah saw Israel's judgment but did not take it seriously. In verse 11 Jeremiah told Judah that Israel was more righteous than she was.

When we have been warned and still choose to sin, our judgment will be more severe. When we know what is right and do not do it, we will be judged more severely than those who do not know. The more we are warned, the more we are accountable.

Despite the terrible sin of God's people, Jeremiah was to go to them with a message of hope (verse 12). He was to go and ask the people to return to the Lord. "'I will frown on you no longer, for I am merciful,' declares the LORD. 'I will not be angry forever.'" The law of Moses said that the divorced wife could never return to her former husband. In his grace and mercy, however, God still called her back.

While the door was open for her to return to him, the Lord required that she acknowledge her guilt. She was to recognize that she had been unfaithful to him. She had scattered her favors on foreign gods (verse 13). She had offered herself to her lovers under every spreading tree in the land. If Israel and Judah were to experience forgiveness and restoration to God, they would first have to recognize their sin and confess it to him.

Many people have not yet come to this point in their lives. They want a relationship with God but are not ready to recognize their sin and rebellion against him. Sin is a barrier between God and people. It must be recognized and confessed before anyone can experience full restoration with God.

"Return, faithless people," the Lord cried (verse 14). Notice that the Lord did not ignore their sin. He called them a faithless people. He recognized their guilt but was willing to forgive them anyway. "I am your husband," he told them. "I will choose you—one from a town and two from a clan—and bring you to Zion." While not everyone would return, there would be a remnant that would return to the Lord. God promised to provide for them shepherds after his own heart who would lead them with knowledge and understanding (verse 15). God would care for those who returned to him.

In the days that the Lord returned to them, their numbers would be increased in the land. Men would no longer cry out for the ark of the covenant. That ark would no longer even enter their minds. In the context of the Old Testament, the presence of God was revealed between the cherubim on the ark of the covenant. The days would come when the Lord's presence would no longer be limited to the ark. Instead, he would reveal himself in a deeper and more intimate way. The city of Jerusalem would be called the "Throne of the LORD" (verse 17). The presence of God would be revealed with such power that people from every nation would gather in Jerusalem to honor the name of the Lord. No longer would God's people follow their stubborn and evil hearts. God would move in power and renewal in their midst. It seems to me that we have yet to see this powerful move of God among his chosen people Israel.

When God moved in power in their midst, the house of Judah and the house of Israel would be united again (verse 18). They would come from the north to the land that God had given their fathers. Old divisions would at that time be put aside, and God's people would be united as one nation. What is important for us to see here is that the work of renewal brings unity to the body.

Verse 19 shows us God's desire for his people. He told them that he would gladly treat them as sons and give them a desirable land. Their inheritance would be the most beautiful of any nation. God would spare nothing when it came to his children.

What a privilege we have to be the children of God. There is abundant blessing in the Lord. He does not hold these blessings back from us, but delights in showering us with his grace.

God's desire was also that his people would again call him "Father" (verse 19). He wanted them to delight in him and enter into that intimate relationship of dependence and love. God's people did not want that relationship, however. Like an adulterous wife, Israel was unfaithful to her husband, the Lord God (verse 20). Jeremiah reminded his people that they would suffer the consequences of this rebellion. The day was coming when they would weep and plead with God for mercy.

Again, in verse 22 God called his people, through Jeremiah, to return to him. He promised that if they returned to him, he would cure their backsliding. Notice here that they could not heal their own sin; they would need the Lord to do this for them. God would change their hearts and move in power among them. When God touched their hearts, they would be healed of their wicked ways.

There is an important lesson we all need to learn here. We cannot heal ourselves. We cannot change our hearts. God alone can heal our sin and cleanse us. The challenge here is simply to come to him. We do not have to be perfect to come to him. All we have to do is to come in repentance for cleansing and healing. God is more than willing to forgive us and heal our hearts.

Throughout the history of Israel, God's people had gone after foreign gods that had stripped them of the fruit of their fathers' labor (verse 24). God had removed his blessing from their land because of their evil ways. God's people turned their backs on the only salvation and source of blessing they had. Their flocks, herds, sons, and daughters were all suffering the consequences of generations of rebellion against God.

In verse 25 Jeremiah challenged his people to lie down in shame and recognize their guilt before God. They were to allow their disgrace to cover them. They and their ancestors had sinned against God and were guilty. From their youth as a nation, the children of Israel had refused to obey the word of their Lord.

We see in this chapter the incredible grace and forgiveness of God. His people had rebelled against him and deserved to perish. They had broken their covenant with God and had given themselves to the perverse worship of demonic false gods. The Lord God, in his grace, was willing to reach out to them and forgive them if they would return to him. They needed to recognize and confess their sin. It was still not too late. The Lord was still calling out to them to repent and seek him.

For Consideration:

- What does this passage teach us about the love and forgiveness of the Lord?

- In what ways have we, as a society and church, proven unfaithful to the Lord?

- What does this chapter teach us about God's desire for his people?

- What do we learn here about the importance of recognizing and confessing our sin? Can there be full reconciliation with God without recognition of sin?

For Prayer:

- Thank the Lord for the way he desires to love and heal us of our backsliding.

- Ask the Lord to reveal any unfaithfulness in your life.

- Ask him to heal the sins of your nation and call it to himself.

5

A Ruined Land

Read Jeremiah 4

I n the last meditation, the Lord called his people to return to him. The prophecy of chapter 4 began with the same call. In the opening verses of this chapter, Jeremiah told his people what would happen if they did return to the Lord.

Notice how the people were to return to God (verses 1–2). They were first to return by putting aside their idols. They could not return if they were not willing to get rid of their idols. God would not share his people with false gods. Second, the people of God were to return to him in truth, justice, and righteousness.

To return in truth meant that God's people had to be sincere and honest in their repentance. They had to willingly put aside everything false and commit themselves to the Lord God alone.

They were also to return in justice. Justice had to do with their relationship with those around them. They were to be right with each other as they came back to the Lord. Jesus reminded his listeners in Matthew 5:23–24 that if they brought their offering to the Lord and remembered that a brother or sister had something against them, they were first to be reconciled with each before coming to worship God.

God's people were also to come to God in righteousness. Righteousness had to do with being in a right relationship with God. If justice had to do with their neighbors, righteousness had to do with their God. When they returned to God, they were to do so by being obedient to God's will for their lives. They were to confess and turn from all known sin and approach him with upright behavior. If they approached the Lord in this way, the Lord would bless his people, and the nations would notice. Through faithful Israel, the nations would recognize the true source of blessing and glory in the God of Israel (see Genesis 12:3).

God challenged his people, in verse 3, to break up the unplowed ground of their hearts. They had allowed their hearts to become hard and indifferent to the things of God. They were no longer to sow the seeds of the Lord's words among the thorns. Thorns represented sin and rebellion. They were to root out these sinful ways so the Lord's words could grow and produce fruit in their lives. They were to circumcise themselves to the Lord. This circumcision represented the cutting off of their old fleshly ways and thoughts to live in obedience to the Spirit of God and his holy ways.

Notice in verse 4 that the wrath of God would fall on them if they did not wholeheartedly return to him. He would break out against them and burn them like fire because of the evil among them. God would burn against them with a fire that could not be quenched. God's wrath was real, but he was offering his people a chance to escape before it was too late.

In verse 5 God called his prophet Jeremiah to proclaim a warning to the people of God. A warning trumpet was to be sounded as an announcement of God's wrathful judgment. A signal was to be raised in Zion (verse 6). The people were to flee for safety. The guard was warning the people of an enemy heading straight for them.

A disaster was coming from the north. This reminds us of the vision that Jeremiah had in chapter 1 of the boiling pot tipped over toward the south. A terrible destruction was coming to the people of God. A lion-like enemy was ready to pounce on them (verse 7). The destroyer of nations had set out and was heading directly for them. Soon their towns and villages would be destroyed and left without inhabitants.

God's people were to put on sackcloth and wail (verse 8). Sackcloth was usually made of goat's hair. It was very rough and uncomfortable to wear. It was worn by those who lamented their sin. In a way, it was a symbol of refusing comfort and showing how repentant they were for their sins.

The day of the Lord's judgment would be a terrible day. On that day the kings and the officials would lose heart. The priests would be horrified, and the prophets would be appalled (verse 9).

In verse 10 Jeremiah was struck by the terrible nature of what was going to happen to the land. He cried out to the Lord: "Ah, Sovereign LORD, how completely you have deceived this people and Jerusalem by saying, 'You will have peace,' when the sword is at our throats."

Did the Lord really say that the people would have peace? It seems that the best way to interpret this is by understanding the context of the time. Certainly many false prophets in the land proclaimed this message (see 6:13–14). They were filling the people's minds with false hope of security and peace without repentance for sin. They were supposedly the instruments of God to communicate his heart to the people, but the false prophets were only deceiving the nation. Jeremiah, no doubt, heard these prophecies of hope and peace. Maybe he had even believed that this was what the Lord had in store for his people. What the Lord was revealing to him, however, was very different. Instead of peace, there was terror and destruction coming. The people had been deceived in the name of the Lord by the words of false prophets.

While the people were hearing that peace and security was their portion, the reality was very different. A scorching wind from the barren heights was moving its way toward the people of God (verse 11). This was no ordinary wind. This wind was not the gentle type of breeze that would drive away the chaff from the wheat. This wind was too strong to cleanse. It had a very powerful and destructive force. It would devastate and destroy because it was the wind of God's judgment.

Righteous judgment was approaching (verse 13). It advanced like a cloud, silently but loaded with torrential rain. God's chariots of judgment would come with the speed and destruction of a whirlwind. God's people would have no chance to escape. They were destined for destruction.

Once again, the Lord challenged his people to repent of their wicked ways and wash their evil hearts. Though the enemy was approaching, there was still time for them to repent and be saved (verse 14). In the verses that follow, Jeremiah went through a lengthy description of the destruction and devastation that awaited the unrepentant people of God in days to come.

A voice of judgment was heard from the region of Dan. Disaster was being proclaimed from the hills of Ephraim (verse 15). A great army was coming from a distant land, raising a war cry against the nation of Judah (verse 16). This army would surround Judah like men guarding a field, because God's people had chosen to rebel against him (verse 17). The unrepentant hearts and evil conduct of God's people had brought this horrible judgment on them (verse 18). This punishment would be very bitter. It would pierce their hearts and cause them to ache (verse 19). They alone, however, were to blame.

As Jeremiah reflected on the agony and devastation that was going to come to his people, his heart began to break. "Oh the agony of my heart!" he cried in verse 19. Jeremiah's heart pounded within him as he thought about the horrible nature of the judgment to come. It was not easy for the prophet to see and hear the details of this righteous judgment. He took no secret delight in prophesying the condemnation of his own people. Jeremiah's heart broke for the nation of Judah.

Jeremiah could not keep silent because he had heard the sound of the trumpet of God's judgment (verse 19). How could he be silent in light of the disaster that was coming toward the people of God? Disaster would follow disaster (verse 20). Jeremiah could see the whole land in ruins. The tents of the land would be destroyed in an instant. The judgment of God would come swiftly and powerfully.

God looked on his people and declared them fools (verse 22). Like senseless children, they had no understanding. They were skilled at doing evil, but they did not know how to do good. What a sad commentary on the people of God. Though they had no excuse, they lived in ignorance of God and his Word.

As Jeremiah looked around him in his prophetic vision, he saw the earth as a formless mass (verse 23). It was empty. All the lights were gone out of the heavens. The mountains quaked. All the hills were swinging (verse 24). There were no people. All the birds had flown away (verse 25). The fruitful land had become a desert, and all its towns lay in ruins (verse 26). This desolation and chaos revealed that God's wrath against his people was very real. However, he would not completely destroy them—there would be a remnant (verse 27).

In verse 28 the Lord made it clear that his mind was made up about this judgment. There was nothing that would stop it from coming, and so the earth and heavens mourned. God had spoken and nothing would change what he had determined. He would not turn back his anger.

At the sound of his horsemen, the towns would take flight (verse 29). Some of the inhabitants would go into the thickets; others would climb among the rocks to hide from the wrath and judgment of God. The towns would be deserted and abandoned.

In verse 30 God asked his people why they were dressing themselves in scarlet and putting on their jewels of gold. The women were shading their eyes with paint, adorning themselves in vain. The people of Judah, like harlots, were still dressing up to meet their lovers (other nations and their demonic false gods), but these lovers despised them and would turn against them.

In verse 31 Jeremiah heard a cry like the cry of a woman in labor. Under the judgment of God, his people groaned like a woman giving birth to a child. The Daughter of Zion (God's own children) was gasping for breath. She stretched out her fainting hands, crying out in desperation as her life was handed over to murderers. Those murderers were the enemies that God would send against her because of her rebellion.

God's wrath was very real. Jeremiah prophesied that God's people would be judged for their sin and rebellion against him. Their idolatrous evil was extreme and demanded punishment. As his chosen people, they had a covenant obligation to obey God, and he took that obligation seriously. He still does.

For Consideration:

- Why do you suppose we do not hear much about the wrath and judgment of God in our day?

- What evidence is there of the justice and mercy of God in this chapter?

- What does Jeremiah teach us here about how we must return to God? Can we return to God unless we are willing to turn from our sin?

- What does this chapter teach us about the judgment of God?

For Prayer:

- Thank the Lord that he is willing to forgive you of your sin.

- Thank him that he does punish sin.

- Do you know someone who is still under the wrath of God? Take a moment to pray that the Lord would reach out and touch this person.

6

Backsliding Israel

Read Jeremiah 5

The spiritual condition of the land left much to be desired. God called Jeremiah to go out into the streets of Jerusalem to see if he could find just one person who dealt honestly and sought truth. If there was just one person who sought truth, God would forgive the entire city (verse 1). As God looked on this rebellious people, he could not find a single honest individual. The whole nation was steeped in deceit.

This is not to say that the people were not religious. They still had the Lord in their vocabulary. They would swear oaths saying, "As surely as the Lord lives," I will do this or that, but they did not intend to keep these oaths (verse 2). When people swore by the Lord's name, they were calling his judgment on themselves if they violated the oath.

God would not sit back and watch his people live this way. He looked for truth, but there was no truth in the nation. He disciplined his people and struck them, but they did not feel the pain (verse 3). He crushed them, but they refused to be corrected. Instead of listening to the correction, they hardened their hearts and continued in their rebellion, refusing to repent.

As Jeremiah considered the reality of the things the Lord had been telling him, he thought: "These are only the poor; they are foolish, for they do not know the way of the LORD, the requirements of their God" (verse 4). He decided, therefore, to speak to the leaders and the educated people in the land, expecting that they would respond favorably to his plea.

In verse 5, however, Jeremiah discovered that they too had broken the yoke of God and torn off their bonds to him. Notice here in verse 5 that these leaders had torn off these bonds "with one accord." All of them were united in defiance to God's holy laws. The problem of transgression and moral corruption was not unique to the poor; it was also the problem of those in authority in the land. The whole land, with one accord, had turned its back on God.

It was on the whole nation that the judgment of God was going to fall. Jeremiah prophesied that a lion from the forest would attack God's people, and a wolf from the desert would ravage them (verse 6). A leopard was lying in wait near their towns to tear to pieces any who ventured out. These animals represented the fierce enemies of God's people. This judgment would come because the hypocrisy of God's people was very great and their backslidings were many (verse 6).

Notice in verse 6 that the word "backslidings" is in the plural. God's people were guilty of many backslidings. What does this mean? To backslide is to pull away from relationship with God. The Israelites had turned from God and returned to the evil ways of the flesh. In the social, political, and religious arenas, the people were not living in covenant obedience to the Lord.

The Lord asked his people a very penetrating question in verse 7: "Why should I forgive you?" They had forsaken him and worshiped other gods. Though the Lord had abundantly provided them all they needed, they turned their backs on him to commit adultery with the false gods of the other nations. God characterized his people as thronging the houses of prostitutes.

How many times do we see people thronging the sports and entertainment arenas of our day to bow the knee to the gods of pleasure? How many spiritual houses of prostitution do we have in our societies today? These spiritual houses of prostitution are places that take us away from our one true God. They offer us pleasure and satisfaction at the cost of our walk with God.

In verse 8 God compared his people to a well-fed and lusty stallion. Each of them was lusting after another man's wife but rejecting his own wife. The anger of God was on these individuals. "Should I not punish them for this?" God asked in verse 9. Would it not be wrong for him to refrain from judging such crime?

As if speaking to the fierce army that God would use to judge his nation, a call went out in verse 10 for the vines of God's people to be ravaged. His people needed to be awakened to the fact that they were sinning against the one true God. He told the enemy to strip the branches off the vine. These branches were to be stripped because they did not belong to the Lord. They did not belong to him because they had been utterly unfaithful to him. All those branches that did not bear fruit were cut off and disposed of in the fire. These branches were only a hindrance to the productivity of the true vine. The Lord was concerned about the health of his vine. There are times when the Lord will deal severly with his vine to increase its health and fruitfulness. God has any number of ways of restoring the health of his vine.

The false prophets had convinced the Israelites that God would not punish their iniquities (verse 12). The people felt quite free to continue to practice their moral corruption and religious hypocrisy. In their sin God's people had lost their fear of the holy Lord and had forgotten the covenantal curses God had promised to visit on his people for turning away from him (see Deuteronomy 28:47).

Do we live in the fear of the Lord today? Do we believe the lie that we can do what we want and God will do nothing about it? Surely, if we understood the wrath and judgment of God, we would turn from our sins and repent. Even in our day, Satan has caused too many people to believe the lie that they can sin and live in rebellion, and God will do nothing about it.

Satan had his instruments in the false prophets who prophesied nothing by wind (verse 13). The word of the Lord was not in them. The judgment that was coming would consume these evil prophets as well as the people they deceived.

God said that he would make his word like fire in Jeremiah's mouth, and the people would be like wood (verse 14). God told Jeremiah, in effect, that he was going to increase his prophetic authority. The words he spoke would be like fire to those who heard. Earlier in this book, God told Jeremiah that he would uproot and pull down nations (1:10). God was confirming this. God's authority was behind what Jeremiah spoke. Jeremiah's words would be powerful and bring the judgment of God on the nation. His words would be like fire consuming a people of wood.

Because of Judah's sin, the Lord God would bring a distant nation against her (verse 15). This nation (Babylon) was ancient and enduring, and its people spoke a language foreign to the Jews. The quivers that held the enemy's arrows were like an open grave, because the Babylonians were fierce archers (verse 16). All of these men were trained warriors. They would devour the harvest of Judah. They would devour the flocks and the herds (verse 17). The fortified cities in which Judah trusted would also be destroyed. God's disobedient nation would feel the sting of his rod.

In verse 18 Jeremiah reminded his people that the Lord's purpose was not to destroy the whole nation. God would not abandon his people completely. He only wanted to cleanse them and draw them back to himself. This judgment was meant to be a lesson for the generations to come. When people looked back at this time and asked why God did such a thing to his people, they were to know that it was because of idolatry (verse 19). In justice God would send his people to be slaves in the nation whose idols they worshiped. It was the intention of God that future generations would see this judgment and flee from any god but him.

In verse 20 God asked Jeremiah to speak to the foolish and senseless people of Israel and Judah. They had eyes, but they could not see what was happening to them. They had ears to hear, but they could not hear what God was trying to communicate.

"Should you not tremble in my presence?" the Lord asked his people through Jeremiah. Their God made the sand to form the boundary for the sea (verse 22). The sea, though it rolls up against the shore with all its force, cannot cross that barrier. God restrains and controls its limits. But unlike the sea that submits to its boundary, Judah had broken the limits of God's laws.

Jeremiah reminded his people in verse 24 that their Lord (not the idols) controlled weather and gave the autumn and spring rains that assured them of regular harvests. Theirs was an awesome God. He was their source of rich blessing (as seen in his guaranteeing the harvest), and he was also a God of tremendous power (as seen in his controlling of the seas). This was a God to fear. Who would risk offending such a God?

Jeremiah told his people that their wrongdoings had restrained God' blessings (verse 25). Their sins had deprived them of much good. They had become rich and powerful through treachery and deceit (verses 26–27). They were fat and sleek because their evil had no limit. In their greed they did not reach out to the poor or fatherless, as God's law required (see Deuteronomy 26:12; 27:19). Injustice reigned as the people turned their backs on God and his Word (verse 28). Should God simply let these things happen in his land? Surely God would punish them (verse 29).

In verses 30–31 Jeremiah told his people that a horrible and shocking thing had been happening in the land. The prophets were prophesying lies, and the priests were ruling on their own authority. God's people loved it that way because they did not want to hear the truth. They did not want to be under the authority of the Lord. The false prophets did not want to speak the commanding word of the Lord because they wanted to please the people. The priests did not want to submit to the authority of God because they wanted to be their own authority. In all of this, the Lord was cast aside.

Did the people of Judah think that God would not punish them for this? Their national covenant with the Lord God promised blessings for obedience and curses for disobedience (see Deuteronomy 28). God was obligated to avenge himself on such a nation. God pointed out extreme corruption on every level in Judah's society—the prophets, the priests, and the people. How could this end except in social chaos and God's just judgment? In verse 31 Jeremiah asked his people what they would do in the end when the wrath of God fell on them.

We see in this chapter the reality of the wrath and judgment of God. His people had been fooled into believing that he would not judge them. The reality of the matter was that the judgment of the Lord had already fallen on them. God would not destroy them completely, but he would certainly give them serious cause to think about their sin and rebellion. The blessings of God had already been stripped from them, and further punishment was imminent.

This chapter serves as a warning to us as well. We must deal with our sins. We serve the same Lord who judged his people in Jeremiah's day. We need to recognize our own rebellious ways and turn back to our loving and awesome Lord, lest his judgment fall on us as well.

For Consideration:

• Compare your society to the society of Jeremiah's day. Is your society guilty of falling into the same sins?

• Do you see evidence of the church in our day being blinded to the reality of the judgment and wrath of the Lord?

• Are you guilty of living with sin in your life? What keeps the Lord from disciplining you for this?

For Prayer:

• Ask the Lord to reveal to you any sin in your life that needs to be broken.

• Ask the Lord to awaken his church to the reality of his holiness and justice.

• Ask him to pour out on us a zealous spirit of repentance so that we turn from our sins and live for him.

7

Disaster from the North

Read Jeremiah 6

In the last meditation, the Lord reminded his people that if they continued to live in rebellion against him, they could expect to see his wrath and judgment. In chapter 6 Jeremiah reminded his people that this judgment was already coming from the north.

Jeremiah began in verse 1 by challenging his people to flee to safety. They were to leave the city of Jerusalem. The trumpet sounded in Tekoa, and a signal was raised in Beth Hakkerem. Commentators tell us that the name *Tekoa* is very similar to the Hebrew word meaning "to blow." It could be that this city was chosen simply as a play on words.

The trumpet was to sound as a warning of the disaster that loomed from the north. God was going to destroy the Daughter of Zion (a reference to his own people). Notice how God described her in verse 2. She was beautiful and delicate. In God's eyes this is how she was. This does not take away the fact that she was also sinful and rebellious. She was also described as an adulterous wife. Despite her ugly sin, God still cared for her and loved her dearly.

Jeremiah told his people in verse 3 that shepherds with their flocks would come against them. These would come against Judah, pitching their tents and "each tending his own portion." Jeremiah was not speaking about literal shepherds. The context indicates that he was referring to a great army that was about to come from the north to invade the land. The enemy would come to eat all the prosperity of Judah. This army would pitch its tents all around the city of Jerusalem and eventually take it for themselves. The spoils of the land would be divided among these enemy "shepherds."

A call went out to the enemy to prepare for battle against the people of God (verse 4). There would be something strange about this battle. The enemy would want to attack at noon, but the shadows of evening would be already on them. Instead, they would decide to attack at night. This was not normal warfare. Usually battles were fought during the daylight. Here we see the enemy resorting to unusual means to destroy the people of God. Judah's punishment would be at the hands of a cruel people who would do whatever it took to defeat them.

What is very strange about this whole scene is that the Lord God stands behind these enemies in their conquest of his people. We are told in verse 6 that the Lord himself called on the enemy to cut down trees and build siege ramps against the city of Jerusalem. This city was to be punished for her sins because it was filled with social oppression.

As a well pours out an abundance of water, so the city of Jerusalem poured out an abundance of wickedness (verse 7). The sounds of violence and destruction could be heard throughout the city. Zion was sick with sin. Jerusalem was an open wound to the Lord. She was bleeding and not cared for, which left her sick and dying. By forsaking her Lord, she forsook her own healing.

Jeremiah called the inhabitants of Jerusalem to attention. He told them that they were to take warning or God would turn from them. He would not hesitate to make their land desolate so that no one could live in it (verse 8). It should be understood here that under the reigns of David and Solomon, this nation was the envy of the entire world. It was filled with the richness of the blessing of God. But by Jeremiah's time (a few hundred years later), Israel's sin was stripping her of blessing and would ultimately lead to her destruction.

In verse 9 God called for the enemy to harvest his vine, Israel. God's people were to be picked like grapes from a vine. The enemy would come in and strip them of their blessings until nothing was left.

As Jeremiah heard the warning from God, his heart was disturbed within him. In verse 10 he asked: "To whom can I speak and give warning? Who will listen to me? Their ears are closed so they cannot hear. The word of the LORD is offensive to them; they find no pleasure in it."

What a sad commentary on the people of God. They needed to be warned of the coming judgment, but no one would listen. The ears of the people of God were closed to their need for repentance. They would not listen to what God spoke to them through Jeremiah. These people wanted nothing to do with the word of the Lord. Their sin made truth offensive to them.

What a sad thing it is when the people of God find no pleasure in the word of God. The Psalmist spoke often of the great delight he had in the law of the Lord (Psalm 1:2; 119:70, 77, 174). This law was his constant delight. He found himself meditating in it day and night. There were times when his eyes filled with tears because his people refused to listen to this law of God (Psalm 119:136). How much joy and delight do you receive from the word of God? The people of Jeremiah's day had lost all delight in hearing from their God.

Jeremiah warned his people that God's wrath was soon going to be poured out on them (verse 11). This wrath could no longer be contained. It would be poured out on the children in the streets and on the young men gathered together. Both husband and wife would be caught in this flood of God's angry judgment. The old and those weighed down with years would know his vengeance. The whole society would suffer the consequences of sin and rebellion against God. No one would escape. From the youngest to the oldest, all would suffer the holy anger of God. The houses in the land would be destroyed, and their fields would be taken. Even their wives would be given to others (verse 12).

It was certainly not without reason that the Lord judged his people in this way. From the least to the greatest of them, they were all greedy for gain (verse 13). Both the false prophet and the priest practiced deceit (verse 13). These religious leaders dressed the wound of sin of their people as though it were not serious (verse 14). We have already seen that this gaping wound was draining the life out of God's people (see verse 7).

The prophets and the priests, however, simply covered over the fatal wound and told people that peace would come instead of judgment. The reality, however, was very different. Sin must be taken seriously. Because the people were not being told how serious sin was in their lives, they were unashamed of it (verse 15). In their moral blindness, they had even forgotten how to blush. They would be brought down by the Lord because of this.

In verse 16 God challenged his people to stand at the crossroads and ask for the ancient paths. This ancient path was the righteous path that God had shown them from the beginning (the Mosaic covenant). It was the path of obedience and respect for God's word. God's people were challenged not only to find that path but also to walk in it. God promised them that if they walked on that path, they would find rest for their souls.

God's people refused to listen to the word of Jeremiah. Instead, they said: "We will not walk in it" (verse 16). They were intent on continuing in their path of rebellion and disobedience. God sent his prophets to warn them about the dangers of the path they were taking, but they refused to listen (verse 17).

Because they had resisted the word of the prophets, God called for his witnesses to observe his justice. In verse 18 he called the earth to hear what he was about to say. He was going to bring a great disaster on this rebellious people. They had rejected him and his laws, and they would suffer the consequences.

God had no more interest in their hypocritical sacrifices and burnt offerings (verse 20). They had been bringing him incense and calamus (fragrant cane; see Exodus 30:22–25) from distant lands. This did not impress the Lord because their hearts were far from him. Nothing could cover the stench of their evil and wicked hearts.

In verse 21 God told his people through Jeremiah that he would put obstacles before them. All generations and all relationships in Judah would face ruin because God would judge his rebellious people. Fathers and sons alike would stumble, and neighbors and friends would perish.

In verses 22–23 Jeremiah described a great army coming from the north. This army would come with spears and bows. They were intent on war and would show no mercy. They would come against the people of God like a mighty roaring sea as they attacked the Daughter of Jerusalem. Nothing would stop them.

God's people would respond in fear (verse 24). Their hands would grow limp so that they could not use them to fight. Anguish would fill their hearts like a woman in labor. They were warned not to go out to the fields or to walk on the roads because the enemy had a sword and would not hesitate to use it (verse 25). There would be terror on every side. There would be nowhere God's people could turn. God told his people to put on sackcloth and mourn bitterly. They were to roll in ashes and wail because they were about to feel the dreadful impact of the Lord's divine wrath.

In verse 27 God told Jeremiah that he had made him to be a metal tester, and the people were the ore. God wanted to purify his people. Jeremiah, as a metal tester, would soon see the quality of the metal of Judah's spiritual life. He would see that all the efforts of the Lord to purify his people were to no avail. These people were a hard people, like bronze or iron. The billows of God's judgment continued to blow fiercely to burn away the corrupting impurities in his people, but they were not being purified. They were not of precious metal but of hard metal from which the Lord could extract nothing of value. There was no discipline or punishment that could drive away the impurity of Judah's sin. There needed to be another way.

Jesus Christ alone can deal with sin by giving God's people a new nature. The old nature is not capable of good. This is why the Lord Jesus came. He came to offer us another life. His death on the cross can accomplish what no punishment or discipline could ever accomplish—a way to live the holy life that God requires.

For Consideration:

• What is it that keeps us from listening to the word of the Lord today?

- What does this chapter teach us about the seriousness of sin? Do we really understand how serious sin is?

- Was God just in punishing Judah? Explain.

- What was the connection in this chapter between obedience to the Lord and rest for the soul? Have you experienced this in your life? Explain.

For Prayer:

- Ask the Lord to show you just how serious a matter your sin really is.

- Ask the Lord to restore your delight in his word.

- Ask God to renew a spirit of repentance in your land today.

8

Temple Sermon

Read Jeremiah 7

In chapter 7 God asked Jeremiah to go to the temple and speak the word he would give him. By going to the temple, Jeremiah spoke to the religious people of his day. In obedience to the word of the Lord, Jeremiah stood at the gate of the temple and spoke the word God gave him for the people present that day.

Through his prophet the Lord God challenged the religious people of Judah to reform their ways (verse 3). Although they were a very religious people, their hearts were not right before God. Jeremiah told them that if they became obedient, they would be allowed to remain in Jerusalem.

We can only imagine the impact this statement would have had on these people going through the temple gates. They were being told that if they did not change their corrupt ways, their nation and temple would be taken from them. They were so insensitive to sin at this point in their history that they did not even know that anything was wrong.

In verse 4 Jeremiah told those at the temple that day not to trust in deceptive words. They had been hearing glorious sermons from the false prophets about the wonderful temple they had and the security they would always enjoy. Their security was in the temple and their traditions. They believed that as long as they brought their offerings and sacrifices to the temple, they could live any way they pleased. How wrong they were. They would soon discover that they were under the judgment of God.

From verses 5 and 6 we understand that the people who came to the temple were not living righteous lives. God accused them of dealing unjustly with their fellow citizens. They were oppressing the vulnerable in society: the foreigners, widows, and orphans. Some were even guilty of murder and idolatry. Their "Sunday morning" religion did not fool God. He looked at their hearts. These people were hypocrites, and God was angry with them. Only if they reformed their ways would God let them remain in the land he had given their ancestors.

The people coming to the temple had an air of spirituality, but they were trusting deceptive words (verse 8). The prophets and priests told them that their sin was not serious. They were stealing, murdering, committing adultery, committing perjury, burning incense to Baal, and following other gods (verse 9). Yet they still came to the temple to perform their rituals. They came into the presence of a holy God after committing such awful crimes. They were not repentant but believed that the formal rituals protected them from God's wrath (verse 10). In coming to the temple in this manner, they were making it a gathering place for criminals (verse 11). The Lord had been watching them.

God challenged his people to go to Shiloh, where he had first made his dwelling in the Promised Land. We read in Joshua 18:1 that Joshua set up the tabernacle in this town. Because of Israel's sin, however, the Lord had allowed the town to be destroyed and forgotten. The place that at one time was at the center of Israel's worship lay in ruins in Jeremiah's day. What happened to Shiloh would happen to the city of Jerusalem if the people would not repent (verses 13–14). God had already destroyed the northern kingdom of Israel (here referred to as Ephraim), and he would destroy Judah also (verse 15).

Because the people were not repentant, God told Jeremiah that he was not to pray for these people anymore (verse 16). God would not listen to any plea or petition for them. They had been warned repeatedly but had refused to listen to those warnings. It was time for their judgment to begin.

Jeremiah was told in verse 17 to look at what was happening in the towns of Judah and the streets of Jerusalem. Whole families were involved in the worship of the Queen of Heaven (verse 18). It is generally assumed that the Queen of Heaven is a reference to the Babylonian or Assyrian goddess Isthar. The people of Judah were provoking the one true God to anger by their idolatry. Pagan worship involved harmful and shameful acts (verse 19).

The wrath of God was going to be poured out on the land, its inhabitants, and its beasts (verse 20). Everything would suffer because of the unfaithfulness of God's people (see Romans 8:22). Nothing would extinguish the fire of his anger. All of their society would suffer because of this rebellion.

God was looking for something much more than burnt offerings and sacrifices (verse 21). He reminded his people that when he brought them out of the land of Egypt, he not only gave them commands concerning sacrifices and offerings, he also gave them the commandment to obey and walk in his ways (verses 22–23). He also promised their ancestors that they would be blessed in their obedience to him. Israel had concluded that all God wanted was sacrifices and offerings. They felt that they could live the way they wanted as long as they brought offerings and sacrifices to God.

The people of Israel refused to listen to the Lord. They chose instead to follow their own hearts and stubborn inclinations (verse 24). They had lived in rebellion from the time they left Egypt, rejecting the prophets God had sent to warn them. They had become more sinful from generation to generation (verse 26).

God warned Jeremiah in verse 27 that when he spoke these words to the people at the temple, they would not listen. As the people had treated the prophets before Jeremiah, so they would also treat him—they would reject his words. The role of the prophet is not always a glorious one. The prophet is called to proclaim the word of the Lord whether people listen or not.

Jeremiah was to remind the people he met that day at the temple that truth had perished among them and vanished from their lips. The prophets and the priests preached the lies that the people wanted to hear. There was a veneer of religion and spirituality, but there was no truth. The nation was completely corrupt and unfaithful to the covenant with the Lord God.

This was cause for great mourning. Jeremiah called his people to cut off their hair and throw it away (verse 29). This symbolized the Lord cutting off the nation and throwing it far from him. The people of Judah were to weep because the Lord had rejected and abandoned that generation for their atrocities. They had set up detestable idols in the house of God and burned their infant sons and daughters to the fire god Molech at a shrine in Topheth at the south end of Jerusalem (verses 30–31). A whole generation was lost to the holy things of God. What a sad picture God painted through his prophet Jeremiah.

Jeremiah told his people that the day was coming when this pagan shrine would be called the Valley of Slaughter. God himself would unleash his wrath on Judah. There in that valley, Judah would bury her dead until there was no more room (verse 32). The carcasses of the people left on the ground would become food for the wild animals and the birds of the air (verse 33). The Lord would end the sounds of joy and gladness. The voice of the bride and groom in the towns of Judah would be stopped. Instead, there would only be the sound of desolation (verse 34).

God's people clung to their religious activities but were guilty of underestimating the wrath of God against idolatry and child sacrifice. They were going to be severely judged by God for their evil ways.

This chapter challenges us to examine our hearts. Is our faith merely an outward show? God is looking for more than sacrifice and offerings. He is looking for a heart that is sincere and right before him.

For Consideration:

- Is there evidence of the hypocrisy of Jeremiah's day in our society as well?

- Why do we believe that God will punish others for their sin but not punish us?

- Is there evidence of truth perishing around us today? What happens to a society when truth perishes?

- What hope would we have if God did not deal with sin and rebellion?

For Prayer:

- Ask God to give us hearts of sincerity before him.

- Ask God to revive his truth in our day.

- Thank him that he is a holy God who will deal with sin and rebellion.

- Ask God to open our eyes to see things as he sees them in the church today.

9

Why Is There No Healing?

Read Jeremiah 8

Jeremiah had warned the people who had come to the temple that they would lose everything if they did not reform their ways and seek the Lord. In chapter 8 Jeremiah told the people of Judah about the judgment that was coming on them.

He began by describing a scene where the bodies of the dead were being dug from their graves (by enemy soldiers) and exposed to the sun, moon, and stars. Notice that there would be no distinction of people here. The bodies of kings and officials as well as the prophets, priests, and the people in general were all being treated with the same indignity.

What we need to understand here is that this was part of God's judgment for Judah's idolatry. Notice in verse 2 that these bodies were exposed to the sun, moon, and stars that these people had been worshiping. These bodies would not be reburied. They would be left as refuse on the ground. This was a terrible indignity to these human remains.

While these terrible things were happening to the human bodies in the graves, the fate of the living would be equally as terrible. Jeremiah prophesied that the survivors of the coming judgment would prefer to die than to live (verse 3).

Why were these people being judged so severely? Jeremiah began his explanation by asking two questions that really did not need an answer. The first of these questions was this: "When men fall down, do they not get up?" The answer was obvious. A man that falls usually gets back up on his feet. To remain on the ground would be foolish indeed.

The second question was similar: "When a man turns away, does he not return?" A man who gets up to go to work in the morning, does he return home? Or if a man gets lost, does he not try to find his way back? Again, the answer to Jeremiah's question was obvious.

This led Jeremiah to yet another question in verse 5: "Why then have these people turned away? Why does Jerusalem always turn away? They cling to deceit; they refuse to return." If a man who has fallen down gets back on his feet and a man who goes away comes back, why then did God's people not return to him? Why did God's people refuse to return to him?

God listened carefully to what his people were saying. He wanted some indication of repentance, but he did not hear it. They did not repent of their wickedness and return in obedience to God. He compared them to a horse charging into battle (verse 6). Nothing could distract them from charging after evil.

To further illustrate what he was saying, God reminded his people that the stork knew her season. The dove, the swift, and the thrush knew when it was time for them to migrate to warmer climates (verse 7). God's people, however, did not see that it was time for them to return to him and repent of their sins.

God had spoken powerfully to his people, but they did not listen to him. He sent his prophets, but his people rejected them. They were stubborn in their sinful ways. They did not know the simple requirements of God. This was not because they were ignorant of these requirements but because they were rebellious— they wanted their own way instead.

In verses 8 and 9 the people claimed to be wise because they had the law of God. They claimed to be the ones to have and proclaim the truth. They saw themselves as a religious people. The reality was that the sinful scribes handled God's law falsely.

These men made copies of God's law and taught it to the people. The scribes twisted the law to justify their own evil deeds and ease their consciences. Their so-called wisdom would be put to shame (verse 9). They and the people they taught would be dismayed and trapped in the very wisdom they claimed. All of Judah had rejected the word of the Lord.

Because they had turned their backs on the Lord and refused his word, their wives would be given to other men, and their fields to new owners (verse 10). The enemy would come in, rape their wives, and take their land (see Deuteronomy 28:30). Because the spiritual leaders perverted God's word for monetary gain, God would cause them to lose everything they had.

Jeremiah accused the priests and prophets of dressing the spiritual wounds of the people as though they were not serious (verse 11). These prophets and priests told the people that there would be peace when in reality there was severe impending judgment.

These spiritual leaders did not even feel shame in what they were doing. They did not know how to blush (verse 12). The Lord was quite clear in this matter. These people would fall. They would be brought down and punished. God would strip away their harvest (verse 13). There would be no grapes or figs, and the leaves would wither on the trees. God would strip them of his blessings.

Jesus told a parable in Matthew 25 of a man who left his servants to care for his belongings while he went away on a journey. To one servant he gave five talents; to the second he gave two talents; to the third he gave a single talent. In the owner's absence, the servant who received five talents and the one who received two talents doubled their money through careful investment. But the servant who had only one talent buried it. When the master returned, he rebuked the servant who buried his talent. The master took this one talent and gave it to the one who had put his money to the best use. Jesus told his audience that he would give to the person who already had, but he would take away from the person who was not a wise steward of his resources: "For everyone who has will be given more, and he will have an abundance. Whoever does not have, even what he has will be taken from him" (Matthew 25:29).

This is what was happening in Judah. God's people had not been faithful in what the Lord had called them to do. They were going to lose all they had received. This is a challenge for us today as well. Why should God give us more if we have not proven faithful with what we already have received?

In verses 14–15 Jeremiah shows us what the response of the people would be: "Why are we sitting here? Gather together! Let us flee to the fortified cities and perish there! For the LORD our God has doomed us to perish and given us poisoned water to drink, because we have sinned against him. We hoped for peace but no good has come, for a time of healing but there was only terror."

The people would wonder why they were just sitting around when the judgment of God was about to fall on them. They would flee to fortified cities for protection. The walls of the city, however, would not be able to keep them from the wrath of God. They were doomed to perish because they refused to repent of their sin. They were destined to drink the poisoned water of God's wrath. They had hoped for peace, but that peace would not come. They wanted to be healed, but instead they would be terrified by the wrath of God all around them.

Judah could hear the snorting of the enemy horses already moving closer (verse 16). The whole land trembled at the approaching hoof beats. The enemy would be like venomous snakes that could not be charmed. Judah would be bitten and not escape the wrath and judgment of God on her land (verse 17).

In light of this terrible disaster, Jeremiah mourned for the people of God (verse 18). His heart was faint as he could hear the cry of his people in captivity in Babylon. He asked the Lord in verse 19: "Is the LORD not in Zion? Is her King no longer there?" Where was God? What had the people done that he no longer listened to them? In their captivity they would remember the Lord asking himself: "Why have they provoked me to anger with their images, with their worthless foreign idols?"

There was a barrier of sin between Judah and her Lord. God would not share his glory with idols. The Lord had continued to plant the seed of his word in the ears of his people, but they had refused to listen and repent.

The time of the harvest of returning to the Lord had come

and gone, and the people were not saved (verse 20). The time of deliverance was past, and God was ready to judge. His people had not turned back to him, so they would perish in their sin.

Jeremiah felt the terror of this judgment of God on his people. Even as his people would be crushed, so he too would feel that crushing load on him. He asked the question: "Is there no balm in Gilead? Is there no physician there? Why then is there no healing for the wound of my people?" (verse 22).

The resin of the storax tree in Gilead, an area east of the Jordan River, was known for its healing qualities. Why was the wound of God's people left without healing? Why was it that God's people would go through such terrible devastation when God himself was willing to heal and forgive their sin and evil? Why were they so powerless to face the enemy when they had the power of Almighty God at their disposal? Why were they perishing in their sin when the forgiveness of God was there for all who repented?

The answer to this question is simply that they did not take advantage of the forgiveness found in repentance. They lived as poor beggars when the resources of God were at their disposal. They turned their backs on the only source of strength and power. Could it be that the same thing is happening in our day?

For Consideration:

• What keeps us from total surrender and obedience to God?

• Has our society lost the art of blushing for its sin? Explain.

• In what way is the Word handled falsely in our day?

• Is there evidence of lack of blessing in our society? Has our disobedience brought a curse on us?

For Prayer:

• Ask God to open your eyes to any way you are not living in complete obedience to him.

• Ask him to open the eyes of your society to see the result of the disregard for the righteous ways of God in our day.

- Thank the Lord that there is a balm in Gilead. Thank him that there is healing for the hurts of our nation in him.

10

Tears for God's People

Read Jeremiah 9

In chapter 9 Jeremiah continued to prophesy to God's people
of the judgment that was coming on them because they had
rejected the Lord. This was not an easy message to proclaim.
This true prophet felt the impact of his message. Here in chapter 9
we catch a glimpse of the difficulty of his ministry.

In verse 1 Jeremiah cried out in anguish: "Oh, that my head
were a spring of water and my eyes a fountain of tears! I would
weep day and night for the slain of my people." Jeremiah's heart
was broken for his people. He told them that he did not have
enough tears to express his grief. His head would have to be a
spring of water, and his eyes would have to be fountains to express
the depth of grief he felt for them.

Notice also that Jeremiah felt the repulsion of God for sin in
the lives of his people. In verse 2 he expressed his desire to find a
place in the desert where he could go to be away from his people
and their sinful ways. God's people were adulterers. They could
not be trusted. The truth was not on their lips. Jeremiah compared
their tongues to a bow that shot out its lies (verse 3). Like arrows,
those lies hit their marks and did their deadly work. God's people

went from one sin to another and disregarded God and his ways.

Things had become so bad in the land that the people could not even trust those who were closest to them (verse 4). Their brothers were deceivers, and their friends slandered them. There was no one who practiced the truth (verse 5). They were skilled at lying and wore themselves out pursuing sin. The people lived in the midst of deception among others who did not acknowledge God.

In verse 7 God promised to refine and test his people because of their evil. These people were deceptive. They spoke with gentleness only to set traps for their neighbors (verse 8). God saw this hypocrisy, and he would punish them for it (verse 9).

Verse 10 is a picture of the desolation that was to come to Judah. Jeremiah wept and wailed for the mountains. He lamented for the desert pastures, which were once luscious but would become abandoned. The lowing of cattle would no longer be heard in the land. The birds of the air would fly away, and even the wild animals would leave. The whole land would become a desert. The beautiful city of Jerusalem would become a heap of ruins and a place where the wild jackals roamed (verse 11). The towns of Judah would be laid waste so that no one could live in them. This was the result of Judah's dishonesty and rebellion against God.

A call went out in verse 12 to the wise men of the land. They were challenged to consider why these things had happened. Verse 13 makes it very clear that the reason why this judgment fell was because the people had forsaken the law of the Lord, worshiping idols and following the stubborn inclinations of their own hearts.

Because of their sin, God would give them bitter food to eat and force them to drink poisoned water (verse 15). God's people would be separated from the Promised Land and scattered among the nations. God would pursue them with the sword until they were destroyed (verse 16). No doubt, it would be very difficult for the people of Jeremiah's day to understand this type of judgment from their loving Lord God.

God called for the professional mourners of the land because this was a time for great sorrow (verse 17). These women were to come and wail over the people of God. The mourners were to lead the people of God in lamenting over their sin and its consequences (verses 18–19). These skilled women were to teach their own daughters to wail and lament because so much sorrow needed to be expressed over the sins of Judah (verse 20). Death would climb in through the windows and enter into every fortress (verse 21). There was nothing they could do to stop this terror. Children would be cut off in the streets and their young men from the public squares. The bodies of their men would lie in the open fields like refuse, cut down like grain left behind by the reaper (verse 22). No one would gather these bodies. They would be left to decay in the open field.

In those days the strong man could not boast in his strength because his strength would never be able to save him from the anger of God (verse 23). There would be no riches that could avert the wrath of a holy and incorruptible God. There would be only one thing that people in Judah could boast of in the day of judgment—that they understood and knew their God (verse 24).

In the day of the Lord's wrath, we can boast of nothing in ourselves. Our entire boast must be in the Lord, his kindness, justice, and righteousness. Our salvation depends entirely on his kindness. Our only boast can be in the fact that God has reached out to us in mercy and love to forgive and cleanse. Were it not for this kindness, we would all be lost in sin. Our boast cannot be in our wisdom, strength, or wealth. It can only be in the grace and kindness of God.

Jeremiah reminded his people that the day was coming when the Lord would punish all those who were circumcised only in the flesh. The foreign nations around them were uncircumcised, and therefore outside the covenant with God. But Israel, though circumcised in the flesh, was uncircumcised of heart. The people of God had maintained their rituals, but they were as far from God as the pagan nations around them. God looked at the heart. Outward signs and rituals did not matter to him.

You may go to a good church. You may have been baptized. Maybe you are even a leader in your church. The question, however, is this: Are you right with God in your heart? The house of Israel had all the externals, but the people were internally corrupt. God was looking for those whose hearts were sincere.

For Consideration:

- How easy would it have been for the people of Jeremiah's day to accept that, though they were a religious people, God would judge them so severely?

- Here in this section, we see something of the heart of Jeremiah as a prophet. Do you see evidence in your life of God's heart for the lost and backslidden?

- What does this chapter teach us about the importance of a sincere heart?

For Prayer:

- Ask God to give you more of his heart.

- Ask God to give you a sincere heart that is in tune with him.

- Ask God to break any particular hold that sin may have on you today.

- Ask God to move in power among his people today so that they demonstrate truth and righteousness to those around them.

11

God and the Idols

Read Jeremiah 10:1–16

There is to be a difference between the people of God and the people of the world. In this section of his prophecy, Jeremiah challenged his people to observe the foolishness of the nations around them and to avoid their pagan ways. Here Jeremiah set apart the true God of Israel from the false gods of Judah's neighbors.

Jeremiah began in verse 2 by telling his people that they were not to learn the ways of the nations or be terrified by signs in the skies. These nations looked to the skies for answers to their problems. They charted the alignment of the stars and planets in order to interpret national and personal events. The people of God, however, were to base their lives on a very different standard—God's holy laws. They were not to follow after the other nations, looking to the skies and the stars for their direction and guidance.

As believers, we are commanded to turn from horoscopes and fortune telling for direction. Our guidance and confidence should always be in the sovereign Creator of history, the Lord God alone. As his children, we must avoid the deceitful powers of evil.

In verses 3 to 5, Jeremiah showed his people the foolishness of the customs and traditions of the nations. Their artisans cut down trees and shaped the wood into a particular form with a chisel. They would take that piece of wood, adorn it with gold and silver, and nail it down so that it would not topple over. This wooden idol had no power to help itself or the humans who made it.

In verse 5 Jeremiah compared an idol to "a scarecrow in a melon patch," which might keep the birds away from the garden but was useless for anything else. Idols needed to be carried from place to place because they could not walk by themselves. They could not do any harm or any good because there was no life in them at all. False gods could neither bless nor curse humans, so worship of them was futile.

How different was the one true God of Israel. There was no god like him in greatness among Israel's neighbors. His name was mighty in power (verse 6). All the nations of the ancient world knew of his great deeds, and their reverence was his due (verse 7). There was no one like God in wisdom among all the wise men of the kingdoms of that day.

It is hard to miss the comparison that Jeremiah made. The God of Israel was all-powerful while the gods of the nations could not even stand or walk by themselves. The wisdom of the God of Israel confounded the wisest people on the earth while the gods of the nations could not even speak. The God of Israel carried his people's burdens while the gods of the nations were burdens to be carried. There was no comparison between the God of Israel and the gods of the nations. How could anyone in their right mind turn from the true God of Israel to serve powerless idols?

Jeremiah reminded his people in verse 8 that those who served false gods were senseless and foolish. They allowed themselves to be taught by speechless idols when the wisdom of the creator God was at their disposal.

The false gods of the nations were made from gold and silver imported from far-off countries (verse 9). The artisans shaped them and dressed them in the royal colors of purple and blue, but these idols were not kings. The God of Israel, however, is truly God and King. Unlike the idols that had no life, the God of Israel is living and eternal (verse 10). He was not created. As an eternal God, he always existed. He has no beginning or end. He is King forever and reigns over his creation. When he is angry, the earth trembles (verse 10). The ancient nations, with all their power and strength, could not endure the wrath of this awesome God. They were no match for his glory and his power.

The idols of the nations did not create this world. They did not have life in themselves. They could not stand without human intervention. They would also perish with the earth (verse 11). The God of Israel, however, created the earth by his great power, and his great wisdom founded it (verse 12). To this day, scientists are still trying to understand the wisdom that put this universe in place. We know that the God of Israel stretched out this universe by his own understanding. No one taught him anything.

The God of ancient Israel was a God of awesome power. When he thundered, the waters roared (verse 13). We see that power today in the floodwaters that ravage this earth. Nothing can stand against these waters. This God still makes the clouds rise and sends forth lightning. At his command, the winds are brought from their storehouses. He controls the forces of nature, which were created by him and move at his command. Human beings, with all their power and understanding, are powerless against these forces. There is no god like the true God.

The greatest knowledge we have is nothing compared to the knowledge of God. In verse 14 Jeremiah described the goldsmiths who crafted idols as being ashamed of their works. They knew that these idols were frauds. They knew that there was no breath in them. These idols, Jeremiah told his people, were worthless objects of mockery. They were objects to laugh at. No one should take them seriously. When the judgment of God came, these idols would perish. They could not protect their worshippers from the wrath of the holy God of Israel.

The God of Israel was different from the idols of the nations. The Old Testament laws forbade any representation of God (see Exodus 20:4). How could an artisan ever portray the power and majesty of the creator God? The God of Israel was far greater than anything humans could ever portray through their art. Verse 16 described this awesome God as "the Portion of Jacob." He had chosen Jacob to be his special treasure, and he would be Jacob's treasure. He desired to enter into an intimate relationship with

Jacob and his descendants. He called the children of Israel to be his people and promised to be their God. What an honor this was! The Creator of the universe desired to be the personal God of Jacob and his descendants. His favor would rest on them. They would be the tribe of his inheritance. Just to think that God Almighty still wants to enter a deep and intimate relationship with his people is beyond human comprehension.

We can only imagine the reaction of the people of Jeremiah's day to this message from God. They would not have appreciated his comments about their pagan worship of false gods. The Lord called Jeremiah to speak out against Judah's idolatry. Particularly, he was to speak out against the tendency of God's people to fall into the idolatry of their Gentile neighbors and turn their backs on the one true God.

Jeremiah's prophecy challenges us afresh today to look again at the awesomeness of our God and marvel at the fact that he should chose us to be his children. We dare not turn from him to worship lesser things.

For Consideration:

• What idols do we have in our day?

• Consider what Jeremiah said about the idols of his day. How do these truths apply to the idols of our day?

• What causes us to lose sight of the awesomeness of God?

• Have you experienced the depth of relationship that Jeremiah spoke of in this chapter?

For Prayer:

• Ask God to reveal to you the idols that we worship in our day.

• Thank him that he has chosen us to be his people.

• Take a moment to consider the awesomeness of this God we serve. Thank him for who he is and what he has done.

- Thank the Lord that he wants to enter a deep relationship with you as his child.

12

Distress in the Land

Read Jeremiah 10:17–25

In the last section, Jeremiah spoke of the foolishness of idolatry. God was angry with his people because they had turned their backs on him to serve worthless idols. In this next section, Jeremiah lamented the imminent capture of Judah.

In verse 17 the Lord commanded his people to pack their bags. The capital city of Jerusalem had been their fortress for hundreds of years. It had protected them from their enemies and kept them safe and secure. This would be the case no more. Judah had angered the Lord with her evil. The Lord himself would come against her, and the land would soon be under siege. The Lord would bring distress on his people. He would "hurl" them out of the Promised Land (verse 18). The word "hurl" indicates that they would be violently and forcibly removed.

In verse 19 Jeremiah foresaw the people lamenting their condition: "Woe to me because of my injury! My wound is incurable!" they cried. Notice here that their injuries were incurable. Nothing could be done about them. Their rebellion was firmly entrenched and could not be removed. They had committed themselves to sin and rebellion, and there they would remain.

Judah's tents were destroyed. The ropes that supported them were snapped, and there was nothing to hold them up (verse 20). All their supports were gone. Judah was pictured as a mother who had lost her children and had no one to help her rebuild what was destroyed.

Their shepherds were senseless (verse 21). The reference here to shepherds is a reference to the spiritual and political leaders of Judah. They were senseless because they did not inquire of the Lord. They did things in their own way and depended on their own strength. The result was that they did not prosper, and the sheep were scattered. God's people were going into exile. The enemy would come in and take them captive. The leaders were to blame because they had not taken the time to seek the Lord on behalf of the people. Everything would be lost.

How important it is that spiritual leaders understand their role as leaders of God's sheep. They are to be people of prayer as they seek the will of God. They must be humble and inquire of God on behalf of the people who depend on them. Human strength and wisdom is not enough. Leaders must trust in God and him alone.

Notice the result of not inquiring of the Lord in verse 22. There was great commotion in the north because the enemy was already on its way. Babylon was preparing her attack against Judah. The towns of Judah would be desolate and would become a haunt for jackals and wild animals. The once-prosperous nation would become a place where the wild animals freely roamed.

As Jeremiah reflected on what was happening in his prophecy, he was reminded that a man's life is not his own (verse 23). I was reminded of this when I was traveling to a local coffee shop to meet my wife. To this day, I cannot recall what happened. It seems that I blacked out in my car, crashed through a guardrail, and flipped my car over. As I reflect on this accident, I am very much aware that my life is not my own. I have no guarantee of tomorrow. God reserves the right to take my life at any time—any hour of any day.

It is also not for us to determine the length of our own lives. We are not here on this earth for ourselves. We belong to the Lord and must live in the reality of God's absolute lordship over our lives. It is no longer our wills but his that must be done. We must learn to die daily to ourselves and surrender to him. This was a lesson that Israel and Judah had failed to learn. They had lived as they pleased and forgot whose they were.

In verse 24 Jeremiah identified himself with the sins of Judah and cried out to God to correct him. Judah believed she could break God's laws without consequence, but she would soon see how wrong she was. For this reason, Jeremiah cried out: "Correct me, LORD, but only with justice—not in your anger, lest you reduce me to nothing."

If God were to correct us in anger, we would perish. How thankful we ought to be that the Lord God will correct us with great patience and grace. This ought to be the cry of every heart that loves the Lord.

Jeremiah wanted to divert God's anger to the pagan nations that did not know him (verse 25). The nations had already devastated the people of God in the northern kingdom and were poised to come against the southern kingdom of Judah. The severe violence against God's people would not go unnoticed. The nations would be corrected for their evil actions against God's children.

We see here in this section that the Lord will correct his people. Sometimes he will take drastic measures to purge evil from them. In the days of Jeremiah, God's people had forsaken the Mosaic covenant and were living in rebellion. Their shepherds refused to inquire of God, and God's people had fallen into moral corruption. The result was that God's people were lost, and he would send an enemy to devour them. Nothing would be left of their blessings. Jeremiah pleaded with God, on behalf of his people, to correct them gently, lest they be completely destroyed.

For Consideration:

- Jeremiah reminds us here that our lives are not our own. Could it be that you have been living your life as though it were your own?

- Are you ready in your spiritual life to ask the Lord to correct you?

- How important is it that we inquire of the Lord in all that we do?

For Prayer:

- Thank the Lord that he is willing to correct us with gentleness.

- Ask the Lord to give us leaders who inquire of him.

- Ask the Lord to forgive you for the way you have chosen to live your life, as if it were your own to do as you pleased. Surrender yourself afresh to the Lord and his service.

13

The Broken Covenant

Read Jeremiah 11

God had been warning his people through Jeremiah that their end would come, and the enemy was approaching. God's people had turned their backs on him to serve the idols of their pagan neighbors. They had broken their covenant relationship with the Lord God. Here in chapter 11 God reminded his people of the binding terms of the Mosaic covenant, which included judgment for disobedience.

The word of the Lord came to Jeremiah to remind Judah of the terms of the covenant (verse 2). The covenant promised curses for disobedience and blessings for obedience. Jeremiah was to remind the people of the promise of the Lord to curse anyone who deviated from his laws. The terms of this covenant were stipulated and agreed to by the people of God when he brought them up out of Egypt, the land of their bondage (verse 4). God had told them that they were to do everything that he had commanded them. All he asked was that they obey his will. In so doing, they would be his people and he would be their God (verse 4).

What an incredible honor it was to be the people of God. As his people, they would experience his blessing in their lives. His presence would go before them and be on them in all that they did. His protection and guidance would be their portion. Who could come against them when God was for them? After they had experienced severe oppression in Egypt, God promised to stand between them and Egypt or any other enemy who would come seeking their harm. All he was asking in return was that they obey him and repent when they disobeyed.

God reminded Jeremiah that the Mosaic covenant was to be the means by which God would fulfill his promise to Abraham of a Promised Land for his descendants (verse 5). Israel's prosperity in a land flowing with milk and honey was directly linked to her obedience to God and his word. Jeremiah agreed by saying: "Amen, LORD." He was obviously touched by the remembrance of the blessings and intimacy that God had promised Israel so long ago.

God told Jeremiah in verses 6–8 to remind the people of what their ancestors had done. They had experienced the wonderful deliverance of the Lord from the bondage of Egypt. This powerful blessing was a foretaste of what was in store for them in the Promised Land. Despite the evidence of God's blessing and the promises he gave them, they still turned their backs on God and followed the stubborn intents of their hearts. Instead of bringing covenantal blessings on themselves, they brought covenantal curses.

Jeremiah's generation had the advantage of seeing what had happened in the wilderness to those who had disobeyed the Lord. That whole generation perished without ever seeing the fulfillment of the promises God had given them. The people of Jeremiah's day had seen what happened when God's people broke their covenant with him. Despite this understanding, however, they fell into the same sin of stubbornness as their ancestors (verse 10). Both the northern kingdom of Israel and the southern kingdom of Judah broke their covenant relationship with God.

Because God's people refused to learn from their history, they too would also feel the effects of the covenantal curses. Disaster would fall on Jeremiah's generation as well. They would cry out to God, but he would not listen to them (verse 11). Intimacy with God had been broken, so God would refuse to listen to their prayers.

In their day of distress, Jeremiah prophesied that God's people would cry out to their foreign gods, which would not answer. Although their false gods were as numerous as the number of towns in their nation, no idols would be able to deliver their worshipers in the day of God's judgment (verses 12–13).

The sentence on Judah had been passed. A general command went out from God in verse 14: "Do not pray for this people nor offer any plea or petition for them, because I will not listen when they call to me in the time of their distress." Prayer would not do them any good because they were unrepentant. God had already passed his sentence, and no amount of pleading would change his mind. There comes a time when God stops pleading with his people.

Notice in verse 15 that although God's people continued to offer him their empty rituals, he would not accept them. "What is my beloved doing in my temple as she works out her evil schemes with many? Can consecrated meat avert your punishment? When you engage in your wickedness, then you rejoice."

God asked his people what they were doing in his temple. While he still called the people his "beloved," he would not accept their false worship. Did they think that they could break his laws and then bring a sacrifice to substitute for repentance? God would not accept their hypocrisy. He was angry with them, and their punishment would not be averted.

In verse 16 Jeremiah reminded his people that the Lord had planted them and caused them to be like a thriving olive tree. They had once been spiritually productive, but that time had passed. At present, they produced only evil fruit that called for judgment. A mighty storm of God's wrath would come and burn them up. The Lord, who had planted them, decreed their destruction. They no longer brought delight to his heart because they had turned from him to offer their sacrifices to Baal (verse 17).

In verses 18 to 23, God revealed what the people of Judah felt toward Jeremiah. They secretly plotted to kill him, and the Lord revealed this plan to the prophet. Obviously, Jeremiah had not yet finished the work God had called him to do, so he would be preserved from the wrath of the people. Jeremiah compared himself to a gentle lamb being led to the slaughter. He was humanly helpless.

Notice what the people were saying about Jeremiah in verse 19. They wanted to cut him down like a tree, destroy his fruit, and remove any remembrance of his ministry and words. They wanted nothing to do with what he said, and there was violence in their hearts.

Notice the response of Jeremiah to these revelations. In verse 20 he committed his cause to the Lord, who judges righteously and tests the heart. He knew God would do what was right. He did not take this matter into his own hands by trying to speak to the people about misconceptions they might have about his ministry. He did not try to resolve any issues between himself and those who had been offended by his messages. He simply committed the matter to God and entrusted his life into God's sovereign hands.

Some men of Jeremiah's hometown of Anathoth were among those who sought to kill him. They told him that if he continued to prophesy in the name of the Lord, they would kill him (verse 21). God heard what they were saying and chose to punish them. God had promised to protect Jeremiah (1:8), and the Lord was faithful to his word.

In verse 22 God told Jeremiah that the wicked men of Anathoth would die by the sword. Their sons and their daughters would perish in a famine. Not a remnant of them would be left. The death they schemed against innocent Jeremiah would be executed against them. God stood firmly behind Jeremiah, and anyone who rejected him and his message rejected God himself.

We can only imagine how humbling it must have been for Jeremiah to hear this word from the Lord. It would have also been very difficult to watch his own hometown perish because it refused his ministry and the message God had given him. It reminds us how firmly God stands behind his servants.

God's hand was on Jeremiah. The one who had called and anointed him for this ministry would also protect him from the enemy. The God who calls us will also keep us. What a comfort this is to us as we minister in the name of the Lord Almighty.

For Consideration:

- What does God expect of us today as people of the new covenant?

- What does this passage teach us about our responsibility before the Lord? What commitments have you made to the Lord?

- What comfort do you receive from the way God's hand of protection was on Jeremiah?

- What warning is there here for us in regard to respecting God's servants? How can we show disrespect for the servants that God has anointed over us?

For Prayer:

- Take a moment to pray for those that God has placed over you spiritually.

- Ask God to give you the grace to be faithful to your covenant relationship with him.

- Thank him for the protection and blessing he promises to all who continue in obedience to him.

14

Why?

Read Jeremiah 12

Even servants of God have their moments of doubt. The Lord's ways are much higher than our ways. We cannot possibly understand the ways of an eternal and sovereign God. Here in chapter 12, Jeremiah questioned what was happening around him.

In verse 1 Jeremiah began with a statement about the righteousness of God. "You are always righteous, O LORD, when I bring a case before you." That is to say, everything God does is right and holy. He can never be accused of wrongdoing. Evil and sin cannot possibly come from the heart of God. Jeremiah was comforting himself with these thoughts and praises. We need to remember that in the last chapter, God revealed to the prophet that even the people of his own hometown were seeking to kill him. Even though things seemed to be against him, Jeremiah's confidence was still in the Lord his God, who would do what was right. Jeremiah did not question the righteousness of God here, but he did have some questions for God.

"I would speak with you about your justice," Jeremiah told the Lord in verse 1. "Why does the way of the wicked prosper?

Why do all the faithless live at ease?" This question is often asked in Scripture, but never directly answered (see Job 21:7; Psalm 37; Habakkuk 1:12–17). This was particularly difficult for Jeremiah to understand in light of the fact that his own people wanted to kill him because he spoke what the Lord called him to speak.

Jeremiah compared his people to a plant (verse 2). The Lord planted them, and they took root and even bore fruit. The fruit Jeremiah referred to here was not spiritual fruit. Their physical fruit consisted of many children and prosperity in this life. They lived successful, abundant lives and appeared to be productive and comfortable. They spoke about the Lord and his ways, but their hearts were corrupt. Jeremiah wanted to know why these people prospered.

Jeremiah knew that the Lord understood the thoughts of his heart. God knew the confusion his prophet felt as he watched injustice prevail in the land. God saw the wicked prosper even though they sought to kill his prophets. Jeremiah did not understand why this was happening, but he did not question what God was doing.

In frustration, Jeremiah cried out in verse 3: "Drag them off like sheep to be butchered! Set them apart for the day of slaughter!" Jeremiah was frustrated with the evil he saw around him, so he cried out for God to move in justice and deal with this evil. He longed to see evil people removed from the land.

As Jeremiah looked around him, he did see the judgment of God on the land. The land was parched and the grass was withering. The birds and the animals were perishing because the land was not producing the food they needed. The blessing of God had been removed.

Despite the obvious judgment of God already on the land, the people were saying: "He will not see what happens to us" (verse 4). In saying this, the people mocked Jeremiah. They were saying that while Jeremiah made these predictions of judgment, he would not see their fulfillment. They did not believe his predictions, and they were planning to kill him before anything could be fulfilled.

God's response to Jeremiah in verse 5 almost seems to be without pity: "If you have raced with men on foot and they have worn you out, how can you compete with horses? If you stumble in safe country, how will you manage in the thickets by the Jordan?" In other words, if the people of his own land wore him out by their death threats, how could he expect to survive the rest of his ministry? God was telling Jeremiah that things were going to get more difficult for him. The reaction of the people of his hometown was just the beginning. God was calling him to compete with horses instead of men and to survive in the wild thickets of the Jordan instead of in the safe country in which he presently ministered. God was calling Jeremiah to greater and more difficult things. What he experienced in his hometown of Anathoth was simply training for future hardship.

In verse 6 God reminded Jeremiah that his family would not support his ministry. He was not to trust them, even though they spoke well of him. Jeremiah would have to persevere without the support of his family and friends. His ministry would be a lonely one, and God did not apologize for this. He expected Jeremiah to persevere through these tough times, even when he did not have answers to the questions that perplexed him.

In verse 7 God mourned over his people that he would forsake, abandon, and give into the hands of their enemies. His inheritance was the people of Judah, and he would turn his back on them. It is easy to see the grief of the Lord in this statement. The one he was turning over to the enemy was the one he loved. It grieved the heart of God to do this, but justice demanded punishment.

Notice in verse 8 how God's inheritance had turned her back on him. The nation he loved had become like a lion roaring ferociously at him. God's people wanted nothing more to do with him. Those whom he once loved dearly had become so rebellious that he had to turn his heart from them. As he did with his Son, Jesus Christ, on the cross when he bore our sin, God was forced to turn his back on his people.

It is important that we understand here that when God said he hated them, he was telling them that he rejected what they had become because of sin. They were no longer a people in whom he could delight. They roared against him and pushed aside his every effort to approach them. This was what he hated about them.

Judah was compared in verse 9 to a speckled bird of prey. This is very different from the pure white dove of the Song of

Solomon (Song of Solomon 5:2; 6:9). The fact that she was a bird of prey made her an unclean bird, according to the law of Moses. The fact that she was speckled and not pure white was symbolic of the pollution and corruption of her heart. Jeremiah prophesied that other birds of prey would surround her and devour her. Judah wanted to be like the nations, so she polluted herself with their pagan customs and idols. In the end, the very nations she wanted to be like would devour her.

Jeremiah prophesied that shepherds would come ruin the vineyard and trample the fields of Judah (verse 10). These shepherds were not true shepherds. They were pagan leaders sent by God to judge his people. This may refer to the Babylonians who captured and destroyed Jerusalem in 586 BC. These shepherds would turn the pleasant fields into wastelands (verse 11). The land that God had promised his people as a land flowing with milk and honey would become a desert under his righteous judgment.

Destroyers would come over the barren heights of Judah in swarms. They would be instruments of God to judge his people. These destroyers would devour the land from one end to the other. There would be no place of safety (verse 12). While these foreigners would take over the nation of Judah, they would obtain nothing from it. The blessing of God would be removed from the land. Neither God's people nor the foreigners would find blessing in it. They would plant wheat but would gather nothing but thorns. They would wear themselves out trying to plant and harvest but would get nothing for their labors.

God would not forget his people. He would hand them over to the enemy for a time, but he would return a remnant of them to their land. God would uproot these foreigners and would again have compassion on his people (verse 15). He would remember them in their distant land of exile and bring them back to their inheritance. Jeremiah prophesied that the day was coming when God's blessing would again come to his people. He would raise them again to a place of honor.

In verses 16–17 Jeremiah prophesied to the foreigners who would occupy the land of Judah. If they learned the ways of the people of God and turned their allegiance over to him alone, then they would be established in the land when he restored his people after their captivity. These Gentiles could also experience God's blessing through obedience to his laws and live at peace among the people of God. If, on the other hand, they did not listen but turned their backs on the Lord God of Israel, then they would perish and be uprooted from the land.

Jeremiah began this chapter by asking the Lord about the injustice he saw around him. God reminded Jeremiah that he would bring justice in his own time. It grieved the heart of God to judge his own beloved children, but he would still judge them. This chapter also shows us the compassion of God for all nations and peoples. He openly invited them through Jeremiah to turn from their evil ways and join his people in the blessing he delighted to pour on them.

It is important that we note the call of the Lord on the life of Jeremiah. God was stretching his faith. The understanding that there were people seeking his life was not easy for Jeremiah. God told him, however, that this was just the beginning of trouble—God was calling him to deeper waters. The Lord was going to give him even more powerful words to share with other nations. Things were just getting started, so God challenged Jeremiah to get ready for what was to come. God was preparing him for greater things.

For Consideration:

* Have you ever questioned the justice of God? What did God tell Jeremiah about this in chapter 12? Do sinners seem to prosper in our day?

* Compare the attitudes of God and Jeremiah toward the sinner. Is God's patience and love toward the sinner greater than ours is? Explain.

* What does this chapter teach us about the desire of God for the nations?

* How was God preparing Jeremiah for greater things? Have you ever felt that God was stretching your faith? Explain.

For Prayer:

- Thank God that he is a God of justice.

- Thank him that, while he will not hesitate to judge sin, he is a God of wonderful compassion.

- Are you being stretched by the Lord God in your ministry and personal life? Thank him that he is doing this to prepare you for greater ministry. Ask him to give you grace to persevere through this stretching, so that you can be strengthened and better equipped to serve him.

15

Jeremiah's Linen Belt

Read Jeremiah 13:1–11

In chapter 13 the Lord asked Jeremiah to do something very peculiar. He told him to buy a linen belt and put it around his waist. The word translated as *belt* in the New International Version (NIV) is translated differently in other versions. The King James Version (KJV) uses the word *girdle*. The Revised Standard Version (RSV) refers to a *waist cloth*. The New King James Version (NKJV) uses the word *sash*. While it is unclear exactly what the prophet was to buy, it is generally agreed that it was a piece of clothing worn close to the skin. The Lord told Jeremiah that this belt was not to touch water. This meant that the prophet was not to wash it.

In obedience to the Lord, the prophet bought this garment and put it around his waist. It was only when he had obeyed the Lord in this matter that the word of the Lord came a second time to him (verse 3). This cannot go unnoticed. There are times when the Lord does not give us the whole picture. He requires that we be obedient to him in what is already revealed before showing us more. Often we want to see the whole picture before moving forward.

In verse 4 the Lord told the prophet that he was to go to the region of Perath (NIV) or the Euphrates (KJV, NKJV, RSV) and bury the belt in a crevice of a rock. The Hebrew word *Parath* is generally used in Scripture to speak of the region of the Euphrates. If Jeremiah was in the region of Jerusalem at this time, he would have had to travel about five hundred miles (eight hundred kilometers) to be obedient to this command of the Lord. This would have required a very special effort on the part of Jeremiah. It also tells us that God wanted to communicate something very significant in this act.

Imagine that Jeremiah had to submit a report of his activities for that month. What would that report have looked like? He had walked five hundred miles to bury his belt under a rock. In an age of productivity and rush, we need to learn the importance of obedience. What Jeremiah did that day did not seem to be terribly spectacular, but it was what the Lord was asking him to do. At this point, Jeremiah did not even know why he was asked to bury the belt. Only by obeying the Lord would he see the next step.

For many days the Lord did not speak to Jeremiah about this belt (verse 6). The day came, however, when the Lord spoke again to him on this matter. He asked the prophet to return to Perath and dig up the belt. Still Jeremiah did not know why the Lord was asking him to do this. In obedience to the Lord, the prophet returned to get the belt. He dug it up and discovered that it was useless.

Only after he had dug up the belt did the Lord reveal to the prophet the reason for these strange requests. God told Jeremiah in verse 9 that just as this garment was ruined, so he would ruin the pride of the people of Judah and Jerusalem.

God reminded the prophet that his people were wicked. They had refused to listen to the words God had given them through the prophets. They insisted on following the stubbornness of their own hearts. They chose to seek other gods—to worship and to serve them. Because of their evil, these people were like this garment. They were corrupt and useless to God.

Just as Jeremiah had bound this garment around his waist, so God had bound his people to him. They were to enjoy his blessing and rejoice in intimacy with him. Instead, however, they became dirty and corrupt. Their sin and rebellion ruined the relationship they had with God. The fact that Jeremiah was not allowed to wash this garment represented the fact that God's people had refused to wash themselves and keep themselves from the impurity of the world.

Notice also in verse 11 what the Lord said about his people: "'I bound the whole house of Israel and the whole house of Judah to me,' declares the LORD, 'to be my people for my renown and praise and honor.'"

I like to imagine a man purchasing a belt or sash and wearing it proudly as he walks about the town. This is what God said about his people in verse 11. He told Jeremiah that he was proud of his people. He delighted in them and wanted them to bring him praise and honor. In other words, God wanted to reveal himself through this people. He wanted the world to see his grace and compassion in how he dealt with his people. He wanted to reveal his power and his majesty through them to the world. They would be instruments to bring praise and honor to his holy name.

This is what the Lord God wants to do through you and me today. He wants to be proud of us. He wants to reveal his glory through us. He wants to draw close to us and show the world through us who he is and what he can do. What a privilege we have as his people.

It is significant that the prophet went to the region of the Euphrates. This was the region where the Babylonians lived and where God's people would be into exile. Jeremiah traced the steps of the captured people walking into exile, even before it happened. Jeremiah's actions were filled with prophetic symbolism.

While Jeremiah did not understand what the Lord was doing, he was obedient to the Lord's leading. Only as he obeyed was the next step revealed. Through his actions that day, Jeremiah revealed the heart of God for his people. They had failed to honor their communion with the Lord, and, like Jeremiah's belt, they had become useless to God for advancing his kingdom.

For Consideration:

• What does this illustration teach us about obedience to the Lord?

- What does this section of Scripture teach us about what God requires of us? Compare human planning with God's leading.

- Are you at a place in your spiritual life where you can hear and listen to the leading of the Lord? Have there been times when you were so busy with your own agenda that you failed to hear what the Lord was telling you?

- What do we learn here about how God leads us step by step? Is it important that we understand the whole picture before obeying what has been revealed?

- What does this passage teach us about the type of relationship God wants to have with his children?

For Prayer:
- Ask God to help you to be obedient even when you do not see the whole picture.

- Thank God for the privilege we have to represent him, his love, and his power in this world.

- Ask the Lord to reveal any sin that would keep you from experiencing the intimacy he wants with you.

- Thank God that his ways are different from ours. Ask him to give you the courage and faithfulness to be obedient even when things are not clear, like Jeremiah.

16

Pictures of Judgment

Read Jeremiah 13:12–27

I n this section of prophecy, the Lord painted a number of pictures of the judgment that was going to come on the people of God in the days of Jeremiah. We will look at these pictures individually.

Wineskins (verses 12–14)

The first picture God gave to Jeremiah was a picture of a wineskin. Jeremiah was to tell the people that every wineskin should be filled with wine. God told Jeremiah that the people would say that they already knew this. What God meant, however, was very different from what the people understood.

For the people of Judah, a full wineskin meant that they would have all they needed for their drunken lifestyle. This was not what God meant. For God, the land was the wineskin that he would fill with the wine of his wrath (verse 13). From the ordinary citizens of the land to the kings, prophets, and priests—all would be filled with this drunkenness. God's people were going to be judged. That judgment would be so terrible that they would stumble and fall under it like drunkards falling on the street. They would be overwhelmed not with wine but with the fierce wrath of God.

In this first picture, we see that the Lord was going to pour out his anger on his people. Judah was already being filled with the wine of God's wrath like a wineskin about to burst. God's people would drink the cup of his fury.

Darkness (verses 15–16)

The second illustration God gave to Jeremiah was one of darkness. Jeremiah called Judah to give glory to God before he covered her with darkness. God's people were to turn their hearts back to the Lord, repenting of their sinful ways, or he would plunge them into thick darkness.

What was the nature of that darkness? The Lord described an individual walking on the darkening hills where the path was very dangerous. The light was turned into dense darkness and deep gloom. Without the necessary light, this individual would plunge to certain death.

When God withdraws his light from a society, there is no hope. It is plunged into the darkness of moral and spiritual decay. All blessings are removed and destruction is the inevitable result. This was what Jeremiah prophesied to Judah.

Scattered Flock (verses 17–20)

The third picture in this section was of a scattered flock. Notice the grief in the heart of the prophet as he drew this particular image for his people. He wept bitterly, and tears ran down his cheeks as he thought about the flock of Judah being taken captive. The Judeans were a proud people who felt they did not need God. The king and the queen were called to humble themselves because their reign was about to end (verse 18). The cities of the Negev in the south, the farthest from the approaching enemy in the north, would be captured. All of Judah would be carried away into captivity.

God's people were to look to the north and see the enemy approaching. The enemy would take their property and hold them captive in a strange land. The shepherds of God's people were asked in verse 20: "Where is the flock that was entrusted to you, the sheep of which you boasted?" The Lord would hold the leaders of Judah accountable.

Labor Pangs (verses 21–22)

The next picture was of a woman in labor. The children of Israel should have known that if they turned their backs on God and conceived evil, the day would come when they would feel the labor pain of his judgment. Judah had cultivated forbidden political alliances with the neighboring lands. She had been seduced by them and had become pregnant with the sinful ways of these nations. Judah, who had flirted with evil, would suffer the labor pains of God's judgment as she gave birth to her child of sin.

The Stain of Sin (verses 23–27)

The Lord asked two simple questions: "Can the Ethiopian change his skin or the leopard its spots?" These questions did not need an answer. It is obvious that it is impossible for individuals and animals to change the color of their skins. What point was God making here? God was telling his people that they were so accustomed to sin that they could no more change their ways than a leopard could change its spots. They were trapped in their evil ways with no escape. They were incapable of doing what was right and pleasing to God. Their whole nature was corrupted.

We need to understand that this is a picture of us as well. There is no way that we can change the sinful human nature. We can try if we want, but we will never be able to change the sin that reigns in our flesh. Nothing that comes from our old fleshy nature will ever please God. It takes the miracle of salvation for this to happen. When the Lord Jesus came to this earth, he came to give us a life that pleases God. He came to place his Holy Spirit in us so that we could serve him in the Spirit and in truth.

Because the people of Judah had forsaken God and turned from him, they would be scattered like chaff driven by the desert wind (verse 24). Because they had turned from God to serve idols, he would humiliate them to their neighbors. God would lift up their skirts and expose them. The lifting up of the skirt was symbolic of their secret sins being revealed. The Lord saw Judah for who she really was. God saw everything. Judah could hide nothing from her Lord. And the day was coming when all her sins would be uncovered before the world as well.

In this section we see many different prophetic pictures of the judgment of God's people. They would be filled with the drunkenness of God's wrath. Darkness would overcome them. Like a flock, they would be scattered. They would feel the pangs of labor as they suffered the consequences of the sin they had conceived in their hearts.

There was nothing they could do to change their evil ways, yet God asked them in verse 27: "How long will you be unclean?" He could ask this only because there was a way for them to be clean. Only as they turned to God would they know the power to live as they were called to live. The phrase "How long will you be unclean" was in reality an invitation to turn to God and his ways. It was an invitation to live in victory. It is an invitation that each of us needs to hear afresh today.

For Consideration:

- Consider each of the pictures of judgment here in this passage. What do they teach us about God's view of sin?

- Can you see evidence in your own society of the darkness Jeremiah spoke about?

- What challenge does this passage bring us regarding our need of a solution to our sin? Can we become righteous by human effort?

- Why do we remain in sin when there is a solution?

For Prayer:

- Thank God that he has made a provision for our victory through the Lord Jesus Christ.

- Take a moment to pray for those who are still under the judgment of God. Ask God to set them free.

- Thank God that he has set you free from the judgment of your sin.

17

Drought in the Land

Read Jeremiah 14

In the last chapter, we saw several pictures of judgment. Here in chapter 14, God spoke to his people about a series of droughts that had devastated the land during the days of Jeremiah. God's people had failed to see the connection between what was happening with the weather and their spiritual condition. This drought had not happened by chance. The Lord had promised to curse the land in this way for covenant violations (see Deuteronomy 28:23–24).

In verses 2–6 we catch a glimpse of the drought that had touched the land in those days. The territory of Judah mourned. The cities were in despair. A cry of desperation went out to the once-glorious city of Jerusalem. The nobles sent their servants to gather water, but there was none. The servants returned with empty jars. The land was in misery. The nobles covered their heads in humiliation and shame.

In verse 4 we read that the ground was so dry that it had cracked. There was no rain to grow the crops, so the farmers were in despair. They too covered their heads in mourning. Even the animals of the field felt the impact of this terrible lack of rain.

The doe deserted her newborn fawn because there was no grass to feed it (verse 5). The wild donkey panted in search for water and grew weak with thirst (verse 6). There were no pastures to feed in because the hand of the Lord was against the land.

The people cried out to God. We hear their cry in verses 7–9: "O LORD, do something for the sake of your name. For our backsliding is great; we have sinned against you" (verse 7). There is nothing like tragedy to bring us to an awareness of our sin and frailty.

In verse 8 the people of Judah cried out to God as the "Hope of Israel" and their "Savior in times of distress." While they had ignored him prior to this time, now they reached out to him. "Why are you like a stranger to us?" they asked God. They accused God of being like a traveler who stayed only one night. This kind of traveler had no personal interest in the people of the community. This was how the people of God were describing him. They were saying that the Lord had no concern for them. He was just a stranger passing through.

"Why are you like a man taken by surprise," they asked God in verse 9. A man taken by surprise is a man whose guard is down. If you want to defeat a man who is stronger than you are, you need to find a moment when you can take him by surprise. Judah claimed that God was like a man with his guard down. He was caught at a moment of weakness. In the mind of these Israelites, this was the only way they could explain why God was not looking after them. They believed that God was under obligation to save them because they were his children. There was tremendous pride in this belief.

God's response to these people was frightening. He heard their pleas and cries and spoke to Jeremiah about them. These people loved to wander. They did not restrain their feet from sin, but then cried out to him in their despair. God went on to tell Jeremiah that he would not accept their cries. Instead, he would remember their wickedness and punish them for their sin. In verse 11 God told Jeremiah that he was not even to pray for the well-being of his people. God would not listen to any prayers for them. Even if the people fasted, God would not listen to their prayers. He would no longer accept their burnt offerings and their grain offerings as sacrifices for sin. He was determined to destroy them by famine, sword, and plague (verse 12).

We cannot take this response of the Lord lightly. In their moment of despair, the people cried out to God, but God would no longer listen. Their judgment had come, and nothing could reverse that judgment. They had been given every opportunity to return to the Lord, but they had refused. They would suffer the consequences.

As Jeremiah listened to these harsh words from the Lord, he questioned what his fellow prophets were saying to Judah. It appears that the other prophets were telling the people that there would be no famine. Instead, they would experience lasting peace in the land (verse 13). This obviously was what the people wanted to hear, but it was contrary to the word of the Lord.

Jeremiah was very concerned about this because the message he was hearing from God was not what the other prophets were prophesying. God told Jeremiah in verse 14 to tell the people that these prophets were lying. God had not sent them, but they used his name anyway. They spoke false visions, demonic perversions, and delusions of their own minds (verse 14). The words these spiritual leaders spoke were a complete misunderstanding of the covenant.

God told Jeremiah that the prophets who said that there would be no sword and famine would themselves perish by the sword and famine. God also told him that the people to whom these false prophets had been prophesying would be thrown dead into the street with no one to bury them. They would be victims of the sword and famine that these prophets said would not come.

Jeremiah would weep day and night for the plight of his people (verse 17). The virgin daughter, the loved one of God, would suffer a grievous wound. She would be dealt a crushing blow. As a virgin, Judah had never known a foreign oppressor.

The devastation in the land would be extensive. As people walked through the country, they would see evidence of those slain by the sword. Jerusalem would be ravaged by famine. Both the prophets and the priests would be forced to leave the land they loved and be exiled to a land of strangers. The reality Jeremiah saw was very different from what the false prophets had predicted.

Jeremiah was alone in preaching a message of truth.

In verse 19 Jeremiah cried out to God about the judgment he saw coming. "Have you rejected Judah completely? Do you despise Zion?" he asked. The false prophets had misled the people saying that peace would come. The people had hoped for a healing but would only find terror.

In verse 20 Jeremiah confessed the wickedness of his people. They were guilty of great sin before God. In the day of God's wrath, Judah would cry out to God not to despise her. "Do not dishonor your glorious throne," they would plead. This is quite possibly a reference to the kings that God had set up to rule over them. "Remember your covenant with us," they would pray. The people would cry to the Lord in this time of judgment. While they had been unfaithful and abandoned God, they would ask him not to be unfaithful to them. While they had broken their part of the covenant, they would beg him not to break his.

In verse 22 Jeremiah spoke of how God's people would soon acknowledge that their idols could not bring rain. They would recognize that the rain they so desperately needed came only from God. In their idolatry they had cried out to their pagan fertility gods to give them an abundance of crops and rain. Soon they would realize that their false gods had failed them, and they would cry out to one true God.

We see here in this chapter that a day of judgment would come for those who had turned their backs on God. God would purge the evil of idolatry from his people during their exile to Babylon. God would not be taken for granted. He was under no covenantal obligation to come to the rescue of those who had turned their back on him. Despite the obvious judgment of God on the land, false prophets were soothing the fears of God's people and telling them that they had nothing to worry about. The spiritual leaders brushed over the seriousness of sin. There was no repentance, and this brought God's judgment on the land of Judah.

For Consideration:

• What does this chapter teach us about opening up our hearts to God while we can still hear him?

- What does this chapter teach us about testing all prophecy? How do we test the word that is being spoken in our day?

- Could it be that there are things happening in your land that are the direct result of sin and rebellion against God? Give some examples.

For Prayer:

- Ask God to give us hearts that will hear him when he speaks to us.

- Ask the Lord to give us real discernment to distinguish truth from the error that is being spoken in our day.

- Ask the Lord to break our hearts before it is too late.

18

Difficult Words

Read Jeremiah 15

I t is relatively easy to read the words of the prophet Jeremiah and not understand the difficulty he had in proclaiming these words to his people. His ministry, however, was a very difficult one. We catch a glimpse of this in chapter 15 as we listen in on a conversation between God and his prophet.

The chapter begins in verse 1 with a powerful statement from God to Jeremiah. "Even if Moses and Samuel were to stand before me, my heart would not go out to this people. Send them away from my presence! Let them go!" Earlier, in chapter 14, the Lord told Jeremiah that he was no longer to pray for Judah. God was telling him here that even if Moses and Samuel were to pray for Judah, he would not hear their prayers. God's people were going to be expelled from his presence.

God continued in verse 2 to tell Jeremiah that when the people asked him where they were to go, he was to tell them that they would all go to their appointed judgment. All those who were destined to death would go to death. Some were destined for the sword and others to starvation. Others were destined to live and be taken into captivity. God had a specific judgment for each individual.

God decreed that there would be four kinds of destroyers to his people (verse 3). The enemy's sword would kill people, and then the corpses would be dragged away and eaten by dogs, birds, and wild beasts. God decreed that even his people's corpses would suffer shame.

God would humiliate his people before the other nations. God would do this because of what King Manasseh did in Jerusalem (verse 4). Manasseh was very evil and led Judah into massive idolatry. Scripture states in 2 Kings 21 that this king set up altars to the foreign gods in the temple of the Lord and desecrated this holy place. He practiced sorcery and consulted mediums. He sacrificed his own son to the pagan gods and shed much innocent blood in Jerusalem. He led Judah into more evil than was practiced in the pagan nations around them.

When the Lord brought evil on his people, who would pity them (verse 5)? Who would mourn their loss? Who would even come to them and ask them how they were doing? The answer to this was obvious. No one would really care. God's people would pass away from this earth with no one to mourn their passing.

The people of Judah had rejected the Lord (verse 6). They did not repent of their backsliding. They kept walking in their evil deeds even though the Lord kept calling them back to obedience and blessing. Because they did not listen, the Lord would lay hands on them to destroy them. "I can no longer show compassion," he declared. What horrible words these are! Judah was going to be judged. Nothing would stop the wrath of God at this point. There had been times in the nation's history when Moses had pleaded for the people, and God had withheld judgment (see Exodus 32:9–14). But this would not be the case for Judah at this point. Even the prayers of Moses would not have changed God's heart toward Judah.

In verse 7 Jeremiah told his people that they would be winnowed with a fork. They would be shaken and disciplined until the chaff of sin was removed from them. To do this, God was going to bring bereavement and disaster. Widows would become more numerous than the sand of the seashore (verse 8). The people would be destroyed at noon, the hottest part of the day, when fighting usually came to a halt. God would strike them without compassion and pity. Mothers of young men would perish as the hand of the Lord came mightily on them. Anguish and terror would be on all sides. Mothers would grow faint and breathe their last breath. Their sun would go down while it was still day (verse 9). In other words, they would die before their time. They would be disgraced and humiliated. The survivors of this judgment would fall by the sword. God's wrath would be vented on his people.

We catch a glimpse here of the reality of the anger of God. He is a God of love and compassion, to be sure; but he will not hesitate to demonstrate his anger and wrath on those who turn from him.

As Jeremiah listened to what the Lord said, his heart was broken. "Alas, my mother, that you gave me birth" he cried out in verse 10. Jeremiah wondered why he had been born into a world of such sorrow and injustice. "I have neither lent nor borrowed, yet everyone curses me." The prophet was saying that he had given no cause for anyone to hate him, but they still cursed him and rejected his ministry.

The Lord listened to Jeremiah's lament and responded. In verse 11 God promised to deliver Jeremiah from the hands of his enemies. The day was coming when his enemies would no longer curse him. Instead, they would plead with him. We are not told here why they would plead with him. Could it be that they would recognize that he alone was preaching the truth. Would they come to him, begging him to plead with God on their behalf?

God reminded Jeremiah of the certainty of the judgment that was going to come on the land. "Can a man break iron?" God asked (verse 12). The iron mentioned here referred to the nation of Babylon which would attack Judah from the north. God's people would not be able to break this iron yoke.

All of Judah's wealth would be taken from her as plunder. This would happen because of her sin. God's people would lose all they had and be taken from their land to live enslaved in a land of strangers. The wrath of God would burn against them because of their evil. God reminded Jeremiah that the time for judging his people was very near.

As Jeremiah reflected on the words of the Lord, he again thought about the reaction of the people to this message. He spoke to the Lord about this. Jeremiah pleaded for the Lord to remember him, care for him, and punish his persecutors. Sharing these words with the people of God would come at a cost for Jeremiah. He would not make any friends by speaking these words; he would only make enemies. He cried out to God to protect him as he took this message to Judah. He reminded God of how much he had already suffered for his obedience. He pleaded with God not to take him away. It is not clear what Jeremiah meant here. He may have meant that he did not want to die at the hand of his own people, or he may have been telling God that he did not want to be sent away in exile along with his people.

Jeremiah continued to place his case before the Lord. "When your words came, I ate them; they were my joy and my heart's delight, for I bear your name, O LORD God Almighty," Jeremiah said to God in verse 16. Jeremiah eagerly took hold of God's word, which is one of life's greatest blessings. There was a real joy in his heart to be the instrument to bring God's word to his people. With that calling, however, came great responsibility. The words Jeremiah brought to his people were difficult words.

God asked Jeremiah to live a particular lifestyle. He was not to fellowship with profane revelers (those who mocked the Lord). That is to say, he did not go to the pagan celebrations of his people. He sat alone because the hand of the Lord was on him. His calling demanded a certain lifestyle. Because the whole nation had turned from the Lord, Jeremiah did not have friends with whom he could share his holy lifestyle. He was alone, and he felt the pain of this loneliness from time to time.

Notice in verse 17 that Jeremiah stated that God had filled him with indignation. What was this indignation? It was anger for the things that angered the heart of God. Not only did God give the prophet words to speak, he also gave him his heart. Jeremiah spoke from a heart that felt what God felt. The weight of this heaviness was very difficult to bear at times.

In verse 18 Jeremiah cried out, "Why is my pain unending?" The prophet could not seem to get away from the pain of his message and the pain of loneliness. His wound seemed to be grievous and incurable. Jeremiah went as far as to say that God had become like a deceptive brook and a stream that failed. In other words, God had not come to his rescue. Jeremiah did not feel the refreshment of God at this point in his painful ministry. Jeremiah was complaining of the burden he bore.

God listened to Jeremiah's complaint and replied in verse 19. He told Jeremiah to repent of his sin of falling into self-pity. The Lord's grace was sufficient for Jeremiah, if he would turn to the Lord again (see 2 Corinthians 12:9). If the prophet would repent of his sins, as he was calling the people of Judah to do, God would refresh and restore him and continue to use him as his prophet.

This passage has become quite personal to me. Some time ago I found myself in Jeremiah's situation, grumbling and complaining about how things were going in my ministry. At that time the Lord clearly led me to this passage. I was powerfully struck by the way God told Jeremiah that if he repented he could be restored and continue to be his spokesman. As I reflected on what God was saying to Jeremiah, the Lord showed me the connection between what God was doing in Jeremiah's personal life and his ministry as a prophet. I remember the Lord speaking to my heart and making me understand that until Jeremiah could learn to trust what God was doing in his life, he could not trust God enough to be his spokesman. If Jeremiah was going to be a true prophet of God, he needed to learn how to trust God—not only in what he said but also in what he was doing in his life. Jeremiah needed to repent of his lack of trust and confidence in the ways of God in his life.

Jeremiah had expressed his feelings about the isolation he felt in ministry and his loneliness, but God did not change this situation. He had called Jeremiah to a ministry of isolation. He was not to let the people's response to him drag him down emotionally. If Jeremiah repented, the Lord would make him as indestructible as a bronze wall to protect him from his enemies (verse 20). God would rescue him from all his foes and redeem him from the grasp of the cruel.

God told Jeremiah to stop complaining. We are led to believe that he would not be restored to full ministry as long as he grumbled against what the Lord was doing in his life. How many times do we grumble and complain about the way things are in our ministries? This passage reminds us that grumbling will only hinder the blessing of God in our lives and ministries.

God did not take away the problems that Jeremiah was going to face. Instead, he promised to strengthen the prophet to face his problems. The people would continue to fight against him, but God would protect him so that they would not overcome him. God would rescue him in his time of need and save him from the hands of the wicked.

We see here that Jeremiah's ministry was not an easy one. It was filled with severe difficulties and trials. God did not take those difficulties away from him. Instead, God promised to protect and strengthen him in his time of trouble. Jeremiah was encouraged to accept his assignment and not complain. It was sufficient for him to know that he was in the will of God.

For Consideration:

* What evidence is there that the ministry of Jeremiah was very difficult?

* Have you ever found yourself grumbling and complaining about things in your life? What is the challenge of this passage for you?

* What is the challenge in this passage to those who face opposition in ministry? Does God promise that things will always be easy in ministry?

* What burden has God given you in ministry?

For Prayer:

* Ask God to help those who are going through a difficult time in ministry. Ask him to protect them and fill them with his joy.

* Ask God to forgive you for the times when you have been guilty, like Jeremiah, of grumbling and complaining.

19

The Life of the Prophet

Read Jeremiah 16

Very often the prophet in the Old Testament was not only called to speak the word of the Lord but also to act it out symbolically. God told Hosea to marry an adulteress to symbolize the relationship God had with his people (Hosea 3:1). He told Ezekiel to lie on his side for a prolonged period to represent the captivity (Ezekiel 4:4). God told Jeremiah to live a lifestyle that reflected the judgment that was coming on Judah.

Notice here in the first few verses what God expected of Jeremiah as his prophet. In verse 2 God told Jeremiah that he was not to marry and have children. God told him the reason for this in verses 3 and 4.

Children born in the land in those days would perish. Some would die of disease and would not be mourned for or buried. Instead, they would lie as refuse on the ground. Others would die by the sword and famine. Their dead bodies would be food for the birds of the air and the wild animals of the earth. This was the destiny of all who were born in those days. The anger and judgment of God was on the nation as a whole. These would be fearful days to raise a family. God wanted to spare Jeremiah from such a burden. The fact that Jeremiah did not have a wife could have symbolized that God did not have an intimate relationship with Judah. The fact that Jeremiah did not have children could have symbolized the loss of holy progeny among God's people.

Notice as well that Jeremiah was forbidden the privilege of going to a funeral, and he was not to mourn or show sympathy for those who had died. We can only imagine what the people of his community thought about this when the prophet showed no sympathy for their loved ones who passed away. The reason for this is given in verse 5. God's blessings had been taken from these people because of their sin. God would show no pity on them when the enemy came. The people of Judah would die and lie on the ground without being buried. No one would grieve for them. Jeremiah was to symbolize this by not grieving for the dead or going to funerals.

Mention is made in verse 6 of people cutting themselves and shaving their heads for the dead. These were pagan mourning rituals. The cutting of oneself was strictly forbidden in Leviticus 19:28: "Do not cut your bodies for the dead or put tattoo marks on yourselves. I am the LORD."

On the day of Judah's judgment, there would be no mourning rituals. Notice as well, that there would be no effort to console those who grieved. In verse 7 Jeremiah told his people that no one would offer food or drink to comfort and console the mourner when the enemy came.

In verses 8 and 9 the Lord told Jeremiah that he was not to enter into a place of feasting. This would rule out weddings and banquets of any kind. The Lord told Jeremiah that the reason for this was that soon all sounds of joy and gladness would be broken. The happy voices of the bride and the bridegroom would be heard no more. By refusing to go to these celebrations, the prophet was showing the people that these things would soon disappear from the land.

The lifestyle that Jeremiah lived was bound to capture the attention of the people. They would eventually ask him to explain his actions. God told Jeremiah what to say to the people when they asked these questions.

Jeremiah was to tell the people of Judah that they were even more wicked than their ancestors who had forsaken the Lord and worshiped other gods. The prophet was to say that they followed the stubbornness of their own hearts and refused to obey the Lord. The Lord would give them over to their sinful ways. He would cast them out of the land he had given to their ancestors and send them to a foreign land. In exile they would worship foreign gods day and night. God would no longer show them his favor.

Two things need to be noticed in verse 13. First, notice that the people were so far into their sin that they no longer even recognized that they were guilty. They had to ask the prophet to explain to them what they were doing wrong. Their sensitivity to God and his purposes had been dulled. They had become so accustomed to their sinful ways that they no longer understood right from wrong.

Second, notice how God gave his people to their sin. Because they had turned their backs on God and refused to return to him, the Lord left them to their evil ways. He removed his blessings from their lives and left them to serve their foreign gods (see Romans 1:21–25).

God will not always stop us from sinning. There are those who believe that if God did not want people to sin, he would stop them. This is not the case. He gives people the choice to accept him and walk in his ways or to reject him and walk in darkness. Jeremiah was to tell God's people that they had willingly chosen to reject their God.

We see from verses 14 and 15 that though God would punish his people, he would not completely forsake them. The day was coming when the Israelites would no longer refer to their deliverance from Egypt as their greatest rescue, but would refer to their deliverance from Babylon and "all the countries where he had banished them." While God would judge his people, he would not punish them forever. He would rescue them in his time and restore them to their land.

First, however, exile would come. God would send enemies, here described as fishermen and hunters, into their land to catch his people (verse 16). These enemies would search out the mountains and the hills of the land for their prey. They would leave no stone unturned or crevice unexplored in order to capture God's people.

Nothing was hidden from the eyes of a sovereign and almighty God. These hunters would be the instruments of God to punish his people for their sin.

Because the Israelites had defiled the Promised Land with their lifeless idols, they would pay double for their sin (verse 18). For some time God had extended mercy to give his people a chance to repent, but that time was over. The day had come when they would answer to God for their evil deeds. The fact that they would have to pay double indicated the severity of their sin and their full punishment.

In verses 19–20 Jeremiah prophesied that the days were coming when nations from the ends of the earth would come to the God of Israel (the refuge, fortress, and strength of Israel) and confess their sin of idolatry. People from every nation would come saying: "Our fathers possessed nothing but false gods, worthless idols that did them no good." The nations would be convicted of their false religions and come to the God of Israel as the one true God. They would come to understand that the gods that they made with human hands were not true gods. There is only one true God.

We are seeing this in our day as people from every tribe and nation turn to the Lord Jesus for salvation. Jeremiah told his people that in those days the Lord would teach the nations his power and might (verse 21). They would know him as LORD.

We see from this chapter that there are times when the Lord asks far more of his servants than simply to share the message he gives them—he calls them to a lifestyle. Jeremiah's life was to reflect the message he preached. We also discover that the Lord will sometimes hand us over to our sinful ways. He does not force us to obey but will hold us accountable to him for any disobedience. Ultimately, God will restore all his chosen people to himself.

For Consideration:

• Does your lifestyle reflect the message you preach with your lips?

- Would you be willing to make the sacrifices that Jeremiah made for his ministry?

For Prayer:

- Thank the Lord that he opened the door for us as foreigners to enter into a relationship with him.

- Ask God to give you ears to hear him so that you do not become hardened in your sinful ways.

- Thank him that though he sometimes hands us over to our sinful ways, he does not reject us forever.

- Ask God to help you to pursue a lifestyle that brings honor to his name and the ministry to which he has called you.

20

The Evil Heart

Read Jeremiah 17:1–13

J eremiah had been warning his people about their sin and its consequences. The sin of God's people was so deeply rooted that God spoke of it in verse 1 as being engraved with an iron tool on their hearts. This meant that their sin could not be quickly erased. It would not be easy for God's people to change their habits and practices. Instead of God's laws being written on their hearts, sin was written there.

Notice that the sins of the Lord's people were also engraved on the horns of their pagan altars (verse 1). In other words, God's people were committing sacrilege at pagan altars instead of worshiping the true God at his bronze altar in the temple. The sins of God's people were permanently inscribed on the pagan altars where they went to worship false gods.

Jeremiah told his people in verse 2 that their children remembered the evil ways of their parents. That is to say, the children of Judah learned idolatry from their parents. Evil was passed from one generation to the next. Not only were parents guilty of forsaking God's laws, but they also taught their children to follow their example.

The land the Lord God had set apart for himself had become polluted. Its inhabitants had turned their backs on him and his ways and taught their children to do the same. God would deal with this evil in their hearts. Jeremiah prophesied in verse 3 that God would give away their mountain (on which the city of Jerusalem was located), their treasures, and their high places (where they worshiped their foreign gods). These would be given as plunder to the conquering nation.

Through their own fault, the people of Judah would lose the inheritance that God had given to them (verse 4). They would be taken away from their land and would become slaves in a foreign country (Babylon). By their evil they had kindled the anger of God. That anger would burn against them forever. This is not to say that the Lord would never renew his offer of love and forgiveness to their descendants. But the judgment of these people, however, would be final. God would no longer plead with them to repent. They would suffer the consequences of their sin.

In verse 5 God spoke of the difference between the person who trusts in human strength and wisdom and the one who trusts in God. It is important that we understand what God was saying here. God was not simply telling Judah that the person who trusts in human strength will not get as far as the one who trusts in God. He made it very clear that there is a curse on those who turn from him. God's people had forsaken their covenant in which he had given them his laws and blessings. They had turned to false prophets, idols, and other nations for wisdom and protection and had brought God's curse on themselves.

God's desire for us is to acknowledge him as Lord and surrender to his righteous ways. How many times have we turned to our fellow humans for help and not consulted God? How many times have we trusted in human wisdom and not listened to the wisdom of Scripture? Jeremiah tells us that there is a curse on those who depend on human frailty.

Jeremiah went on to show his listeners the destiny of the one who trusts in the flesh for strength. That person would be like a bush in the barren desert, far away from the streams of water that could nourish it and cause it to grow. The desert bush is small and fruitless. This is the destiny of the person who trusts in human resources. That person will not see the prosperity of the Lord but live in the parched places of the earth where nothing grows. The people of Judah felt that they could do things on their own. They did not see their need of God and his guidance and power. We can very easily fall into this trap as well. This path, however, leads to barrenness and fruitlessness. How we need to understand just how much we need the Lord and his wisdom.

The one who trusts the Lord is blessed (verse 7). According to Jeremiah, that person would be like a tree planted by the waters, drinking deeply from the plenteous supply. When the heat of difficulty came, these individuals would not fear. They would have an infinite supply of strength and wisdom in God, their source. They would be fruitful at all times.

The people of God had turned against the strength of the Lord. They chose to reject him and placed their confidence in their own wisdom and strength. They failed miserably as will anyone who relies on human ability. Why do we turn from the abundant supply that God provides and instead trust in the limited and frail strength of humans?

God answered that question in verse 9: "The heart is deceitful 'above all things' and beyond cure." These are powerful words about the human heart. Commentators tell us that the word used for *deceitful* here is from the same root as the word *supplanter*. Jacob's name came from this same root. Jacob was a deceiver. He stole his brother's birthright and his blessing. He also tricked his father-in-law by breeding the spotted sheep and keeping them for himself. The story of Jacob is one of dishonesty and trickery. This is what comes naturally to the human heart.

Notice that the Lord told his people that there is nothing more deceitful than the human heart. It is deceitful above all things. The heart is the source of many lies and treacherous ways. It has also been the cause of terrible deeds done in the history of this earth. The human heart in its natural condition is deceitful and evil.

God said another thing here about the human heart—it is incurable. People cannot change the nature of the human heart. It is for this reason that the Lord told his people that he would give them a new heart (see Ezekiel 11:19). The old heart cannot be fixed.

Although people do not understand their own hearts, God does. The Lord searches the heart and is the final judge of human motivations (verse 10). This ought to strike reverent fear in us. Jeremiah went on to say that the Lord God is going to reward each person according to his or her deeds, as each rightly deserves. What chance would we have if God were to search our hearts and minds in their natural states? God would certainly curse us. This natural heart is wicked and cannot please God. We have seen that the sinful human heart is beyond cure. We need a new heart. Only God can give us that new heart, and we must cry out to him for it.

In verse 11 we see another example of the sinfulness of the human heart. Here Jeremiah spoke of the person who gains riches through injustice. Greed is one of the fruits of the wicked human heart. Jeremiah compared this person to the partridge that hatches eggs that are not hers. By stealing eggs, she enjoys the fruit for which others have labored. God will punish thieving individuals whose ill-gotten gains will desert them in the end. God will not allow them to fully enjoy the fruit of their evil hearts. Judah would be taken away from her land, and the prosperity she had gained through evil and corruption would desert her, leaving her barren and empty.

Jeremiah concluded this reflection on the evil heart by reminding his listeners that the sanctuary in Jerusalem was God's glorious and exalted earthly throne (verse 12). The sanctuary was where God dwelt among his people. It was there that Israel could find God. All who came to that sanctuary seeking God would find hope. This was an open invitation from God to his people for them to find all they needed in his presence.

All who turned away from him and his sanctuary would be put to shame. Their names would be written in the dust because they had turned their backs on the springs of living water. Have you ever written your name in the dust on the ground? If you have ever done this, you know your name will not be there very long. The slightest wind will blow the dust away. The rain will come and wash it away. Those who trust in the flesh are like this. They will quickly be blown way and be no more.

No wonder God tells us that those who trust in the flesh are cursed. The heart in which we trust is desperately wicked. It is deceitful and greedy. The challenge here in this passage is for us to seek the Lord and his ways. We cannot trust our own wisdom. We must come to the sanctuary and seek the wisdom and heart of God. We must learn to seek him in everything. We must learn to mistrust our own wisdom and strength and turn to God for his.

For Consideration:

• What does this section teach us about the human heart?

• Can you see evidence of this evil heart in yourself?

• How can we learn to trust more in the Lord?

For Prayer:

• Ask the Lord to teach you how to rely more on him in everything you do.

• Ask him to forgive you for the times you have trusted in your own wisdom and not surrendered to him.

• Thank the Lord that he has given you a new heart if you have trusted the Lord Jesus as your Savior. Ask him to help you to live out of that new heart.

21

Broken Sabbath

Read Jeremiah 17:14–27

Jeremiah had been reminding his people of the hardness and deceitfulness of the human heart. This was not an easy message to preach. Not many people like to think that their hearts are desperately wicked and beyond repair. This word of the prophet would not be well received. We can be sure that Jeremiah's faithfulness in preaching the word of God did not make him many friends. In this next section, Jeremiah again shared openly with God concerning the pain in his heart.

Jeremiah began in verse 14 by asking the Lord to heal and save him. The work to which Jeremiah was called was difficult. He felt the abuse of the words that were hurled at him. He felt the sting of the insults and the pain of rejection. There were times when his heart and soul were downcast and weary. He had nowhere to go with this pain except his Lord. Notice, however, that he believed that the Lord could heal him. "Heal me, O LORD, and I will be healed," he said. His confidence was in his God.

Notice, as well, in verse 14 that Jeremiah did not cease to praise the Lord in his time of difficulty and trial. "You are the one I praise," he told God. Praising God is sometimes difficult for us to do in our trials. Jeremiah, however, continued to trust in the Lord and praise him as his deliverer even when people hurled insults at him and sought to kill him.

We catch a glimpse of what particularly was causing pain in the life of the prophet Jeremiah in verse 15. Jeremiah told the Lord that the people were asking him why the word of the Lord was not being fulfilled. Jeremiah had been pronouncing judgment on the people of God, but that judgment had not yet come. Therefore, the people of Judah doubted his word. There was a sense of disbelief and mockery in the words of the people. Jeremiah proclaimed these words in faith that the Lord would bring them to pass. In the meantime, he suffered the rebuke of the people.

Jeremiah reminded the Lord that he had not run from being his shepherd, despite the ridicule of the people. As a shepherd, Jeremiah had fed the people on the word of the Lord and warned them of the judgment that was coming. The people rejected those words, but Jeremiah did not give up preaching.

There is a lesson here for those of us who have felt weary in the work of the Lord. Let us not look to the results as the motivation for our ministries but to the Lord and his call on our lives. Has the Lord called you to the ministry you are doing? Then, do not lose heart. Like Jeremiah, look to the Lord to heal and save you, and remain faithful.

There is something else we need to see in this verse. When people mock us, it is easy to become bitter. Like Jonah, we begin to preach the judgment of the Lord with certain pleasure. We want to see these people condemned. Jeremiah told the Lord in verse 16 that he did not desire the day of despair. He did not secretly long to see his people judged, even though they sought his life. He wanted them to repent and avert God's judgment. Jeremiah opened his heart to the Lord and asked him to examine his motives in preaching. His motives were right. He ministered out of compassion and love, and God knew this.

Jeremiah pleaded with God not to be a terror to him, for in God alone was the prophet's place of refuge. In what way could God have been a terror to him? Could it be by abandoning him in this time of difficulty in ministry? Was Jeremiah pleading with God not to abandon him in this lonely time?

In verse 18 Jeremiah asked the Lord to put his persecutors to shame. He asked God that terror and disaster fall on them so that they would be destroyed with double destruction. How are we to understand this verse in light of what Jeremiah said in verse 16 about not desiring the day of despair? Maybe we need to understand this in the light of a parent's discipline of a child. A parent does not secretly delight in punishing a child but will not hesitate to do so for the good of the child. In the same way, the Lord God does not delight in punishing his children. He longs for them to repent and turn from their evil ways. We read in Ezekiel 18:31–32: "Rid yourselves of all the offenses you have committed, and get a new heart and a new spirit. Why will you die, O house of Israel? For I take no pleasure in the death of anyone, declares the Sovereign LORD. Repent and live!"

While the Lord took no pleasure in the death of the wicked, he would not hesitate to judge. Could it be that the prophet Jeremiah realized that, for the good of Judah and the glory of God, judgment needed to be pronounced? Judah had broken her covenant, and the Lord had to discipline his people with the promised curses for rebellion.

Having poured out his heart, Jeremiah listened to the response of God. In verse 19 God told him to stand at the gates of Jerusalem. From these gates he was to proclaim the word the Lord would give him. God did not seem to address Jeremiah's concerns here. He responded to Jeremiah by giving him a further message for the people. His absence of words to Jeremiah personally ought to be seen as the Lord indicating that everything was as it should be.

What was the word that God had for the people of Judah at this time? It was a word about the Sabbath. Jeremiah was to announce that God's people had broken the Sabbath laws (verse 21). They were not to bring a load into the city on the Sabbath. They were not to bring a load out of their houses on the Sabbath or do any work on that day. This was the commandment of the Lord to their ancestors (see Exodus 20:8–11). The people of Jeremiah's day had not been living in obedience to this command of God.

There was a blessing attached to this law. If the Israelites obeyed what the Lord told them about the Sabbath, then Jerusalem would be secure and inhabited forever (verse 25). True worship would be restored at the temple as people would come from all around to bring their offerings of praise as the Lord required. God's blessing would again be on his people if they chose to repent of their sins and return in obedience to the Mosaic covenant. If, on the other hand, they refused to obey the word of the Lord, then the Lord would send an unquenchable fire to consume the city. That fire would come in the form of the Babylonians who would kill the Davidic kings and destroy the temple and the city.

We see that the ministry of a prophet was not always an easy one. Jeremiah had many enemies, but he was willing to persevere despite the difficulties. His example is a challenge to us. This section calls us to persevere and be obedient, no matter the cost.

For Consideration:

• What do we learn from the experience of Jeremiah in this section? Should we expect ministry to be always easy?

• Have you ever felt discouraged in your ministry? What challenge do you receive here in this passage?

• What is the connection between obedience and blessing in this chapter?

For Prayer:

• Ask the Lord to give you the encouragement necessary to persevere in the ministry to which he has called you.

• Thank the Lord that when there seems to be no one else to go to in your moments of pain and trial, he is always there for you.

• Thank the Lord that you can openly share your heart with him.

22

At the Potter's House

Read Jeremiah 18

In this section of the book of Jeremiah, the Lord spoke to his servant and told him to go the house of a potter. Notice that the Lord did not tell Jeremiah why he was to go to the potter's house. The reason would become clear in time. Jeremiah would not understand what the Lord wanted from him until he was obedient. The same thing was true for Philip who was called into the desert to witness to the Ethiopian in Acts 8:26. It was not until he was obedient to the initial prompting of the Lord that he would receive further direction. Many times, we want to understand everything before obeying, but God asks us to take one step at a time. Until we are obedient to the initial leading, God will not lead us the rest of the way. God made it clear to Jeremiah in verse 2 that it was at the potter's house that he would receive his next message.

When Jeremiah went to the potter's house, he watched the potter form an object from the clay. As he watched, something went wrong, and the potter simply reshaped the clay in his hands. This is what God wanted Jeremiah to see. There was a lesson in how the potter took a misshaped object of clay and reformed it. What is important for us to note at this point is the great sovereignty of God. God had chosen to use the potter that day, but the potter was not aware that he was going to be used of God to communicate a spiritual truth to the prophet Jeremiah. From the potter's perspective, all he knew was that the piece he was working on became flawed and had to be reshaped. There are times like this in our own lives. Like the potter, we cannot see that the misshaped piece of clay in our hands is actually going to accomplish great things in the kingdom of God.

The timing was perfect. Jeremiah arrived in time to see exactly what he needed to see. The activity of the potter that day was in the hands of the Lord. How frustrated we can become with the little things that seem to get in our way each day. Even as I sat down this morning in a coffee shop to work on this chapter, a man came over and spoke to me for about an hour. How was I to view this? Was this simply an interruption of my plans or the hand of a sovereign God leading that man to me for encouragement? What we see in this incident with the potter is that the Lord God is sovereign over the events of life.

When Jeremiah had seen what he needed to see, the word of the Lord came to him. God told him that Israel was like the clay the potter formed on the wheel (verse 6). God could do whatever he wanted with his nation. As human beings, we would like to think that we are in control of our lives, but this is not the case. I was reminded of this in a recent car accident. A simple trip to the coffee shop ended with my car overturned in a ditch. In the weeks that followed, God showed me that I was not in control of my life. God has the right to shape my life as he determines. He brings whatever he wants into my life to shape me into the person he desires me to be. The challenge for me is to become a willing lump of clay and to trust the Heavenly Potter to do what is right.

God told Jeremiah in verses 7–8 that if a nation was destined for judgment because of its sin and then the nation turned from its evil ways, God reserved the right to reshape its future. He could choose to be compassionate and forgive that nation of sin and rebellion. If, on the other hand, a nation under the rich blessing of the Lord turned its back on him, God could change his blessing into a curse. Instead of continuing to bless that ungrateful nation, the Lord would judge it. Like a potter, he could reshape a nation's destiny according to its sin or righteousness.

In verse 11 the Lord reminded Jeremiah that he was preparing disaster for the people of Judah. He challenged the people to repent and turn from their sin so they did not have to be destroyed. If they turned from their evil ways, they could again experience the blessing of the Lord. God was willing to repent of the evil he planned to do against them if they would turn to him. Through Jeremiah, the Lord pleaded with his people to return to him.

God knew the response of the people to this plea even before it went out to them. They were stubborn and insisted on doing evil. They would not listen to what the Lord God said through Jeremiah (verse 12). Even though God knew the response of the people, he still sent Jeremiah so that they would be without excuse when judgment came. God had warned them of judgment and called them to repentance time after time. By rejecting repentance they sealed their judgment.

In verse 13 God asked his people to inquire among the nations to see if anything like this had ever happened before. God asked if waters ever stopped flowing from the snowy caps of the mountains. While a wise person would never abandon a fresh supply of water, God's people had abandoned him in search of worthless idols. God reminded his people in verse 15 that these idols caused them to stumble on the ancient path and walk in ways that were not smooth. That ancient path was the Mosaic covenant. That path represented God's holy ways and his unique purposes for his people. They stumbled on the righteous path when they were seduced by pagan religions and the lies of their false prophets. Idolatry led God's people on a path of evil and spiritual destruction. Because of this, their land would be laid waste. People who passed by would shake their heads in wonder at the destruction of such a great nation. All this would take place because the house of Israel had chosen to break their covenant and live separate from God's ways. They refused the path that God had laid out for them. As a consequence, God would scatter them like dust blown by an east wind, and he would turn his face from them.

This word was not well received by the people of Jeremiah's day. They responded quite violently against him and his message. Verse 18 tells us that they chose to plot against him and listen instead to their corrupt priests and false prophets. These priests and false prophets did not see any cause for alarm. They taught the people that God would not judge them as Jeremiah had said. Jeremiah's enemies attacked him with hateful words.

Notice the claim made here: "The teaching of the law by the priest will not be lost, nor will counsel from the wise, nor the word from the prophets." The people saw no need for Jeremiah. The people thought they had everything they needed: the law, their own prophets, and their own wise men. The people of Judah really did not understand their spiritual need. Sin had blinded them to the truth of God that Jeremiah spoke. They had faith in their religious rituals and did not understand why they needed anything else.

Jeremiah pleaded with God to hear what these individuals were saying about him (verse 19). Their words hurt him very much. "Should good be repaid with evil?" Jeremiah asked. "Yet they have dug a pit for me. Remember that I stood before you and spoke in their behalf to turn your wrath away from them" (verse 20).

Jeremiah called out to God to judge the people. His words were harsh in verses 21 and 22: Let their children die in a famine. Hand them over to the sword. Let their men be killed and their wives become childless and widows. Let their young men die in battle. Let the invaders come suddenly against them because they have dug a pit for me. Don't forgive their crimes. Overthrow them and deal with them in your anger because they have plotted to kill me.

How are we to understand this outburst from Jeremiah? Was the prophet feeling sorry for himself and seeking revenge? Were these words the angry outburst of the flesh? Could it be that what we are seeing here is not a sinful outburst but rather a judgment of the Spirit of God? It is better to see these words as a prophetic judgment from the Lord. Under the inspiration of the Holy Spirit, Jeremiah pronounced the judgment of God on his own people. God's righteous wrath is real. God's judgment would powerfully fall on the people of Judah because they rejected him and his holy purposes by rejecting Jeremiah's prophecy.

God's people had every opportunity to return to the Lord and his holy ways, but they refused. The Lord would have willingly reshaped them into a vessel of honor, but because of their refusal to repent, they would be destroyed. They alone were to blame.

For Consideration:

- What do we learn here about God's control of all the events of life? What comfort does this bring you?

- Have there been times in your life when God used what appeared to be a tragedy to accomplish good? Explain.

- Jeremiah reminded his people that God was willing to change their destiny depending on their response to him and his word. What do you think would be the result if your nation turned to the Lord?

For Prayer:

- Ask the Lord to help you to be willing clay in the hands of the Master Potter.

- Thank the Lord that he is in control of the events of your life. Ask him to give you the grace to trust his plan and purpose.

- Ask the Lord to give you grace to persevere like Jeremiah under the trials and difficulties that come your way.

23

The Valley of Ben Hinnom

Read Jeremiah 19

After the incident at the potter's house, the Lord asked Jeremiah to buy a clay jar and go the Valley of Ben Hinnom located to the south of the city of Jerusalem. He was to go particularly to the entrance of the Potsherd Gate. In this area jars were made for use in the temple. According to the Lord's instructions, Jeremiah took the elders of the city with him.

When they arrived in the Valley of Ben Hinnom, Jeremiah told the elders that the Lord was going to bring a great disaster on that particular place. God reminded the elders that the people of this valley had forsaken him. They had burned sacrifices to foreign gods and filled the place with blood. They had burned their sons in sacrifice to Baal (verse 5). God's people had stooped so low as to offer their own children on pagan altars to honor the false god Baal. God brought the elders of the land to the center of this evil practice and pronounced his judgment on them and that place.

Jeremiah told the people that this place would no longer be called Topheth or Ben Hinnom but the Valley of Slaughter. Topheth was located to the south of the Valley of Ben Hinnom. It was there in particular where the children were sacrificed on the altar. The name *Topheth* may come from the Hebrew word for "drum." This may have been because drums were beaten in the pagan ceremonies there.

God was going to judge this place because of its evil. There would be a slaughter in this place that would be remembered for a long time. This slaughter would not be the slaughter of innocent children sacrificed to the pagan gods but of those who had practiced these horrible deeds.

God would ruin the plans of the people of Judah (verse 7). They had great plans for evil, but God would foil those plans. Instead of receiving prosperity by their pagan rituals, these idolaters would be massacred at their worship centers. Their carcasses would be given to the birds of the air and the beasts of the field. Their land itself would be devastated. They would be brought so low that they would resort to cannibalism. In order to survive, they would eat the flesh of their sons and daughters (verse 9). These would have been difficult words for the elders of Jeremiah's day to receive.

After Jeremiah spoke these words, he was to break the jar he had brought with him to the valley. He was to do this in the presence of the elders to symbolize what would happen in that place—God would smash the people and the city. Judah would be broken beyond repair (verse 11). The dead would be buried in Topheth until it was full. There would be a great slaughter at this site of blasphemy and atrocity.

The great city of Jerusalem would become like Topheth in the Valley of Ben Hinnom (verse 12). There the human and animal carcasses of pagan sacrifices were thrown over a cliff. At the bottom of that cliff, a fire burned continually to consume the remains of the sacrifices along with other refuse from the city. As the elders stood there with Jeremiah, they could very likely see the smoke of that fire. The smell of burning flesh would have filled the air as they listened to what Jeremiah was saying. All their senses would have been activated as Jeremiah pronounced the coming judgment of the Lord.

Topheth became a symbol of punishment. It was a place where the fire never stopped burning. It was a place of burning flesh and uncleanness. This is what God would do to the city of Jerusalem.

The city of glory and hope would be devastated and defiled like Topheth.

Jeremiah's words to the elders were very powerful that day. Then the prophet went to Jerusalem and there prophesied to the ordinary citizens the same judgment he pronounced in Topheth. In verse 15 Jeremiah stood in the court of the temple to proclaim the judgment of God: "Listen! I am going to bring on this city and the villages around it every disaster I pronounced against them, because they were stiff-necked and would not listen to my words."

We can be sure that this was not what the people of Judah wanted to hear. Jeremiah stood alone in his judgment of the nation. We have to admire his courage as he prophesied these words to the people who came into the temple. These were days of great idolatrous blasphemy and atrocity. The people of Judah were blinded by their sin. They would sacrifice their children to Baal and then come to the temple of God to hypocritically perform the Mosaic ceremonies. They hated Jeremiah because he confronted them with their sin and God's imminent and holy judgment.

For Consideration:

- What does this chapter teach us about the evil of God's people in the days of Jeremiah?

- What can we learn about the righteousness of God's judgment?

- What does this chapter teach us about human sinfulness and how far we can run from God and his ways?

- What are the sinful practices of your nation?

For Prayer:

- Thank the Lord for his patience with us.

- If you know the Lord Jesus as your Savior today, thank him that he has saved you from your sin and the wrath to come.

- If you do not know the Lord Jesus as your Savior today, ask him to forgive you for your sin and to make you his child.

- Ask God to bring a spirit of repentance to your land so that it turns from evil to God.

24

Jeremiah in Stocks

Read Jeremiah 20

Jeremiah had prophesied judgment in the Valley of Ben Hinnom. From there God called him to the temple to proclaim that the city of Jerusalem would be judged and become like Topheth, a place of fire and human sacrifice. This message was not well received.

One person in particular was offended by what Jeremiah was prophesying. A priest by the name of Pashhur heard the prophecy of Jeremiah and felt he needed to do something to keep Jeremiah from spreading this word any further. As the chief officer in the temple, Pashhur had Jeremiah beaten and put in stocks. The stocks were instruments of restraint and torture with five holes into which the hands, feet, and the head of the prisoner were placed. He was left for a certain time in this very uncomfortable position. According to verse 3, Jeremiah was left in these stocks until the next day.

When Pashhur released Jeremiah from the stocks, Jeremiah had a word from the Lord for him: "The LORD's name for you is not Pashhur, but Magor-Missabib" (verse 3). *Pashhur* means "largeness" or "security on all sides." *Magor-Missabib*, on the other hand, means "terror on all sides."

God had seen what Pashhur had done to his servant Jeremiah, and God would deal with this in his own time. The day was coming when Pashhur would experience terror in Jerusalem when the Babylonians broke through the city wall. Pashhur would watch as the Babylonians killed his people and took others, at the point of the sword, into exile. He would watch as these enemies took the wealth of Judah's king as plunder to Babylon. The treasuries would be emptied as Pashhur looked on in horror. Jeremiah told Pashhur in verse 6 that he and his family would go into exile and never return to Jerusalem. There he would be buried along with all those he had deceived by his false prophecies.

It is important to note that Pashhur would not be alone in his exile. He had deceived many people with his false comfort. Many Judeans would travel along with him to Babylon because of his deception and trickery. We see here the power of false teachers.

The apostle John told of the dangers of false leaders in 2 John 7–8: "Many deceivers, who do not acknowledge Jesus Christ as coming in the flesh, have gone out into the world. Any such person is the deceiver and the antichrist. Watch out that you do not lose what you have worked for, but that you may be rewarded fully." According to John, evil leaders can cause people to lose what they have worked to achieve. In particular, John mentioned the rewards of the believer. In other words, false teachers can cause us to walk a path that will bring shame to us as we stand before God on our day of judgment.

Here in the book of Jeremiah, we see how Pashhur the priest, though respected in his position, was leading his people astray with words of false comfort. He would be held accountable to God for what he was doing. How important it is for those of us who are in positions of spiritual authority to recognize the power we have in that position for good or for evil.

Repeatedly in this book, we see glimpses of the heart of Jeremiah. He found no pleasure in speaking words of judgment to his people. The words he prophesied were not well received by the people of his day. As God's prophet, he needed to be willing to suffer to communicate the truth of God. In this next section, we again see the pain he felt in his lonely ministry.

In verse 7 Jeremiah poured out his heart to God: "O LORD, you deceived me." The word *deceive* can also mean "to persuade." It may be better to understand the word in this sense. God had clearly told Jeremiah when he called him that his message would not be accepted. God had made it clear to him at different times that the ministry would be difficult. God had not tricked Jeremiah into this ministry. Jeremiah knew something of what he was getting into, but the actual experience of it was difficult to bear. He had been ridiculed and mocked ever since he started proclaiming God's word of judgment. Jeremiah had just been publicly humiliated by being beaten and placed in the stocks by Pashhur. He felt the physical and emotional pain of this cruel treatment, and his heart cried out to God.

"Whenever I speak, I cry out proclaiming violence and destruction. So the word of the LORD has brought me insult and reproach all day long," Jeremiah told God in verse 8. I am sure that the prophet would have preferred proclaiming the love and blessing of God to an obedient people. However, God called him to proclaim judgment and destruction to a hardened and rebellious people, and so Jeremiah made many enemies. People did not like to hear what Jeremiah was saying. As a result, they began to insult and mock him. According to Jeremiah in verse 8, this was happening all day long. For Jeremiah there did not seem to be any reprieve from the harsh treatment and rejection. He was bombarded day after day with these abuses, and he was discouraged.

There were times in Jeremiah's life when he wondered if he would be better off not to speak any longer in the name of the Lord. Every time he determined that he would no longer speak the Lord's prophesies, the words of God would burn like fire in his bones and he could not hold them in. He spoke because he was compelled by the Spirit to speak. He could not hold these words in even when he tried. Such was the nature of the call of the Lord on his life.

If God has truly called you, then you too will experience this same burden. Try telling a man called to be an evangelist to stop sharing Christ. Try telling someone gifted in acts of mercy and compassion not to reach out to those in need. Those who are truly called can no more stop sharing or exercising their calling than they could stop breathing. When God calls, he also burdens. That burden is so great that we will willingly suffer the abuse and insults that come our way. This was the experience of Jeremiah.

The exercising of his calling caused Jeremiah terror on all sides (verse 10). He could hear his enemies whisper, "Report him! Let's report him." The sense here is that they were seeking to find anything they could to use against him. They were waiting for him to slip so they could jump on him. They wanted to hear him say something they could use against him to sentence him to death. They were like lions waiting to pounce on their prey. Jeremiah felt them watching his every move. He knew they hated him. Every word of judgment he spoke made them hate him even more.

Jeremiah realized, however, that while everyone was against him, the Lord was with him like a mighty warrior (verse 11). God would not let him down. Jeremiah had very few friends in this life, and he had no wife. God had told him not to attend funerals or parties. He had few companions, but he had the Lord. Jeremiah's God was a mighty warrior. What could people do to him? Jeremiah entrusted himself into the hands of God. He believed that his enemies would stumble instead of him. His enemies would eventually fall and be disgraced. God would watch over him and care for him. Jeremiah's confidence was in the Lord, his God. Without this confidence he would surely have given up.

In verse 12 Jeremiah asked the Lord to let him see vengeance on his enemies. He did not take matters in his own hands but waited on the Lord to exercise justice. He committed his cause to God and left it there. He then persevered in what God had called him to do. His heart rejoiced and sang praise to God who rescues the needy (verse 13). We can only admire his dedication and commitment to the Lord in this matter.

Verses 14–18 are somewhat difficult to understand in light of what precedes them. Jeremiah had just said that he committed his cause to the Lord who rescues the needy. In verse 14, however, he cursed the day in which he was born. In verses 16 and 17, he cursed the man who announced his birth to his father.

How are we to understand this sort of cry from Jeremiah who had committed his cause to the Lord? Was Jeremiah bemoaning his lot in life? Was he lamenting all the problems he had as a prophet? It seems to me that Jeremiah was not so much speaking here about his own personal problems with his enemies as he was speaking about the devastation of the nation he loved. As God revealed to him what was to take place in Judah and Jerusalem, Jeremiah's heart was broken. He not only announced the judgment of God, he also felt the pain of that judgment. He wondered why he had been born to see this terrible judgment of God. He could handle those who hated him and wanted to kill him—this he had given to the Lord. The severe and righteous judgment of his rebellious nation, however, was much more difficult to bear. He took no delight in the messages he spoke. It broke his heart to have to tell his people that the city they loved would be devastated. He believed what God told him, and it hurt him deeply. This is the heart of a true prophet of God.

For Consideration:

- What does this passage reveal about the reality of struggles in ministry? Will we always be appreciated as servants of God?

- Consider the perseverance of Jeremiah. What example does he give us to follow?

- Jeremiah's messages affected him deeply. Do you feel the reality of the messages you preach?

- What gifts has the Lord given you? Do you feel compelled, like Jeremiah, to use them?

- What problems do you face in ministry? Have you committed these matters to the Lord?

For Prayer:

- Ask the Lord to give you a burden for the ministry to which he has called you.

- Thank the Lord for his promise of protection and guidance in your calling.

- Ask the Lord to forgive you for the times you were unwilling to persevere like Jeremiah. Ask the Lord for his strength to be faithful.

- Ask God to show you something of the fire in his bones that Jeremiah felt regarding his ministry. Ask God to give you a deeper burden to use the gifts he has given you.

25

Zedekiah's Inquiry

Read Jeremiah 21

As Jeremiah had prophesied, King Nebuchadnezzar of Babylon came and laid siege to the city of Jerusalem. King Zedekiah of Judah was afraid of what would happen should the enemy gain entrance to the city. He sent a delegation to the prophet Jeremiah to inquire of the Lord about what would happen. Despite what Jeremiah had been prophesying, the king still wondered if the Lord God would do something miraculous to deliver Judah from enemy hands.

The delegation sent to Jeremiah consisted of two priests in particular: Pashhur and Zephaniah. (It should be noted that this Pashhur was not the same man of chapter 20 who put Jeremiah in stocks.) This delegation approached Jeremiah and asked him to seek the Lord about the situation in the nation. The hope was that the Lord would deliver Judah from Nebuchadnezzar's attack by some great wonder. The priests knew the stories of how the Lord had done great things in the past and wanted to see him do so again.

It is interesting to see how these individuals, who had turned their backs on Jeremiah all the time he had been prophesying, came running to him when the words he spoke were proven true. Jeremiah told the delegates that the Lord had determined to judge the city. The weapons of war they were using against the Babylonians would be turned against them. The Babylonians would gain entrance into the city. The Lord himself would fight against his people with anger, fury, and great wrath (verse 5). God would strike down both people and animals with a plague. The enemy would seek and find those who survived the plague and put them to death by the sword, showing no pity or compassion on them at all.

In verse 8 Jeremiah told Pashhur and Zephaniah that God was giving them two options. They could resist the punishment of God through Babylon and perish by the sword, famine, and plague, or they could submit to Babylon and live. If they remained in the city and defended it, they would die. If, on the other hand, they surrendered to God's judgment and went voluntarily into captivity, they would live.

This would not have been an easy word for the people of God to receive. God was asking them to give up what was dear to them. This really did not make sense to them. Why would God take away all he had promised to them and their ancestors? What kind of witness would they be to the world if, as God's people, they were defeated and lost everything? How could the glory of God be revealed to the world in their defeat at the hands of the Babylonians?

In verse 11 God spoke directly to the royal house of Judah. God challenged the king and his administrators to govern with justice every morning and to rescue the one who was being robbed from the hands of the oppressor. Through Jeremiah, the Lord reminded the king that he was guilty of injustice. God saw the deeds of his hands and challenged him to repent of his evil. God was not going to overlook these matters. The sin of the land needed to be punished. If Zedekiah did not repent of his evil, the Lord's anger would break out like an unquenchable fire on Judah.

Jeremiah was called next to speak to the citizens of Jerusalem. God addressed their pride in particular. The inhabitants of Jerusalem lived on a rocky, protective plateau. They had come to feel confident in themselves. "Who can come against us? Who can enter our refuge?" they said (verse 13). Their confidence was in themselves and not in the Lord. That pride separated them from the Lord. The Lord would reward them according to what their deeds deserved. He would kindle a fire that would consume everything and leave them with nothing. Their pride would be broken, and they would come to realize that without God they had nothing.

We see here the pride of God's people. God called the king to humble himself and administer justice in the land. He called the people to turn from confidence in themselves to confidence in God. The delegates that King Zedekiah sent to Jeremiah did not hear the words they wanted. They had hoped for a miraculous sign from the Lord, but instead they were told to submit to their enemies and go into exile. God would not spare them from invasion. Babylon was his instrument of judgment. The people of Judah would live only if they surrendered to Babylon and the righteous discipline of God.

But God had not completely forsaken his people. He would return to them in time. They had sinned and turned from him, so they would be punished as Jeremiah had prophesied.

For Consideration:

- How easy is it to fall into the pride we see in Jerusalem? How often do we find ourselves trusting in our own strength and wisdom?

- God was going to use Babylon to discipline his people and judge them for their sin. Have you ever found yourself fighting something the Lord wanted to use in your life to accomplish his purpose? Explain.

- God will punish sin. We see in this chapter that there came a time in the life of his people when God would no longer come to their aid. Is God always obligated to come to our aid? Explain.

For Prayer:

- Ask the Lord to give you the grace to accept his purposes for your life.

- Ask him for discernment of what he is doing in your life through the trials that come your way. Ask him for wisdom to learn the lessons he wants to teach you.

- Ask him to break any pride that stands between you and him.

26

A Word to the King

Read Jeremiah 22

The prophet Jeremiah spoke in chapter 22 to three kings of Judah. To understand this chapter, we need to know something about the kings who reigned during this time.

Jeremiah prophesied from the reign of Josiah to the reign of Zedekiah. Josiah was a good king and brought many positive reforms to the nation of Judah. He was killed in a battle against Egypt (2 Kings 23:29). His son Jehoahaz (also known as Shallum here in this passage) became king in his place. Shallum or Jehoahaz reigned for three months and was taken captive to Egypt (2 Kings 23:31–34). His brother Jehoiakim was placed on the throne by Pharaoh Neco of Egypt (2 Kings 23:34). During the reign of Jehoiakim, Nebuchadnezzar invaded Judah. Jehoiakim was subjected to him but eventually rebelled. When Jehoiakim died, his son Jehoiachin took his place. He reigned for three months and was taken into captivity by Nebuchadnezzar, who then placed Zedekiah on the throne. Zedekiah was the last king of Judah (2 Kings 24:16–17). He would go into exile in Babylon. This period was a very difficult time for the people of Judah.

A Word to Shallum (Jehoahaz)

In verse 1 Jeremiah was called to go to the royal palace and speak the word of the Lord to the king and his officials. From verse 11 we understand that Shallum was king at this time.

In verse 3 the Lord challenged Shallum to do what was just and right. He was to rescue the oppressed from the hands of the one who had robbed him. He was to treat the foreigner, the widow, and the orphan in the land with respect. God commanded him not to shed innocent blood in the land. This tells us something about the situation in the land under the reign of Shallum. God was not pleased with the evil that was taking place under his reign. He called Shallum to account for his actions.

Along with this challenge to reform his ways came a warning. God reminded the king and his officials that if they obeyed him, then kings would come through the city riding on their horses and chariots. This was a promise of victory and blessing. If, on the other hand, Shallum and his officials refused to listen to the words of Jeremiah, then God swore by himself that the palace would become a ruin. The blessing and prosperity of the government depended entirely on the king's obedience to the word of the Lord. This is a very sobering thought.

In verse 6 God reminded the king that, although the royal palace was as beautiful as Gilead and as majestic as the summits of Lebanon, it would soon become like a desert and an uninhabited town. If the leaders continued in their evil ways, the Lord would send destroyers from the foreign nations against them. These foreigners would cut off their fine cedar beams and burn them. Those cedar beams were very likely part of their palace and temple. These wonderful buildings would be burned to the ground. On seeing this terrible destruction, people from the surrounding nations would ask, "Why has the Lord done such a thing to this great city?" (verse 8). The Lord reminded them that the answer to this question was quite simple. The Lord allowed the enemy to come in and destroy the land because his people had forsaken their covenant with the Lord God and worshiped other gods.

Shallum (whose name means "retribution") was told not to weep for the dead king or mourn his loss (verse 10). This very likely referred to his father, King Josiah, who was killed in battle against Pharaoh Neco of Egypt. Instead of mourning for his father, he was to mourn for those who would go into exile and never return to Judah. This would be his own destiny. After only a three-month reign, Pharaoh Neco took Shallum into exile to the land of Egypt. Shallum would never return to his homeland. Jeremiah told Shallum that he would die in exile (verses 11–12).

Shallum's father died in defense of his country. King Josiah had died an honorable death in the land of his fathers. Shallum, however, would be humiliated. He would not have an honorable death but would suffer the humiliation of exile and banishment from his homeland.

In verses 13–17 we catch a glimpse of the attitude of Shallum. "Woe to him who builds his palace by unrighteousness," the Lord told him. God rebuked him for building his great palace without paying his laborers. In doing so, he was guilty of breaking the law of Moses: "Do not take advantage of a hired man who is poor and needy, whether he is a brother Israelite or an alien living in one of your towns. Pay him his wages each day before sunset, because he is poor and is counting on it. Otherwise he may cry to the LORD against you, and you will be guilty of sin (Deuteronomy 24:14–15).

In his pride Shallum demanded his people make a great palace for him. Notice in verse 14 that he wanted it to be spacious with large windows, paneled with cedar, and decorated in red. Seeing that Shallum only reigned for three months, we wonder when he had time to begin this great project. Obviously, this was one of the first objectives of his reign. He wanted to live in luxury and ease. This was his heart. Notice what God said about this in verse 15: "Does it make you a king to have more and more cedar?" Somehow, Shallum believed that if he lived in luxury, he would gain the respect and admiration of his people.

God pointed Shallum to the example of his father, Josiah. His father did what was right, and the Lord blessed him. God reminded Shallum of how his father defended the cause of the poor. Those who know and love the Lord will be righteous before him and support justice among the people (verse 16). This was what the Lord was expecting from the kings of Judah, but this was not the heart of Shallum. Instead, he had chosen to extort, shed innocent blood, and oppress his people to obtain his own ends. His eyes were set on doing evil. For this the wrath and judgment of God were on him.

A Word to Jehoiakim

Concerning Jehoiakim, the next king of Judah, Jeremiah prophesied that no one would mourn his death. Pharaoh Neco placed Jehoiakim on the throne; and during his reign, Nebuchadnezzar of Babylon invaded Judah. His was a very troubled reign. In verse 19 Jeremiah prophesied that he would have the burial of a donkey. He would be dragged outside the city and left for scavengers to feed on. No one would lament the passing of his splendor.

These would be difficult days in the life of the people of God. Jeremiah was called to go to Lebanon and Bashan and cry out for the towns of Judah. All their allies would be crushed. God had warned the people of Judah of the judgment to come, but they would not listen. They had been a rebellious people from the time of their youth. A great wind would drive their leaders away and put them to shame. That wind would be in the form of an enemy that would invade them. The people would groan like a woman in labor under the heavy discipline of the Lord (verse 23).

A Word to Jehoiachin

The final word of this prophecy came to King Jehoiachin. He reigned for only a few months before he was taken into exile to Babylon. Jeremiah told Jehoiachin that even if he were God's signet ring, he would be pulled off. The signet ring was a ring that carried the authority of the king. Official documents were stamped with this ring. A person who wore this ring spoke for the king. Even if Jehoiachin were God's chosen representative, God would cast him down. He would be handed over to the enemy. He and his mother would be hurled into the land of the Babylonians. They would never return to their homeland and would die in exile.

Jehoiachin was described as a broken pot that nobody wanted. He would be recorded as childless. None of his descendants would ever sit on the throne. Instead, they would perish in the land of exile.

In this passage Jeremiah reminded his people that difficult times were coming. Their kings would be sent into exile, and they would lose everything they had. They would be judged because of their sin. In particular, God held Judah's kings accountable for oppressing the poor and needy.

For Consideration:

- What is the connection here between obedience to the Lord and prosperity in the land? What would happen in your land if obedience to the Lord God became a priority?

- What does this passage tell us about the control of the Lord over the events of our day? How much were these kings really in control of the events of their lives?

- What does this passage teach us about our responsibilities as leaders? How can our actions affect those under us?

For Prayer:

- Pray for the leadership of your land. Ask the Lord to turn their hearts to him.

- Thank the Lord that he is in control of the events of our lives.

- Thank the Lord that he is a God who sees and judges sin. Thank him that truth will triumph in the end.

27

Careless Shepherds and Lying Prophets

Read Jeremiah 23

Chapter 23 begins with a challenge to the shepherds of the land. The term *shepherds* refers to the kings and officials whose responsibility it was to care for the general needs of the people of God. The kings and the officials were accountable to God for the poor and the needy in the land. They were to assure that justice was administered in the land. Theirs was a very important work.

The shepherds of Jeremiah's day, however, did not care for the people. "Woe to the shepherds who are destroying and scattering the sheep of my pasture!" the Lord said in verse 1. Those who were responsible for the well-being of the people of God were actually destroying them.

God told them in verse 2 that he would punish them because they were not taking care of his sheep. God held these leaders personally responsible for how they treated his people. How important it is for us to understand this. If you have been called as a shepherd of God's people, you cannot take this responsibility lightly. God holds you accountable for the well-being of his flock.

Notice that the flock had been scattered to various nations. This had happened because of sin. The leaders of Judah had not guided the people away from sin. The Lord still loved his people. He would not abandon them in their time of need. He promised in verse 3 to bring them back from the countries of their exile. He would again settle them in their own land where they could once more be fruitful and productive.

God promised in verse 4 to place different shepherds over his people who would properly care for them so that they would no longer live in fear. None of the sheep would go missing, and every one of them would be tended with special care. Under the leadership of the old shepherds, the flock had been scattered. These new shepherds, however, would lovingly protect God's flock.

God would raise up a shepherd as a righteous Branch. We need to see several important details in this passage about this man.

This righteous Branch would be a Davidic king who reigned wisely and did what was just and right in the land. In the day of this king, Judah would be saved and Israel would be kept safe (verse 6). His name would be "The Lord Our Righteousness." Ultimately, there is only one person who could bear this name. The Messiah, the Lord Jesus Christ, alone could bear this name. He was called here The Lord Our Righteousness not only because he was righteous and perfect in all his ways but also because he is our righteousness. He alone is our hope of a right standing with God.

In the history of God's people, they had often looked back to the land of Egypt and their delivery from bondage under the leadership of Moses. The Lord reminded them in verses 7 and 8 that the days were coming when they would look back to their deliverance from other countries. They would no longer speak about their release from Egypt but rather about their release from the land of the north and other countries where the Lord had banished them. The leaders of the house of Israel had not taken care of God's people. They had allowed them to break the Mosaic covenant and not repent. This led to their exile and banishment from the land as the covenant required. These evil shepherds had been careless in their efforts to provide for and protect the sheep.

The result was devastating, and God's people were scattered to other countries. God, however, had not abandoned them. The day was coming when he would remember them and bring them back to the land he had promised their ancestors.

Jeremiah moved from a word about the careless shepherds in the land to the prophets of the day. Notice in verse 9 that Jeremiah's heart was broken by what he saw in the land. What he shared was not mere words but his broken heart. Notice the effect the word he carried had on him. He stumbled like a person drunk with alcohol, and his bones trembled within him because of the word that the Lord had given him. Jeremiah shared God's burden with deep intensity of feeling.

As Jeremiah looked around him, he saw that the land was full of adulterers (verse 10). This adultery was primarily spiritual in nature. God's people had abandoned him to serve other gods. Because of this, the land was under a curse. It was desolate and barren. The pastures were withered, and the soil no longer produced its fruit.

Notice that the prophets were busy at this time using their authority unjustly. Instead of directing the people in the holy ways of the covenant, the false prophets directed the people in evil paths of idolatry. Because of this wickedness, the Lord had devastated the land. The prophets did not warn the people that they were under a curse. The godless priests even brought their evil practices into the temple of God. The Lord warned them through Jeremiah that they were on a slippery path leading to their own destruction. They would be banished to darkness (verse 12).

Instead of leading the people along the path of truth, the false prophets of Samaria (the capital city of the northern kingdom) had prophesied by Baal. They had not spoken the word of the Lord but the word of demons. God accused the false prophets of Jerusalem (the capital city of the southern kingdom) of committing spiritual adultery and living a lie (verse 14). These prophets strengthened sin among God's people by pretending to speak for the Lord. Because these prophets did not speak truthfully, the land quickly became like Sodom and Gomorrah, the wicked cities that the Lord destroyed in the days of Abraham (see Genesis 19).

God held these prophets accountable for the evil that had spread through the land. They should have spoken up for righteousness and confronted sin among the people. They should have spoken the word of the Lord, but they refused. They chose to be popular with the people and cater to the lusts of their own flesh. God told them through Jeremiah that they would eat bitter food and drink poisoned water (verse 15). God accused the false prophets of being the source of the evil that had spread throughout the land.

Jeremiah challenged the people not to listen to false hopes from the prophets (verse 16). They were prophesying visions that did not come from the Lord. They spoke lies from their own minds, instead of truth from the mouth of the Lord.

The prophets of Jeremiah's day were telling those who despised the Lord that they would have peace. They told those who lived in the stubbornness of their hearts that no harm would come to them. This pleased the rebellious people. These men prophesied lies in order to gain popularity and favor with the people. These prophets had not entered into the council of the Lord to hear from him. They simply announced pleasant messages that the people wanted to hear. The words they spoke were from their own minds and according to their own understandings. Their prophecies of peace were not from God.

In verse 19 Jeremiah warned the prophets that the storm of the Lord would suddenly break out against the wicked. His anger would not turn back until it had accomplished his purpose. God took this matter of false prophecies very seriously. God did not send these men, yet they ran with a message. He did not speak to them, yet they stood in front of the people and prophesied. In verse 22 Jeremiah declared that if only they had stood in the Lord's council, they could have turned many people from their sins.

Jeremiah reminded the prophets that God saw what they were doing. There was nowhere they could go where he could not see their deeds and hear their words. "'Am I only a God nearby,' declares the LORD, 'and not a God far away?'" (verse 23). He heard and saw everything that went on. These evil prophets could not hide from him.

The prophets claimed to have dreams, which they prophesied to the people, but these messages were not from God. These were false prophets who spoke lies out of the delusions of their own minds (verse 26). These prophets had their own agendas. They prophesied believing that what they spoke would cause people to forget the Lord. They saw the Lord and his ways as a hindrance to their evil intentions. They wanted God's people to follow the idolatrous ways of Baal, and so they spoke words that would ease the consciences of God's rebellious people.

In verse 28 the Lord declared: "Let the prophet who has a dream tell his dream, but let the one who has my word speak it faithfully. For what has straw to do with grain?" This meant that, in the end, the truth would be revealed. The day was coming when the empty straw of these false prophets would be distinguished from the nourishing grain of the true prophets. The true word of God is like a fire that consumes and like a hammer that breaks the rock to pieces.

Jeremiah told the false prophets in verse 30 that God was against them for stealing words from one another while declaring that their messages were from the Lord. Although Jeremiah did not explain what he meant, it might be that he was speaking of how false prophets would steal prophetic words from true prophets and then proclaim those words as though they had received them directly from the Lord. What is clear here is that the false prophets were resorting to trickery to look authentic to the people. God accused them of wagging their tongues and saying "the LORD declares" while they actually prophesied false dreams and led God's people astray.

In verse 33 God told Jeremiah that if the people asked him what the oracle or burden of the Lord was, he was to tell them that the Lord would forsake them. He was to tell the lying prophets in particular that if they spoke again in God's name, the Lord would punish them (verse 34).

In verses 35–40 God told the prophets that they were not to speak to the people because the message they spoke was not from the Lord but from their own minds. The Lord would punish them for perverting truth and misleading the people. The Lord told the lying prophets that he would forget them and cast them away from him. He would bring everlasting shame to their city.

The Lord was very angry with the spiritual leadership of the day. They had not been faithful to him and his word. Instead, they wandered from the path of righteousness to serve themselves. God held them accountable for speaking lies while claiming to speak for the Lord. The result was that all of Judah would be punished and brought to shame.

For Consideration:

- As preachers of the Word of God, how easy is it for us to speak our own minds and not the word that God wants us to share?

- Consider the temptations of spiritual leaders to seek the approval of others. Do you see evidence of this even in your own life?

- To what extent is the spiritual leadership of your land responsible for the condition of your nation? Explain.

For Prayer:

- Ask the Lord to raise up a new generation of prophets who speak only the word of the Lord.

- Thank the Lord for those shepherds of our land who have been faithful to God in caring for the sheep.

- Take a moment to pray for your spiritual leaders, asking that they would remain faithful to God in the work he has called them to do.

28

A Basket of Figs

Read Jeremiah 24

I n chapter 24 Jeremiah had a vision of two baskets of figs placed in front of the temple of the Lord. Let's consider what was happening at this time in the nation of Judah.

King Jehoiachin, his officials, and many skilled workers were captured by the Babylonians and taken to Babylon. King Nebuchadnezzar of Babylon set up Zedekiah as king over the people who remained in the land of Judah. Zedekiah did what was evil in the eyes of the Lord (see 2 Kings 24). He rebelled against Babylon and was captured. His sons were slaughtered in his presence and his eyes blinded. He was then led in chains to Babylon.

In his vision Jeremiah saw two baskets of figs (verse 1). These baskets were placed in front of the temple. The first basket contained very good figs, like those that ripened early. Some commentators see this as a reference to the firstfruits offering, which was dedicated to the Lord from the harvest (see Exodus 23:16). The other basket contained figs that were so bad that they could not be eaten.

The Lord explained to Jeremiah what the vision meant. The

good figs represented the people who had gone into exile in the land of Babylon. God promised to watch over these people and bring them back to their land. They would be planted again in their land, never to be uprooted.

God also promised to give these people a heart to know him. He would be their God, and they would know him with all their heart. He would move in power in the lives of those who had gone into exile. God's hand was on them for good.

This prophecy would have been a real encouragement to the people of God in exile. They had lost everything, and this word would have lifted their spirits. God would not abandon them in their time of trial but use this trial to accomplish something good. This exile would make them a people who loved the Lord.

In verse 8 God told Jeremiah that the bad figs represented King Zedekiah, his officials, and the survivors of the Babylonian siege of Jerusalem. They had rebelled against Babylon, the instrument of God's discipline. Jeremiah had told them to surrender to Babylon and not fight against what God was doing. But they refused the Lord's counsel and brought greater judgment on themselves and the nation. God promised that wherever they went, they would be an object of cursing and ridicule (see Deuteronomy 28:36–37). God would send the sword, famine, and the plague against these rebellious people until they were destroyed. Like the basket of bad figs, they were of no use to God.

This chapter challenges us to submit to the discipline of God in our lives. It reminds us that God has our best interest at heart when he disciplines us. It is important for us to let God accomplish his perfect will in us. The circumstances he sends our way are for our good. They are intended to mature us in righteousness and justice. Like Zedekiah, however, we often grumble and complain about what God is doing. God calls to us through this passage to trust him and believe that what he is doing in us is for our good and his glory.

For Consideration:

- Can you remember times in your life when the Lord used trials to mature you? What did he accomplish through those trials?

- What comfort do you take in the fact that there is nothing that happens in life that God cannot use for your good and his glory?

- What struggle are you facing right now in your walk with God? What is your reaction to that struggle? What does this passage teach you about grumbling and complaining about the situations that God brings your way?

For Prayer:

- Thank the Lord that he is sovereign over the trials in your life.

- Are you going through a struggle right now? Ask the Lord to teach you what you need to learn through this struggle. Thank him that he is going to use it for your good.

- Ask the Lord to forgive you for the times you have grumbled and fought against his purpose in your life.

29

The Cup of the Lord's Wrath

Read Jeremiah 25

This prophecy of Jeremiah came in the fourth year of King Jehoiakim, 605 BC. This was also the first year of King Nebuchadnezzar and the year he first invaded Judah. The prophecy not only concerned Judah but also Babylon and many other nations. Jeremiah spoke here to the nations of the earth and expressed God's international purpose. Jeremiah began by reminding his people that for twenty-three years, he had prophesied to them, but they had not listened to him. We must admire Jeremiah's dedication here. How long would you persevere without seeing results? It is relatively easy to minister when we are being encouraged by results, but it is not so easy when we see nothing for our efforts. For twenty-three years, the people of Jeremiah's day not only rejected his message but also mocked him and sought to kill him.

Jeremiah was not the only prophet that the Lord had sent to his people. He had sent them many other prophets, but the people had also rejected those prophets. Through his faithful prophets, the Lord had warned his people that if they repented of their evil ways and obeyed the covenant, they could remain in the Promised

Land that the Lord God had given them. If they stopped provoking the Lord to anger with their idolatry, then the Lord would keep them from harm. However, God's people would not listen to these prophets. Instead, they continued in their evil ways and brought judgment on themselves.

Jeremiah warned the people of Judah that because they did not listen to the Lord their God, he would bring Nebuchadnezzar and the nations of the earth against them (verses 8–9). They would become an object of ruin and ridicule. God would banish joy and gladness from their land. The voice of the bride and the bridegroom would no longer be heard; the millstone would no longer grind its produce, and light would be removed. Their sin would make their land desolate, and there would be nothing to celebrate. For seventy years they would serve Babylon while their own nation lay in ruins. Sin is a terrible thing. It strips us of the blessing and favor of God.

Jeremiah reminded the people that while God would punish them for their sins, he would not forsake them forever. When the seventy years of judgment were over, God would return to them and extend his hand of favor to their children. After seventy years the Lord would punish Babylon. God would destroy Babylon as a nation. All the prophecies written in the book of Jeremiah would come to pass (verse 13). We have here the stamp of God's approval on the prophetic writings of Jeremiah. None of the words of this prophecy would be left unaccomplished.

In verse 15 God told Jeremiah to take the cup of the Lord's wrath, figuratively, from his hands. Jeremiah was to make the nations drink from that cup. He did this by proclaiming the word of the Lord to those nations. That word was a message of wrath and judgment. The cup of the Lord's wrath would cause the nations to stagger and go mad because of the sword of destruction the Lord would send among them.

In obedience to the Lord, Jeremiah prophesied to the nations. Perhaps symbolically in a vision, he took the cup and had representatives of each nation drink the Lord's wrath. Jeremiah prophesied first against the city of Jerusalem and the towns of Judah that they would become a place of ruin and an object of scorn and cursing.

Jeremiah next prophesied against Egypt and other foreign nations of his day. Verses 20–26 list the nations that God would destroy. Further details of these prophecies to the nations can be found in chapters 46–51. These nations would drink from this cup of God's judgment. They would become sick and would never rise again. God's judgment against Judah was part of a larger judgment against the evil nations of the earth (verse 26). Ultimately, this global judgment would not be complete until the end of time. God reminded the nations through Jeremiah that he had already begun to judge his own people. If he did not hesitate to judge his own covenant people, he would surely not hesitate to judge those he had no relationship with (verse 29).

Jeremiah prophesied that the day was coming when the Lord would thunder from his holy place. He would roar like a lion against the nations. Like a person treading out the grapes, God would shout in victory over the nations and bring his judgment against them. Disaster would spread from nation to nation. The slain would be everywhere (verse 33). No one would mourn them. They would lie on the ground like refuse (see Revelation 19:11–21).

The leaders of the nations were called to weep because their people would be scattered (verse 34). The leaders would have no place to escape from the judgment of the Lord when he, like a fierce lion, destroyed the nations (verse 38).

These were not easy words for the prophet Jeremiah to proclaim. As the Sovereign over all the earth, God would judge the nations. He holds them all accountable to him. How important it is for us to be right with him today. He is an almighty and all-powerful God. His wrath is fierce and righteous. What a joy it is for us to know that through the Lord Jesus Christ our sins have been forgiven. We stand before this holy and awesome God cleansed and loved. Instead of his wrath, we know his wonderful blessing.

For Consideration:

- Consider the faithfulness of Jeremiah to his difficult ministry. Would you be willing to persevere like Jeremiah under such severe circumstances?

- Would you consider that Jeremiah had a successful ministry? What makes a ministry successful?

- What does this passage teach us about the sovereignty of God over all the nations of the earth?

- What does this passage teach us about nations that have never heard the gospel? Are they accountable to God?

For Prayer:

- Ask the Lord to enable you be faithful to him and the ministry he has called you to do.

- Thank the Lord that he is a sovereign God to whom all nations will one day bow the knee.

- Thank him that through his grace you know him personally today.

- Ask God to raise up men and women who will go to the nations with the message of salvation.

30

Jeremiah's Life Is Threatened

Read Jeremiah 26

I t was early in the reign of King Jehoiakim that the Lord called
Jeremiah to go to the courtyard of the temple and speak a
particular word to the people who had gathered there. The
Lord clearly told Jeremiah to prophesy the entire message and not
leave out anything.

Verse 3 reminds us of the Lord's intentions in sending this
word with his people. It was his desire that those who listened
to Jeremiah would turn from their evil ways and so avert God's
punishment. It was not the desire of the Lord that his people
be destroyed. His justice, however, demanded that their sin be
punished if they did not repent. Through his prophet Jeremiah, God
called his people to return to him. He longed to be compassionate
and forgiving, but Judah would not repent.

Jeremiah was to tell the people that if they did not listen to the
Lord and follow his law, then God would make their nation like
Shiloh. The region of Shiloh had been, at the time of Samuel, the
location of the tabernacle of God (see 1 Samuel 4). In the days
of Jeremiah, however, Shiloh was deserted and barren because
of God's judgment. If Judah did not repent, the nation would

become like Shiloh, and the capital city would become the object of cursing and ridicule to the nations (verse 6).

The people of Jeremiah's day felt secure in their land. They did not believe that God would ever destroy Jerusalem or the temple because they believed that these were sacred sites—God's dwelling place on earth. Verse 7 tells us that the priests, the prophets, and the people were all present when Jeremiah spoke this word of judgment from the Lord. When Jeremiah had finished, those present seized him and said, "You must die." They thought Jeremiah was a false prophet and was blaspheming against the holy places, a crime punishable by death. Verse 9 tells us that after hearing Jeremiah, the people crowded around him with evil intentions.

The situation in the temple got so bad that news of what was happening reached the city officials. When they heard of the uproar, they came to the temple to intervene. Officials took their place at the temple gate where court cases would be heard. Jeremiah was put on trial.

As Jeremiah stood before the people, the priests and prophets brought charges against him. They told the officials that Jeremiah deserved to be sentenced to death because he spoke out against the city (verse 11). This was considered treason.

Jeremiah listened to these accusations and then spoke in his own defense. In verse 12 he reminded the crowd that he had not come to this temple of his own will. He had come because the Lord sent him. The words he spoke were the words the Lord told him to speak; they were not the inventions of his own mind. Jeremiah did not back down here. He spoke with confidence and boldness in the Lord: "Now reform your ways and your actions and obey the LORD your God. Then the LORD will relent and not bring the disaster he has pronounced against you," Jeremiah told the people in verse 13. Even in the face of death, Jeremiah remained true to the word of the Lord. He did not apologize for speaking the truth.

Having said these things, Jeremiah placed himself in the hands of his accusers, telling them to do with him whatever they wanted. He was willing to lay down his life for the word he had spoken to them. He reminded them in verse 15, however, that if they killed him, they would be putting an innocent man to death and bringing the guilt of his blood on themselves and their city.

After hearing Jeremiah's defense, the officials and all the people spoke to the priests and the prophets and told them that they did not think Jeremiah should be put to death. They believed that what he had spoken was from the Lord (verse 16).

It should be noticed here how quickly the people changed their opinion. Prior to this, they had surrounded Jeremiah telling him that he deserved to die. Then they began defending his life. It seems they were motivated by the fear of what might happen to them if they were wrong, but they were not ready to change their lifestyles and repent of their sins.

As Jeremiah's fate was being debated, some of the elders of the land added their input. They remembered some similar examples from their history. The intention here was to bring some unity to this much-divided group.

The first example the elders cited to the people was the example of the prophet Micah. Quoting from Micah 3:12 the elders reminded the people present at Jeremiah's trial of the words of a previous prophecy: "This is what the LORD Almighty says: 'Zion will be plowed like a field, Jerusalem will become a heap of rubble, the temple hill a mound overgrown with thickets'" (verse 18). This proved that Jeremiah was not the only one to prophesy against the city of Jerusalem. What Jeremiah said was exactly what Micah had spoken earlier. This word from the elders gave some credibility to Jeremiah's message.

The elders reminded the people of what happened in the days of Micah. Hezekiah was king of Judah at that time, and he did not put Micah to death. Instead, he feared the Lord and sought his favor. The result was that the Lord relented of the disaster he had intended for his people. In light of this, the elders reminded the people that they needed to be very careful about what they did with Jeremiah and his words. They were about to bring a terrible disaster on themselves by killing Jeremiah and rejecting the word the Lord had given him.

The elders cited another example to the people in verse 20. This was the example of the prophet Uriah who also prophesied the same things Jeremiah prophesied against the city of Jerusalem.

But Uriah's situation was handled quite differently. When King Jehoiakim and his officials heard the words of Uriah, they sought to put him to death. Uriah heard of the plot against his life and fled to Egypt. Jehoiakim sent Elnathan and some other servants to Egypt to bring him back. They captured Uriah and brought him back to Jehoiakim, who killed him and buried him in a plot of land reserved for the poor and common people.

It is somewhat difficult to understand what the elders were trying to get across here. In the case of Micah, the elders were obviously challenging the people to be careful lest they kill Jeremiah and bring the wrath of God on themselves. Here in this second example, Uriah the prophet was killed. What we need to understand is that the two examples mentioned here happened in the reigns of two different kings. In the reign of Hezekiah, because he spared the life of Micah and heeded the prophet's word, God's blessing came to him and the nation. It was obvious, however, that Jehoiakim's reign was very different. Babylon was a constant threat to him and stripped him of much wealth. The people knew the difference between these two reigns. Were the elders insinuating that part of the reason the nation was suffering was because Jehoiakim had killed Uriah? Was God judging Judah because of the murder of one of his prophets? If this was the case, it would have been very dangerous for the nation to risk killing Jeremiah.

Verse 24 tells us that Ahikam the son of Shaphan supported Jeremiah, so he was not handed over to the priest. In 2 Kings 22 we read the story of how earlier in the history of God's people, Shaphan the scribe brought the recently rediscovered Book of the Law to King Josiah. The reading of this Book of the Law transformed the nation of Judah. Ahikam, as the son of Shaphan, would have been very much aware of his father's work and its impact on the nation. As a result, Ahikam stood firmly behind Jeremiah.

We see in this chapter the incredible protection of God on the life of Jeremiah. God surrounded him in his time of need. Jeremiah's life was spared because God had not finished with him. We must admire the spiritual courage of Jeremiah to place his life in the hands of the Lord. He would willingly die to proclaim the word that God had put on his heart. May the Lord give us the courage to be faithful to the ministries he has given us.

For Consideration:

- What do we learn here from the example of Jeremiah who risked his life to proclaim the truth of God?

- Consider the people in this section who quickly changed their allegiance from one opinion to another. What do you suppose was motivating this change of allegiance?

- What encouragement do you find here concerning the protection and guidance of God in your life?

For Prayer:

- Thank the Lord for the way he protects his servants.

- Ask the Lord to give you the courage of Jeremiah to stand up for the truth.

31

Nebuchadnezzar's Time

Read Jeremiah 27

I have always taken great comfort in the fact that I serve a sovereign God. This God is Lord over all the events and circumstances of my life. He rules supreme in the history of this world. All things are in his hands, and he uses all events to accomplish his purpose and will. In a mysterious way, this happens while still giving us a free will to choose the course of our own lives.

We see in this passage the great sovereignty of God over the nation of Babylon. While Babylon chose to invade the nation of Judah of her own free will, God used this to discipline his people. When the discipline of his people was over, the Lord released them from the domination of Babylon. God was in complete control of every circumstance in the lives of his people.

This particular word of prophecy came during the time of Zedekiah, the last king of Judah. It should be noted here that both the King James Version and the New King James Version state that this prophecy came during the reign of Jehoiakim and not Zedekiah. The manuscripts available to us are not clear on this matter. Verses 3 and 12 do make it clear that the prophecy was delivered during the reign of Zedekiah. Jeremiah 28:1 is also quite important in this regard. It begins with the following statement: "And it happened in the same year, at the beginning of the reign of Zedekiah king of Judah" (NKJV). So while there is some debate as to the exact time of the prophecy, the prophecy itself is very clear.

In verse 2 God asked Jeremiah to make yokes of straps and crossbars and put them around his neck. Jeremiah was to act out his prophecy so that the people would get the significance of what he was saying.

In this particular situation, the prophet was to send God's word of judgment to five surrounding nations through their envoys who had come to Judah to visit Zedekiah. We know that the pressing issue of the day was Babylon. Nebuchadnezzar was an immediate threat. Had these nations gathered to see what could be done about this threat? If this was the case, then it was an ideal opportunity to communicate God's word to many nations at once.

Jeremiah told these envoys that they were to tell their masters that the God of Israel made the earth with his great power. He also made all the people and the animals that are on it. As a sovereign God, he has the right to give it to whomever he chooses (verse 5). Although these nations had been fighting against Babylon, in reality, it was God they needed to deal with. While it was true that Babylon was conquering their lands, it was the Lord who gave Babylon the power to conquer. Jesus said a similar thing to Pilate in John 19:10–11. Jesus reminded Pilate that God controls all power (see also Psalm 62:11 NKJV).

God told Jeremiah to announce to the envoys that the Lord was going to hand their countries over to Nebuchadnezzar. Even the wild animals would be subject to him. All nations would be held in subjection to him, his son, and his grandson. According to God's plan, Babylon would also be judged and conquered. This would happen when God was finished using Babylon as his weapon of judgment.

At this point in history, it was the purpose of Almighty God that the nations submit to Nebuchadnezzar and his domination. If they did not place their necks under his yoke, God warned that he would punish them with the sword, famine, and plague until they were destroyed.

There are times when the will of the Lord is very difficult for us to understand. Sometimes we fight for things that God wants to take from us. There are times when the Lord calls us to submit to his yoke of discipline. God has his perfect ways of teaching us righteousness. Don't run from the yoke that God brings into your life. Let him accomplish his perfect will and teach you through it.

In verse 9 Jeremiah told the envoys that they were not to listen to their prophets, diviners, dreamers, mediums, and sorcerers. These individuals were telling the people that they would not serve the king of Babylon. Jeremiah boldly told the envoys that these individuals were lying to them. You can imagine that these words would not have gone over too well with these foreign visitors. Not only was Jeremiah telling them to submit to Babylon, but also he was telling them that their spiritual leaders were deceiving them. Jeremiah stood alone here. You can imagine the amount of faith Jeremiah needed to have in his God. All the other spiritual leaders of Judah and her neighbors were prophesying that they would not be led into captivity. Jeremiah stood alone with God in his words to the contrary.

Jeremiah told the envoys that if they bowed their necks under the yoke of Babylon and accepted this domination, God would let them remain in their land and farm it (verse 11). God's ways are different from ours. It is important for us to trust in his sovereign purpose even when we do not understand what he is doing and his ways seem strange to us.

What Jeremiah prophesied to the nations he also announced to his own king (verse 12). He challenged Zedekiah, as well, to surrender to Babylon. If the king would not submit to the purpose of God in this, he and his people would die by the sword, famine, and plague. Just because they were God's beloved people, did not mean that they would be exempt from his discipline.

Jeremiah challenged Zedekiah not to listen to the words of Judah's false prophets. They claimed to prophesy in the name of the Lord but were liars. They prophesied like the prophets and mediums of other nations that Jerusalem would not be captured. Judah's false prophets deceived the people. They spoke in the name of the Lord, but the Lord did not send them. Because the king and the people wanted to believe the lying prophets instead of repenting and returning to the Mosaic covenant, the people of Judah would be banished from their land and perish.

In verse 16 Jeremiah shifted his attention to the priests of Judah, who were concerned about the temple. They too had been listening to the lies of the false prophets. Babylon had already seen the value of the temple articles and had already taken many of these articles to Babylon. The priests were very concerned about this and had consulted the false prophets who told them that very soon these articles would be brought back from Babylon. Jeremiah told the priests, however, that this was incorrect. These articles would not be coming back soon but would remain in Babylon for a long time. Jeremiah challenged the priests also to serve the king of Babylon. Only in submitting to Nebuchadnezzar would their lives be saved. By refusing the discipline of the Lord, they would bring disaster on themselves.

Jeremiah called the prophets in verse 18 to pray that the furnishings of the temple would not leave the temple. This would only be possible, however, if these prophets stopped prophesying lies in the name of the Lord and the people in Judah repented and returned to the Lord.

In verses 19–22 we see that there were still some articles in the temple that had not yet been taken by the king of Babylon. The pillars, the basin, movable stands, and other furnishings remained in the temple for worship. These articles were not taken away when Jehoiachin was taken into exile. Jeremiah told the priests that these articles would be taken when Nebuchadnezzar returned for more objects of value. They would remain in the land of Babylon until the Lord determined it was time to return them to his people. Judah would be stripped of everything, but, according to the divine plan, these things would be restored to Judah when she returned from exile (see Ezra 1:7–11).

These treasures would be reserved for those who returned from the exile. The enemy would not be able to keep what God had allowed them to take away. In time, when God's people had learned their lesson, these temple treasures would be returned to them. We see this principle at work in the life of Job in the Old Testament. Satan stripped him of everything he had, but it was all restored to him when God accomplished his purposes in Job's life. The enemy cannot keep what God has given to us. He may take it for a time but God will restore it to us in his time.

For Consideration:

* What does this passage teach us about the sovereignty of God?

* What do we learn here about how God can use our trials to accomplish his good?

* Have you seen God using trials in your life to accomplish much good? Explain.

* In this chapter we catch a vision of Jeremiah who willingly stood before envoys, priests, mediums, and false prophets to proclaim a message they contradicted. Are you willing to stand alone on the truth of God like Jeremiah?

For Prayer:

* Thank the Lord that he is a sovereign God who is in control of all things.

* Ask the Lord for grace to submit to his purposes in order to learn from the trials he sends your way.

* Ask the Lord to give you the courage of Jeremiah to stand firm and faithful even when you are alone.

* What has the enemy succeeded in taking from you as a believer? Ask the Lord to restore the blessings Satan has stripped from you and your church.

32

Hananiah the Prophet

Read Jeremiah 28

I n chapter 27 the Lord asked Jeremiah to make a yoke and to go to the envoys who had come to Judah from many nations and to tell them that they were to submit to the king of Babylon. As you can imagine, this message would not have been well received. The strongest reaction to this message came from a prophet named Hananiah.

In the fourth year of the reign of Zedekiah, the prophet Hananiah spoke to Jeremiah. Notice here that Hananiah spoke this word in the presence of the people in the temple. This word was intended to be a public rebuke to Jeremiah.

According to Hananiah, it was the will of the Lord to break the yoke of Babylon; whereas, Jeremiah told the people that they were to place their necks under the yoke of Babylon. Hananiah told them that the yoke would be broken within two years, and all the temple articles that Nebuchadnezzar had removed would be restored. King Jehoiachin and all the exiles would also return within those two years. This prophecy contradicted what Jeremiah said. Jeremiah had prophesied that this exile would last for seventy years: "'This whole country will become a desolate wasteland,

and these nations will serve the king of Babylon seventy years. But when the seventy years are fulfilled, I will punish the king of Babylon and his nation, the land of the Babylonians, for their guilt,' declares the LORD, 'and will make it desolate forever'" (25:11–12). In contradicting this prophecy, Hananiah publicly placed himself in opposition to Jeremiah.

Jeremiah responded to Hananiah's prophecy in verse 6: "'Amen!' said Jeremiah. 'May the Lord do so!'" Jeremiah longed to see his people freed from the bondage of Babylon as much as Hananiah. He wanted to see the articles of the Lord's house returned to Jerusalem. He took no delight in seeing the land and people destroyed by Babylon. God's people had been guilty of horrible sin and had turned their backs on their holy Lord. Despite their guilt, Jeremiah longed to see forgiveness and reconciliation.

While this was Jeremiah's heart cry, he knew that what Hananiah spoke was not God's will for his people. Jeremiah reminded Hananiah and the people that from early times true prophets had prophesied war, disaster, and plague. Jeremiah's messages were similar to those of God's prophets of the past. Hananiah was prophesying peace, not war and famine. Jeremiah told him that the truth would be revealed when the events came to pass. Jeremiah did not feel any need to defend his prophecies. He simply placed the matter in the Lord's hands. Time would tell who was right.

After hearing what Jeremiah said, Hananiah took the yoke Jeremiah was wearing and broke it in front of the people (verse 10). Then he told the people that God would break the yoke of Babylon within two years. Jeremiah did not debate the issue any more with Hananiah.

We must admire the courage of Jeremiah before Hananiah. He knew what God had asked him to say, and he was secure in this. Jeremiah did not feel the need to defend his name and his reputation before Hananiah when he was accused of being a false prophet. Jeremiah did not fall into the snare of the enemy here. He left the matter in the hands of the Lord and walked away. It was not for him to defend his reputation. We need to learn this lesson in our own lives and ministries. God himself will take our defense in his own time.

Not long after this event, the Lord spoke to Jeremiah and asked him to speak to Hananiah. He was to tell Hananiah that though he had broken Jeremiah's yoke of wood, God would put a yoke of iron in its place, which would not be so easily broken (verse 13). God surely would force the nations to serve the king of Babylon. Even the wild animals of the land would fear this king and submit to him. This is what the Lord had determined, and there was nothing that would stop him from accomplishing his purposes.

As for Hananiah, the Lord had never sent him, and yet he had prophesied in the Lord's name and persuaded his nation to believe his lies (verse 15). Jeremiah told Hananiah that the judgment of the Lord would fall on him. Through Jeremiah, the Lord told Hananiah that he would remove him from the surface of the earth. Shortly after Jeremiah's prophesy, Hananiah died—the Lord judged him for the falsehood he had spread in Judah. The whole nation saw Hananiah's judgment and knew him to be a false prophet.

What strikes me here is the way God defended his true servant. Jeremiah did not need to defend himself. God did a much better job than Jeremiah could have. The prophet left this matter in the hands of the Lord and continued to preach as he was called. Notice how serious a matter it is to stand against those the Lord sends to speak his word. God does not take it lightly when we rebuke his servants. The Lord defends and cares for those who belong to him.

For Consideration:

• Have you ever found yourself in a situation where you felt the need to defend your honor? Why is it hard in these times to leave this matter in the hands of the Lord?

• How can we recognize the difference between a true prophet and a false prophet?

• How easy is it to criticize our spiritual leaders? What does this passage teach us about the danger of this practice?

For Prayer:

- Ask God to give you the courage to let him defend you. Place yourself in his hands and trust him to be your defense.

- Ask the Lord to forgive you for the times you have spoken evil against his servants.

- Ask the Lord to give us more men and women like Jeremiah who will stand firm on the truth of the word of God.

33

Jeremiah's Letter

Read Jeremiah 29:1–14

C hapter 29 tells us the details of a letter written by Jeremiah to the people who had gone into exile in Babylon. Some of Jeremiah's prophecies were originally written out for God's people to read.

The letter was addressed to the elders, prophets, priests, and people who Nebuchadnezzar carried away into captivity. It was written after Jehoiachin and his mother had been taken into exile. Notice in verse 2 that Nebuchadnezzar had taken all the artisans from the land. All these well-educated and skilled individuals were useful to him in Babylon to advance his kingdom.

This letter was sent to the exiles by means of two individuals by the names of Gemariah and Elasah. Gemariah was the son of Hilkiah, who had discovered the Book of the Law, and Elasah was the son of Shaphan, who had read the contents of the Book of the Law to King Josiah (see 2 Kings 22:8–10). Obviously, these men had the same respect as their fathers for the Word of the Lord. It was to these men of faith that Jeremiah entrusted his letter.

In his letter Jeremiah challenged the exiles to build their houses and settle down in the land of Babylon. They were to plant their gardens, to marry, and to find spouses for their children so that they could have descendants. The Lord expected the Jews to increase in number during their exile. Obviously, from these words, Jeremiah was reminding the people that they were going to be in exile for a long time; whereas, Hananiah the false prophet had told them that they would be in exile for only two years. Other false prophets also believed this.

Notice as well that Jeremiah told the people that they were to seek the peace and prosperity of their new city. They were to pray that the Lord would prosper and bless the city of their exile. If it prospered, they would also prosper. There is a very important lesson here for us to understand. God had called his people to this time of exile. In their exile, they had to make a choice: they could either become bitter or make the most of their situation. If they continued their rebellion against God's discipline in Babylon, their suffering would only increase and their exile would be miserable. On the other hand, they could learn to rejoice in their new environment. They could build homes and see their children marry and establish families. They could cultivate the land and enjoy the produce and other blessings God would give them.

What is your trial today? Like the exiles of Babylon, you too have a decision to make. You can become bitter and angry with God and others during your trial. This will only be to your own harm. On the other hand, you can accept that God has allowed this trial for a reason and rejoice in what he promises to do through it in your life. You can turn your trial into a blessing by your attitude. To fight against what God has allowed will only cause more frustration in the end.

In verse 8 Jeremiah warned the people about the false prophets among them. He told the exiles not to listen to the dreams and visions of these men. These evil spiritual leaders spoke lies, though they claimed to speak for the Lord. The God of Israel never sent them to prophesy; they spoke in their own authority.

Jeremiah reminded the people again that they would be in exile for seventy years (verse 10). Only after these seventy years had been accomplished would they see the fulfillment of God's promises to them. This was a long time to wait. Many of those who had gone into exile would never return to their homeland. A whole generation would pass. God had finished with the generation of Jeremiah's day. He had pleaded with them to repent, but they had refused to listen. Now they would be punished. His call would be renewed to their children, but the rebellious generation was under the discipline of God and would never return to the Promised Land.

God had not forgotten his covenant promises to them as a people. He had plans to give them a hope and a future (verse 11). The time was coming when their children would call on the Lord, and he would listen to their cry. They would seek him wholeheartedly and find him. The Lord would gather them from all the nations and restore them to their land. For a time, the Lord hid his face from his people, but he would not forget them. They would again hear his call. Jeremiah reminded the exiles that God still loved them deeply and had a wonderful plan for them.

This passage challenges us in our walk with God. It is a call to each generation to surrender fully to the Lord. It reminds us that the Lord will not abandon us. Jeremiah challenges us to trust God in the trials we face in this life. He encourages us to make the most of the times of discipline. We can become bitter and angry, or we can learn to rejoice in what God is doing. We can be confident that God has not abandoned us in our trial. His plans for our good will never change. He promises to care for us, minister to us in our need, and bring us out the other side. There are rich blessings for us on the other side of our exile.

For Consideration:

- What trial are you facing today? What is Jeremiah's challenge to you in this trial?

- Have you been making the most of the Lord's discipline? Are you taking Jeremiah's advice and learning to rejoice in it?

- What is the promise here for those who are going through a personal exile?

- What is the present challenge of God to your generation? Has your generation been faithful to that call?

For Prayer:

- Thank the Lord that he will not forget us in our personal exile.

- Ask the Lord to help you rejoice in your trials.

- Take a moment to pray for the witness of your generation for the cause of the Lord.

- Take a moment to pray for the next generation. Ask God to equip them to be a powerful witness for him.

34

A Word to the Exiled Prophets

Read Jeremiah 29:15–32

This section of the book of Jeremiah describes the content of a letter that Jeremiah sent to the exiles in Babylon. In the last meditation, we saw how Jeremiah encouraged the people in exile to build their homes, find spouses for their children, and cultivate the land. He reminded them that they would be in the land of Babylon for seventy years. Jeremiah challenged his people to make the most of their situation. In the remainder of his letter, Jeremiah spoke specifically to the prophets who had gone into exile.

Jeremiah knew what those who read his letter would say. He knew that they would question why they should listen to him when they had prophets with them in exile. These false prophets misled the people by prophesying that the exile would soon be over and they would quickly return to the land of Judah. Jeremiah, on the other hand, told them that this was not the case.

Jeremiah prophesied that Judah would be abandoned. The Lord God would send a sword, famine, and plague against the people who remained in Judah. He compared them to bad figs that could not be eaten. This goes back to the vision Jeremiah had in chapter 24. There Jeremiah was told that those who remained in Judah and did not go into exile would be like a basket of bad figs that were worthless. God would pursue them with sword, famine, and plague and make them to be an abomination in the eyes of the kingdoms around them. God would scatter those who chose to remain in Judah. They would suffer an even worse fate than those who accepted God's discipline and went into exile.

The exiles probably envied those who had remained in Judah. God told them, however, to flourish in the land of exile and that their homeland would become deserted. Jeremiah painted a picture of desolation while the false prophets painted a picture of restored prosperity in their homeland in a few years.

These exiles were just as guilty of not listening to the Lord as those who defiantly chose to remain in the land of Judah. God had a word for these exiles. In particular, he had a message for the false prophets there.

Jeremiah spoke first to the prophets Ahab and Zedekiah (verse 21). According to this verse, these prophets had been speaking lies in the name of the Lord. Because of these lies, the Lord said that he would hand them over to Nebuchadnezzar who would put them to death. Their punishment would be public for everyone to see. Everyone would know that these prophets had not spoken the truth. People living in exile would use the example of these prophets as a curse. They would say, "The LORD treat you like Zedekiah and Ahab, whom the king of Babylon burned in the fire" (verse 22).

Jeremiah then revealed something about the evil lives of these prophets. They had done terrible things in the land of Israel. In verse 23 Jeremiah said that they had committed adultery with their neighbors' wives and had spoken words that God did not tell them to speak. Notice how these two sins were placed together in this verse. While we understand the terrible nature of the sin of adultery, Jeremiah reminds us that the sin of speaking lies in the Lord's name is just as evil.

In verse 24 Jeremiah spoke also to a false prophet by the name of Shemaiah who had sent a letter from Babylon to the people in Jerusalem. This letter condemned Jeremiah and the things he had written to the people in exile. Shemaiah's letter had been sent to

Zephaniah the priest.

In this letter Shemaiah stated that Zephaniah, as priest in charge of the house of the Lord, had the responsibility of dealing with any madman who acted like a prophet (verse 26). This was a clear reference to Jeremiah and revealed Shemaiah's opinion of God's true prophet. The letter told Zephaniah to put Jeremiah in stocks and neck-irons because Jeremiah was only posing as a prophet. Shemaiah told Zephaniah of the letter that Jeremiah had written to the exiles, telling them to build their homes and settle in the land of Babylon.

When Zephaniah received the letter from Shemaiah, he read it to Jeremiah. God told Jeremiah to send another letter to the exiles exposing Shemaiah as a lying false prophet (verse 31). The Lord promised to punish Shemaiah and his descendants. This family would perish and never see the good things that the Lord would do for his people. This would happen because he had preached rebellion against God.

This reminds us that Jeremiah was often rejected. The false prophets who lived with God's people in exile taught that Jeremiah was a madman and not a true prophet. They tried to undermine his ministry by questioning his authority. Even when the prophecy of Jeremiah came true about Judah being exiled in Babylon, these false prophets still refused to believe the truth. Even in their time of exile, God's people were being misled.

For Consideration:

• What does this passage teach us about God's concern for the truth?

• What does this passage teach us about the seriousness of speaking as God's representative?

• What opposition did Jeremiah face during this time? How was God going to deal with that opposition?

For Prayer:

- Take a moment to pray for those whom God has placed in spiritual authority over you. Ask God to enable them to speak the truth.

- Ask the Lord to give you discernment to recognize the difference between the false ideas of people and God's sovereign will and purpose.

- Ask God to give you something of the perseverance of Jeremiah, who seems to have been opposed everywhere he turned.

35

Israel and Judah Restored

Read Jeremiah 30

Over the last few meditations, we have seen how the prophet Jeremiah reminded the people who had gone into exile that they would be there for seventy years. They were to make the best of this time of discipline. They were not to lose heart but to recognize the sovereign hand of God in their trial and learn to rejoice in what the Lord was doing. In this chapter Jeremiah reminded his people that God had not forsaken them in their judgment. The day was coming when he would restore their blessings.

God told Jeremiah to write this particular prophecy in a book. In this way, many would profit from it. The days were coming when God would bring his people back from exile. He would restore to them the land he had given to their ancestors. Verse 4 tells us that this prophecy concerned both Israel and Judah. Some commentators find here a reference to the severe suffering of God's people during the end times described in Matthew 24 and the book of Revelation.

In verses 5–6 Jeremiah painted a picture of individuals in tremendous pain and suffering. The prophet used the picture of a woman in labor, about to give birth. Her cries could be heard throughout the land. These were cries of fear and terror. Even the strong and brave were holding their stomachs, like a woman in labor. Their faces were pale as if they had lost all hope in life.

Jeremiah described a time of great suffering, like no other (verse 7; see also Matthew 24:21). Jeremiah may have been referring to the events that surrounded Judah's removal from her land at the hands of the Babylonians, or perhaps he was including a future reference as well. Notice in verse 7 that while the people of Israel and Judah (here referred to as Jacob) would face this trouble, they would also be saved out of that trouble. God would not completely abandon his people.

Jeremiah told his people that God would break the yoke off their necks and tear off their bonds. Jeremiah told them to submit to the yoke of Babylon, but the time was coming when the Lord would remove that yoke. They would no longer be enslaved by foreigners but instead would serve the Lord their God and David their king (verse 9). God would raise up another David to be their king, and no one would make them afraid (verse 10). This reference to David pointed the people to the Lord Jesus Christ, who would come as a descendant of David to be their eternal and true King.

As they faced the discipline of God in Babylon, they were not to fear or be dismayed. Their trial would not be easy, but God would be with them. He would deliver them and bring them out of the land of their exile. Jacob's descendants would again have peace and security because God would save them.

Notice in verse 11 the difference in how God treated his people and how he treated the unbelieving nations. While God's people would be punished, they would not be destroyed. God's hand was on them to discipline them, not to annihilate them. God's justice demanded that they be punished because of their sin, but God would have compassion on them. This was not the case for the unbelieving nations, which God would one day completely destroy.

As believers, our sins have been forgiven, and our future is assured. Nothing can take us from the Lord. While the Lord may at times discipline us, we will not be abandoned or destroyed. In his judgment he will remember that we are his children. On the other hand, there is finality to his judgment of the unbeliever. Hell is very real and a place of eternal punishment. The judgment of the unbeliever is forever.

While God's discipline of the believer is not final, it can still be very painful. The Lord had inflicted an incurable wound on his people (verses 12–14). There was no one to intercede for them, and the Lord was not listening to their cries. All their political allies had deserted them.

God reminded his people in verse 15 that this discipline was the result of their sin. God took no pleasure in disciplining his people. This discipline was not without reason: it was intended to cleanse and purify. Jeremiah reminded his people in verse 16 that while they were being disciplined because of sin, God would sustain them through that discipline. Anyone who dared to harm them would have to answer to God. Those who devoured them would themselves be devoured, and those who plundered them would be plundered. Though he disciplined his people, God would also protect and keep them. He knew what they could handle and would carefully measure the discipline his people needed without destroying them.

I have personally experienced my share of the discipline of the Lord. There have been times when I wondered if I could handle what he was doing in me, but God has always brought me through each trial. Never once has he left me. We can be absolutely assured of his grace in the trials he uses to train us.

God promised to restore the health of his people and heal their wounds (verse 17). God would restore Jacob's fortune and again have compassion on his people. Their city would be rebuilt. Their palace would stand tall in its proper place in Jerusalem. Songs of thanksgiving and rejoicing would be heard in the land God had given to his people. God would restore his blessing to them. He would multiply their descendants so that they would be as numerous as in the days of old. Their towns and cities would be established and strong, and God would again be their defense. He would also punish those who had oppressed them.

Notice in verse 21 that God would give them a leader from their own nation who would be devoted to God. This may be a reference to the Messiah, the Lord Jesus. He would be uniquely close to the Father and perfectly devoted to him. He would be a perfect leader for his people.

Verse 21 brings us a challenge from God: "Who is he who will devote himself to be close to me?" The context of this verse is the leader whom God would raise up from among his people. What the verse has to tell us is that the leader that God is looking for is one who will devote himself to the Lord.

More than education and experience in life, we need men and women who will devote themselves to being close to God. The enemy fears those who are close to God because he knows that they are in a place of communion and power. Many things can keep us from drawing close to the Lord. I have found myself so busy in ministry that I had no time to draw close to the Lord. If this is what has happened in your ministry, you may need to take some time to seek the Lord afresh. It is only in intimacy with God that you will be effective in ministry.

The invitation was extended to God's people. The extent of blessing they would experience would depend on their willingness to devote themselves to being close to the Lord. The question Jeremiah asked is still valid in our day. Who will devote himself or herself to be close to the Lord? May God make this the highest priority of our lives. This path is not easy. There will be times when the Lord will have to discipline us to purge away things that keep us from him. The Holy Spirit of God, who is dedicated to drawing us close to the Lord, will complete the work of God in us (see Philippians 1:6; 2:13).

The Lord promised to be the God of his people. He would burst out in a storm of wrath on the nations (verse 24). That storm would cleanse the nations. God's anger would not turn back until it had accomplished everything he intended to accomplish, according to his eternal plan.

Jeremiah reminded his people in the closing verse of this chapter that the day would come when they would understand what he was telling them. At this point in Judah's history, what Jeremiah was prophesying was difficult to understand. God's people were experiencing the harshness of God's discipline in exile, and their land was devastated. In time, however, when they looked back, they would understand what their just and gracious God had been doing in their lives.

Maybe you are going through something difficult right now, and you do not understand what God is doing. You are experiencing his discipline and cannot see how this is going to be for your good. In time, however, all will make sense.

For Consideration:

- What does this passage teach us about the discipline of the Lord?

- Where is God when we are facing our trials? What does Jeremiah teach us about this?

- How can you devote yourself to being close to God? What distracts you personally from spending time with the Lord?

For Prayer:

- Thank the Lord that he is not only in control of the events of your life but will also use them to draw you closer to himself.

- Thank the Lord that he will never abandon you in your trial. Thank him that he promises to take you out of your trial when he has accomplished the purpose for which he sent it.

- Ask the Lord to give you patience to wait on him to accomplish his purpose in your time of difficulty.

- Ask the Lord to give you a heart devoted to being close to God.

36

Renewed Promises for Israel

Read Jeremiah 31:1–17

J eremiah had reminded the exiles that the time was coming when the Lord would return to his people and restore their fortunes and blessing. Jeremiah continued on this theme in chapter 31. While chapters 30–33 do refer to the return of the Judean exiles from Babylon, many commentators see here a far-distant reference to the end times and a restoration of the nation of Israel in a millennial kingdom.

The time was coming, Jeremiah told his people, when God would be the God of Israel, and they would be his people. This merits some consideration. While God had always been the God of Israel, his people had not always recognized him as such. While Israel had always been God's people, there was a time when God chose to withdraw his presence from them. In their exile they did not experience the reality of God being their God. There was a day coming, however, when God would return to them. As a people, they too would return to their God with all their heart. The intimacy between God and his people would again be restored. They would truly be his people, and he would truly be their God—not in words only but in reality.

The day was coming when those who had survived the sword of Babylon would find favor with God in the desert. This was where the people of God were at this point in their history. The desert is a barren and dry place without the blessing of God. There in the desert they cried out to God for deliverance. They were broken and alone. Jeremiah reminded them that God would hear their cries and restore them. God's favor would again be on them, and they would find rest.

God had not forgotten his people in their trial. He loved them with an everlasting love. It was true that, at this point, they were not seeing that love, but even their terrible sin and rebellion could not quench his desire for them.

God was going to restore his people. The day was coming when they would again take up their tambourines and dance with joy (verse 4). They would again plant vineyards on the hills of Samaria and enjoy the fruit of their labors.

In that day the watchmen of Israel would call the people of Israel to worship. Who were these watchmen? Ezekiel was called a watchman who proclaimed the word of the Lord to his people (Ezekiel 3:17). The watchmen were the spiritual leaders of the land. Worship and praise would again resound from the nation of Israel. God's people would shout forth his praise and proclaim his deliverance to the whole earth.

That same call goes out to you and me today. We who have been delivered from bondage are to be a people of praise and thanksgiving. We are not to be ashamed to let our praises be heard. We have much to thank God for as a people delivered from sin. God has been good to us. He has remembered us in our weakness and sin. He has set us free, and we are to proclaim his praise.

God promised here a wonderful deliverance to Israel. God would bring back a people from the nations (verse 8). Wherever they were scattered, God would bring them to himself. Ultimately, God's kingdom would extend to the far corners of the earth. God's Spirit would move through every tribe and nation, gathering a people to himself. Notice that among those who would be restored to the Lord would be the blind, the lame, the expectant mothers, and women in labor. A great throng of people would return to the Promised Land, and God would be concerned for every one of them, regardless of their condition.

Jeremiah prophesied in verse 9 that his people would return weeping and praying to the Lord. Could it be that they would weep out of repentance? Notice here that they would pray as they returned. Their hearts would be seeking God and his purposes. They would be seeking his forgiveness and restoration. God would renew and revive them.

God promised through Jeremiah to lead his people beside streams of water. There they would be refreshed as they walked with him. He would lead them in level paths where they would not stumble. As a loving father, he would care for them.

Jeremiah called on the nations to hear what God was doing for his people (verse 10). The God who scattered his people would also return them to the land he had promised them by covenant. He would buy them back from the hands of those who had taken them into exile. He would rescue them from the hands of those who were strong.

It is important that we see how the Lord wants the whole world to see what he is doing in the lives of his people. Through his people, God reveals himself to the nations. He would restore Israel so that the world could see his grace. He would rescue Israel so that the world could see a demonstration of his power. He would return to Israel so that the world could see his forgiveness and love. The way God deals with his people is a testimony to the world of his character. As God's people today, we are witnessing to the world about what God is like.

What a glorious day it would be when the Lord restored his blessing to his people Israel. They would return to their Promised Land with great shouts of joy proclaimed from the heights of Zion where everyone could hear (verse 12). They would rejoice in the Lord's bounty. There would again be an abundance of grain, new wine, and oil. The flocks and herds would again be blessed and produce much offspring. God's people would be like a well-watered garden. Sorrow would be banished. The young maidens of the land would be glad and express their joy in dancing. Their men, young and old, would see their mourning turned into gladness. God would give them comfort and joy instead of sorrow.

In the phrase "and they will sorrow no more" (verse 12), some commentators see a reference to a future time, because presently Israel is still scattered and languishing. This promise was not completely fulfilled when Judah returned from the Babylonian exile.

In verse 15 Jeremiah painted a picture of contrast to the joyous future of Israel. Rachel, the wife of Jacob (Genesis 30), was used here to symbolize all Israelite mothers weeping for their children slain in the Babylonian conquest of Judah. Jeremiah envisioned Rachel looking around her at the nation that was promised to her descendants and seeing only desolation and barrenness. Her children had been taken from her to Babylon and were no more. In verses 16–17 God spoke comfort to Rachel. He called her to stop weeping. Her work would be rewarded. What was Rachel's work here? Was it not in her giving birth to a nation? Was it her grieving and petitioning God for her children? God was not deaf to the cries of this mother for her children. The day was coming when her cries would be heard and God would restore her children. God reminded her that there was hope for Israel's future.

A day of tremendous blessing was coming for God's people. Jeremiah challenged them not to lose hope in this time of exile. While their trial would be long and painful, God would not forget them. His hand was on them. In time he would return to them, and they would again experience his rich blessing in the Promised Land.

Take courage in the trial you face today. God will not abandon you. He will hear you and, in his own perfect time, come to your rescue. He will yet prove himself to you and through you show himself to the world.

For Consideration:

• What is the Lord showing the world through his dealings with you? Are you a vehicle through which God can demonstrate his power and love to the world?

• What keeps us from being vessels through which God can demonstrate himself to the world?

- Will God abandon you in your trial? What comfort do you find in this passage for your present trial?

For Prayer:

- Ask the Lord to help you to be a willing vessel through which he can work.

- Take a moment to consider the good things the Lord has done in you and through you. Thank and praise him for his goodness and bounty in your life.

- Thank the Lord that he promises not to forget you in your trial. Thank him that he works out all things for our good and his glory.

37

A Renewed Covenant

Read Jeremiah 31:18–40

Through Jeremiah the Lord had been reminding his people that he had a wonderful plan for them. While they were temporarily in a very difficult trial, the time was coming when the Lord would renew his covenant with them and bring them back to the land he had promised to their ancestors. This restoration would involve the people recognizing and grieving over their sin. Jeremiah pictured this repentance as Ephraim (Israel's largest tribe) moaning for his sin.

Ephraim understood that he was being disciplined like an unruly calf (verse 18). He had been rebellious. He had turned his back on God and his ways. The punishment he justly received was because of his sin. Notice, however, that he still cried out to the Lord to restore him so he could return to the Lord and his ways. There are several things we need to see here.

First, notice the compassion of God to forgive a sinner. No matter what we have done, we can come to the Lord for forgiveness. Ephraim knew he could go to God and find mercy.

Second, notice how Ephraim prayed that the Lord would restore him so he could return. Ephraim knew that if he was to return to the Lord, he needed to be restored to a right relationship with him. That meant that things needed to change in his life. He could not continue in rebellion and approach God. He must be willing to bear the Lord's yoke of holy demands.

Third, notice in verse 19 how Ephraim was broken because of his sin. He had been blinded by sin, but the Lord had opened his eyes to see the reality of his need. When he understood his sin, he was ashamed and beat his breast in a symbol of anguish and repentance ("struck myself on the thigh," NKJV). Until we are broken because of our sin, we cannot be renewed in our spirit.

God responded to the repentance of Ephraim with compassion and mercy. In verse 20 God stated that Ephraim (Israel) was his dear son, a child in whom he delighted. There were times when the Lord had to speak harshly to Ephraim, but God still yearned for him (literally, "my stomach churns for him"). God's discipline was harsh at times, but it was for Ephraim's good. God disciplined him out of love and compassion. Never once did God ever abandon his deep love for his people. Even in his discipline, God's desire was to draw his rebellious children back to himself.

Jeremiah told his people in verse 21 to set up road signs and guideposts. They were to take note of the road they traveled into exile. The reason for this was that they would return to their homeland by this same route. God wanted to focus their attention on the future restoration. He would not forget them, and his love would never leave them.

The heart of God was grieved as he watched his dear people wander from him. They had been unfaithful to him, but God was going to reach down in grace and do something new among them. Before that could happen, however, they needed to stop wandering and return to him. He asked them how long they would continue in their waywardness. Their sin was a barrier between them and their God.

Notice the new thing the Lord would do in Israel. Jeremiah told his people in verse 22 that a woman would surround a man. There are at least three interpretations of this very puzzling verse.

Some believe that Jeremiah was saying that the hand of God would be so powerfully on his people that the women would be able to defend the nation against its enemies. The woman was surrounding the man here in order to overpower him.

A second view sees a renewal of relationships in the land. The word translated "surround" can also mean "return." Some believe that the verse is saying that the wife would return to her husband. In this interpretation, God's people, the wife of God, were returning to God.

Yet a third interpretation merits mentioning. Some commentators see here a reference to the birth of Christ. God was going to do a new thing in the land. A woman would surround a man. In other words, a man would be conceived in the womb of a woman. It would be through this man that this new thing would happen.

In verses 23–29 Jeremiah prophesied the future prosperity of Israel and Judah. The deserted land of Judah would again see farmers cultivate its soil. Sheep would peacefully roam its pastures and mountains. God promised to refresh the weary and satisfy the faint.

In verse 26 Jeremiah woke from his sleep. From this we understand that this word had come to him in his sleep. He tells us that this sleep had been very pleasant to him. So much of what Jeremiah prophesied related to the fierce judgment of God. But here the prophet saw the love and compassion of God for his people. That dream refreshed his soul. He was happy and content to be able to tell God's people that their God had not abandoned them.

In verse 27 Jeremiah prophesied that the Lord would again plant both the houses of Israel and Judah with people and animals. The deserted land would be repopulated. Just as the Lord had watched over them to uproot them from their land, he would return to them and watch over their rebuilding. The day of blessing was going to return.

There was apparently a proverb among the children born in Babylon that expressed the idea that they were being disciplined for the sins of their parents (verse 29). Their fathers had eaten sour grapes, but it was the children's teeth that were set on edge. If you have ever eaten something sour, you know what happens in your mouth. The picture we see here is the fathers eating sour grapes and the children suffering the consequences. It is true that the sins of our parents do affect us. Jeremiah reminded his people, however, in verse 30 that in the future, justice would be more obvious as each person would suffer for his or her own sin.

In the days to come, God would restore his people to himself and make a new covenant with them. Notice in verse 32 that this new covenant would not be like the old covenant God had made with them through Moses. That old covenant had been broken by Israel's unfaithfulness, and covenant judgment had come. A new covenant had to be drawn up.

In this new covenant, God would put his law in the minds of his people and write it on their hearts (verse 33). The law of the old covenant was written on tablets of stone. This new covenant would be written on soft hearts. The law of God would become part of God's people.

Notice also that under this new covenant, all the Israelites would know the Lord from the least to the greatest (verse 34; see Romans 11:26–27). God would forgive their sin and remember it no more. Under the old covenant, many of the Israelites did not know the Lord. They were part of the old covenant because they were born into the nation of Israel, not because their hearts were devoted to God. However, all who belonged to this new covenant would be forgiven of their sin and personally know and love the Lord.

Those who entered into this new covenant would do so not by physical birth into the nation of Israel but by a spiritual birth into the family of God. The Lord Jesus would come to initiate this new covenant. All who accepted him as their Messiah would enter into a new life. God would, through the work of the Lord Jesus, forgive their sin and restore them to a right relationship with him. He would place his Holy Spirit in their hearts. The Holy Spirit would burn God's law into their lives and empower them to follow his ways. God's people would have an inner commitment to obedience instead of an evil heart that wandered.

In verses 35–37 God assured Israel that he would fulfill the new covenant and confirm his relationship with his people. He reminded them that it would be easier for the sun and the stars to stop shining than for him to forget his people. They and their descendants would be before him forever. God promised that he would not forsake them as a nation. Only if the heavens above could be measured would he forget his people

Verse 40 is of particular interest to us. Jeremiah told his people that the valley where the dead bodies and ashes were thrown would become holy to the Lord. The reference here was to the Valley of Ben Hinnom and in particular Topheth where children were sacrificed to Baal. Jeremiah prophesied about this valley in chapter 19. This place of tremendous evil would be reclaimed for the Lord, never to return to the enemy. All of Jerusalem would one day be holy. Some see the ultimate fulfillment of this to be in the heavenly Jerusalem (Revelation 21:1–5), while others see this as a reference to Jerusalem in a millennial kingdom (Revelation 20:4). What is important for us to note here is that the Lord would restore even the worst places of Jerusalem and make them holy again.

There are many such places in our day. There are strongholds in our lives and in our land that need to be reclaimed for the Lord. The Lord is fully able to restore these places to himself. Let us trust him to do this in our lives and in our cities.

For Consideration:

- What does this chapter teach us about the love and compassion of God for his people?

- What is the difference here between the old covenant made through Moses and the new covenant made through Christ?

- Have you always been faithful to the Lord? What comfort do you find in this passage regarding the compassion and faithfulness of God to repentant sinners?

- What places in your life need to be restored to the Lord?

For Prayer:

- Thank the Lord that in his discipline he does not forget mercy and love.

- Thank him that he will not forsake his children who have wandered from him.

- Do you know someone who has wandered away from the Lord today? Take a moment to pray that the Lord would restore that person to himself.

- Ask the Lord to restore those places in your life and in your land that the enemy has conquered. Ask the Lord to bring them in line with his will and purpose.

38

Jeremiah Buys a Property

Read Jeremiah 32

Their particular events of chapter 32 happened in the tenth year of King Zedekiah of Judah, which was the eighteenth year of Nebuchadnezzar. At this time, the king of Babylon was attacking the city of Jerusalem, and Jeremiah was confined in prison. We should not read this book as an orderly sequence of events. The book of Jeremiah is a series of prophetic messages that do not necessarily appear in the order in which they occurred in his ministry.

Verse 3 tells us the reason why Jeremiah was in prison. King Zedekiah had imprisoned him because of the message he was preaching. Jeremiah had been telling the people that the Lord was going to hand them and their king over to Babylon. Jeremiah had been prophesying that it was God's purpose that they surrender to the Babylonians who were attacking the city of Jerusalem. King Zedekiah said that Jeremiah's message was treasonous, and he imprisoned the prophet so the people would not listen to him and become discouraged.

It was in his prison cell that Jeremiah heard again the word of the Lord (verse 6). God told him that his cousin Hanamel would be coming to see him to make a very particular request. As his closest of relations, Hanamel was going to offer him the opportunity to buy a piece of property. This was common practice in those times. In order to keep property in the family, the nearest relative was given the opportunity to purchase the property. We read in Leviticus 25:25: "If one of your countrymen becomes poor and sells some of his property, his nearest relative is to come and redeem what his countryman has sold."

We are not told why this property was for sale, but we can imagine that things were quite difficult at this time. Babylon's siege of the city would have caused tremendous hardship for the people.

Just as the Lord had said, Hanamel came to Jeremiah in the courtyard where he was confined and asked him to buy this property. Jeremiah knew that it was the will of the Lord for him to buy this field, and he gave Hanamel seventeen shekels of silver for it. The deed for the property was sealed and witnessed. There were two copies of the terms of the agreement: a public copy that was signed and witnessed and a private, sealed copy that contained more specific terms that were not public information. These documents were given to Baruch, Jeremiah's friend. All this was done in the presence of witnesses. Jeremiah gave particular instructions to Baruch, asking him to take the deed and the official documents and put them in a clay jar for safekeeping. Jeremiah then reminded those present that the time was coming when commerce such as this would return to the land.

We need to understand that Jeremiah bought this property as Babylon was conquering Judah. Would you buy a piece of property under similar conditions? God wanted to use the sale of this property to speak to his people. Jeremiah's obedient purchase of the property symbolized that the day was coming when the Lord would return their land to them. Jeremiah acted in faith. He had been prophesying not only that Babylon would conquer Judah and take God's people into captivity but also that the day was coming when the Jews would return from their captivity and again settle in their land. Did Jeremiah really believe what he was preaching? Did he believe it enough to buy a piece of property, trusting God that the day was coming when it would be returned to him? It is easy to preach, but if asked to stake everything on what we preach, would we pass the test of faith like Jeremiah?

When the whole transaction was over, Jeremiah prayed to the Lord. His prayer revealed the struggle he had gone through in order to be obedient. This purchase of property had stretched Jeremiah's faith. In verse 17 he praised God as the sovereign Lord who made the heavens and the earth. There is nothing impossible for him to accomplish. He praised God for being loving, holy, and just. God is mighty in his deeds and will reward all people according to their conduct (verse 19). The God of Israel is a God of miraculous signs and wonders, whose power is known throughout the earth. He demonstrated that power when he brought his people out of Egypt. He showed his love and faithfulness to his people by giving them their land. His people had enjoyed the fruitfulness of that land, but they did not follow the Lord and his ways. God demonstrated his justice and holiness by punishing their sin and unfaithfulness. He brought disaster to the land he had given them (verse 23). In this section of his prayer, Jeremiah reminded himself of God's sovereignty, love, and justice. He reviewed the many ways in which God had proven faithful in the past. He did not understand why God was asking him to buy this property, but, knowing that God's ways are perfect, he was willing to act in faith (verse 25).

Having reminded himself of who God is, Jeremiah expressed his honest feelings about what had just taken place. He reminded the Lord that the city was, at that moment, being captured by siege. Everything was happening just as the Lord had told him it would. While Jeremiah saw that the Lord was accomplishing his purposes, he expressed his concern about the transaction he had just made with his cousin. He did not understand why the Lord had asked him to make this purchase at this time of foreign domination.

It is important for us to realize that Jeremiah did not wait until he understood before obeying. There have been times in my life when I failed to act in faith because I could not understand what God was leading me to do. Sometimes God asks us to obey without understanding. If we wait until we understand everything, we will never move forward.

The Lord spoke to Jeremiah's concerns in verse 26, reminding the prophet that nothing is too hard for him. God told Jeremiah that he was about to hand this city over to the Babylonians, who would set the city on fire. They would do so because God's people in the city had provoked him to anger by serving other gods. Though God had spoken repeatedly to his people, they refused to turn from their evil ways. They defiled the house of the Lord by setting up foreign idols. They sacrificed their sons and daughters to Molech (verse 35). Jerusalem had so aroused the anger of God that he was going to remove the city from his sight.

In verse 37 the Lord told Jeremiah, however, that one day he would restore his people to himself. He would bring them back from all the lands of their punishment and exile. Then they would live in safety. The day was coming when God's people would again recognize him as their God and live as his people. In that day the Lord promised to give them singleness of heart. They would serve the Lord with a heart that was devoted to him alone. They would fear the Lord and teach the fear of the Lord to their children. In that day the Lord would make a new covenant with his people.

The Lord would again rejoice in doing good to his people. He would plant them in the land with all his heart and soul (verse 41). Notice the great joy the Lord has here in doing good to his people. It thrills his heart to minister to them in this way. It is hard for us to imagine why God would so delight in us, but this verse clearly shows us his heart. While his people had turned their backs on him, God still wanted to bless them and shower them with loving kindness. And he would do so.

We can only imagine how these words from the Lord confirmed Jeremiah in the purchase of this property. The Lord reassured him in a time of confusion. The day was coming when Jeremiah would benefit from the land he had purchased. Though the Babylonians were about to take that land away, they could not keep it. God would restore it to Jeremiah and his people. God is ready to restore what the enemy has taken from us as well.

For Consideration:

• What does this chapter teach us about obedience to the Lord?

- Have you had times in your life when you were not obedient because you wanted to understand everything first?

- In this chapter Jeremiah was called to act in faith for what he preached. Do you believe and practice what you preach? Are you willing to stake everything on the truth you proclaim?

- What has the enemy taken from you? Do you believe it is the heart of the Lord to restore what Satan has taken from you?

For Prayer:

- Thank the Lord for the times that he has reassured you in your times of confusion.

- Thank the Lord that there is nothing impossible to him.

- Ask the Lord to enable you to live what you preach to others. Ask him to forgive you for any inconsistency in this matter.

39

God's Promise of Restoration

Read Jeremiah 33

In the last meditation, we saw how the Lord asked Jeremiah to
buy a piece of property to symbolize the fact that in the land
ravaged by the enemy, property would once again be sold and
purchased. God was going to restore his blessing to his people,
Israel.

In chapter 33 another word came to Jeremiah while he was
restrained in the courtyard. He had been imprisoned because of
his prophetic messages about the invasion of Judah by Babylon
and the conquest of God's people.

God described himself in this prophecy as the God who made
the earth and established it. This was evidence of his tremendous
power. This great and awesome God challenged Jeremiah to
call to him, and he would answer him and tell him great and
unsearchable things that he did not know. Notice that this verse
was particularly directed to Jeremiah as a prophet. God's promise
was that he would tell Jeremiah wonderful secrets. This was the
privilege of being a prophet. God reaffirmed Jeremiah's call as
prophet here. God gave Jeremiah an open invitation to call out
to him for the purpose of knowing his heart and his mind. God

promised to Jeremiah that he would use him to speak things that he could never have known were it not for the Lord revealing these truths to him.

What was it that God longed to share with Jeremiah? In verse 4 we see that the Lord had a wonderful plan for his people. The day was coming when the houses and palaces, which had been torn down when Babylon laid siege to the city, would be filled with the dead bodies of men. God would hide his face from the city of Jerusalem because of its terrible wickedness.

While God's wrath against Jerusalem would be very real, it would not last forever. God would again bring health and healing to the city. He would heal his people, both Israel and Judah, and they would enjoy peace and security (verse 7). In that day the Lord also promised to cleanse his people from their sins. He would forgive them for their rebellion against him. It is important for us to note here that it was the Lord who would do the cleansing of his people. Our own efforts to rid ourselves of sin and be acceptable to God will never work. God must cleanse us. Our responsibility is to open our hearts to receive that cleansing and forgiveness.

When the Lord healed their city once again, it would bring great glory to his name. God's blessing would be showered on the city of Jerusalem. The nations would sit up and notice. They would stand in awe and tremble when they saw the tremendous peace and prosperity the Lord would give Jerusalem.

People were saying that the land was a deserted waste, without men and animals (verse 10). God's blessing, however, would again come to that place. Once more, the sounds of joy and gladness would be heard. Offerings of thanksgiving and praise would rise to the Lord from his house. God's people would again give thanks to the Lord their God for his goodness and love. Their sheep would once again graze in abundant pastures and rest peacefully. God would fulfill his promises to his people in Israel and Judah, a unified nation (verse 14). This was what he longed to do. He wanted to bless and renew his people. He saw the sickness of their city and longed to heal it.

That cleansing and healing of the land would come through a Righteous Branch that would sprout from David's line. From the family of David, a great king would bring this healing and cleansing of the nation. This descendant of David would do what was just and right in the land. When he came, Judah would be saved and Jerusalem would live in safety (verse 16). Jerusalem would be called by the name of her Lord. She would be united to him and love him with all her heart. This Branch is none other than the Lord Jesus who came as the Son of God to heal and to forgive. Judah's hope, and indeed the hope of the whole world, is in him alone.

God promised through Jeremiah that one of King David's descendants would always sit on the throne of Israel. Today the Lord Jesus sits at the right hand of the Father (Colossians 3:1). God the Father has lifted him up and placed him above all things. Today his kingdom is not an earthly kingdom but a spiritual kingdom. Some believers, however, look forward to the Second Coming of Christ when he will set up an earthly kingdom in Jerusalem and literally fulfill these promises to Israel.

Notice in verse 18 that Jeremiah told his people that not only would David not lack a descendant on the throne but also the Levites would never lack a man to stand before God to offer sacrifices. While it is easy to see how the Lord Jesus, as a descendant of David, is king forever, what did Jeremiah mean when he told his people that the Levites would always have a man to stand before God to perform priestly duties? Again, we can see this as being spiritually fulfilled in the person and work of the Lord Jesus. He offered the sacrifice of his life for our sin (see Hebrews 7:24–8:2). No more sacrifices are now required. Today Jesus acts as our priest and brings us into the presence of the Father through the sacrifice of his life for us. We may note here that some believers take these verses literally and believe that in a millennial kingdom, the Levitical priesthood will be reestablished to offer sacrifices of worship to the Lord in a temple in Jerusalem.

What a wonderful thing it is to see, even in our day, the spiritual fulfillment of these promises to God's people in the church. The Lord Jesus has taken his throne. He stands before the Father on our behalf as a priest. His sacrifice gives us access to the presence of God.

God assured Jeremiah in verse 20 of the certainty of these promises to a unified and restored Israel. God told the prophet that it would be easier to break the cycle of day and night than for this covenant he was making with Israel to be broken. The promise of God was that he would make the descendants of David and Levi to be as numerous as the stars of the sky and the sand of the seashore. David and Levi were singled out here because of what they represent: the kingship and the priesthood of Israel. All those who belong to the Lord Jesus today are now part of a spiritual kingdom of priests (see 1 Peter 1:4–10). They have bowed the knee to the God of Israel. They join with his true people to worship and honor the God of Israel.

The people in Jeremiah's day were saying that the Lord had rejected his people of Israel and Judah (verse 24). God told Jeremiah, however, that even as he had made a covenant with the heavens and fixed the law of day and night, so he would be faithful to the promise he made with Israel and Judah. He would restore the fortunes of his people through the Messiah who was to come. They would be his instruments to bring great glory to his name in all the earth.

For Consideration:

- What do we learn about the heart of God for his people in this section of Scripture?

- How is Jesus both king and priest for us today?

- We are also called to be priests in our day. What does this mean? Have we been faithful to the Lord in this calling? Have we faithfully represented him?

- Does your city need to be healed by God? Explain.

For Prayer:

- Thank the Lord for his tremendous promise to restore his people and be their king and priest.

- Ask the Lord to show you those areas of your city that need to be healed. Pray that the Lord would bring that healing.

- Thank him for sending the Lord Jesus to be our king and priest. Thank him that as king he is expanding his kingdom throughout the whole earth.

40

Zedekiah and the Slaves

Read Jeremiah 34

In chapter 34 Jeremiah had two messages from the Lord for the people. The first word was directed to King Zedekiah. The second word was directed to the people and concerned the practice of slavery in the land.

These prophecies came when Nebuchadnezzar and his army were fighting against Jerusalem and the surrounding towns. Obviously, there would have been many questions in the minds of the people at this time. Would the Babylonians conquer them? What would the Babylonians do to them? What would happen to the city of Jerusalem? Where was God at this time?

In verse 2 the Lord told Jeremiah to go to King Zedekiah and speak to him. The Lord wanted to warn the king that he would hand the city over to the king of Babylon. Nebuchadnezzar would capture the city, burn it down, and capture King Zedekiah, who would be taken captive to Babylon.

While this was not what Zedekiah wanted to hear, there was a bright spot in this dismal future. God promised that Zedekiah would not die by the sword. He would die a peaceful death in exile (verse 5). His memory would be honored in death, and his people would make a funeral fire in his honor. The nature of this funeral fire is uncertain. Some see a special ceremony with the burning of spices to honor the dead king. We have a reference to this type of funeral fire in 2 Chronicles 16:13–14. Zedekiah would be honored in his death in exile. God was showing him that he would not be forsaken. As the Lord had commanded him, Jeremiah shared these words with King Zedekiah.

In verse 8 the Lord gave Jeremiah another word. This word came after King Zedekiah had made a covenant with the people of Jerusalem to proclaim freedom to all slaves. From verse 9 we understand that these slaves were from their own people. The king and his officials determined to set all Hebrew slaves free. While the decision was admirable, it did not last very long. The slave owners very quickly returned to this practice of taking slaves (verse 11).

The Lord had something to say to his people about this change of mind. He reminded them that he had made a covenant with their ancestors when he brought them out of the land of Egypt. The law of Moses clearly taught that any Hebrews who sold themselves as slaves were to be freed after six years (Exodus 21:1–2). The practice of selling oneself into servitude was a common practice and governed by strict law. When people could not pay their debts, they would sell themselves to a wealthier landowner in order to work off that debt.

Jeremiah reminded the people that the Lord had been pleased with their covenant decision to release their slaves. By not keeping their promise, however, they had profaned the Lord's name, and he was angry with them for this injustice (verse 16). God would punish them, and they would fall by the sword, plague, and famine. They would be despised by the nations around them. God took seriously this matter of breaking covenant laws.

It is important for us to understand here that God takes our commitments seriously. What made this matter particularly offensive to the Lord was the fact that his people had repented and then returned to their sin of oppressing their fellow Hebrews in a time of national crisis. They had come to understand their sin against God and turned from it. By falling again into this sin, they willfully chose to defy God and their covenant. It is one thing to fall into sin through ignorance or weakness; it is quite another to rebelliously return to sin after repentance. For this they would be punished.

God compared these rebellious people to the calf that was cut in two when the covenant was made. This is a reference to a common practice of that time. A calf was sacrificed and cut in half. Both halves were laid side by side. The individuals making an agreement would walk between the halves symbolically saying, "May I be like this calf if I do not keep my agreement." The people making this type of covenant were, in reality, staking their lives on their commitment. God was telling these rebellious people that this is how he would treat them. Because they had failed to keep their agreement with the Lord, they would perish like this calf.

The people of Judah would be handed over to their enemies. Their dead bodies would become food for the birds of the air and the beasts of the earth. Zedekiah, their king would be handed over to the Babylonians. Notice in verse 21 that while the Babylonians had withdrawn from Jerusalem for a time, they would return to fight against it and burn it to the ground. Judah's towns would be laid waste so that no one could live in them.

This came about because God's people had been unfaithful to their commitment to the Lord their God. They had willingly and knowingly turned their back on him. The slavery issue was only one of the issues that led to their downfall. To know the truth and refuse to practice it is worse than not knowing the truth at all. This is what the apostle Peter told his readers in 2 Peter 2:20–21: "If they have escaped the corruption of the world by knowing our Lord and Savior Jesus Christ and are again entangled in it and overcome, they are worse off at the end than they were at the beginning. It would have been better for them not to have known the way of righteousness, than to have known it and then to turn their backs on the sacred command that was passed on to them." Those who know the truth are expected to live in that truth.

For Consideration:

• Have you been faithful to the commitments you have made to the Lord?

- Consider the example of how a covenant between two parties was put in place by means of a calf split in two. Are you serious enough about your relationship with God to walk between those halves of the calf?

For Prayer:

- Ask the Lord to reveal to you any shortcoming in your commitment to him.

- Do you know someone who has wandered from a commitment to the Lord? Ask the Lord to help this person to see the seriousness of this situation.

- Ask God to enable you to be faithful to your commitment to him.

41

The Recabites

Read Jeremiah 35

In chapter 35 the Lord called Jeremiah to speak to a group known as the Recabites. Notice that this particular prophecy came for the Recabites during the reign of Jehoiakim. As we have already stated, the prophecies of this book of Jeremiah are not in chronological order.

There are several things we need to understand about the Recabites. They belonged to a larger tribe known as the Kenites. We read in Judges 1:16 concerning the Kenites: "The descendants of Moses' father-in-law, the Kenite, went up from the City of Palms with the men of Judah to live among the people of the Desert of Judah in the Negev near Arad." This verse tells us some important details about the Kenites. Moses' father-in-law was a Kenite, and the Kenites lived in the Promised Land among the people of Israel. There was a healthy relationship between the Kenites and the Israelites during their history in the land.

In 1 Chronicles 2:55 we learn that Recab was a Kenite: "And the clans of scribes who lived at Jabez: the Tirathites, Shimeathites and Sucathites. These are the Kenites who came from Hammath, the father of the house of Recab." The family of Recab distinguished itself from the rest of their tribe because they refused to drink wine and chose to live in tents (see verses 8–9).

The Lord asked Jeremiah to go to the Recabite family and invite them to the side rooms of the house of God and offer them wine to drink (verse 2). It should be understood that the nation of Babylon was invading the land. The Recabites were particularly vulnerable to the attack of the enemy. Living in tents, they had no defense. Jeremiah invited them into the city of Jerusalem, behind the fortified wall of the city. He also offered them a room in the temple where they would be protected and secure. This however, was contrary to their practice as a family, as their father had commanded them to live in tents. When Jeremiah offered them wine, this too was contrary to their practice as a people.

Jeremiah knew the practices of the Recabites but chose to be obedient to the Lord in this matter. He brought the Recabites into the temple. When they were in the house of the Lord, Jeremiah set bowls of wine before them and offered them a drink.

The Recabites refused to drink the wine that Jeremiah offered them. They reminded him that their forefather Jonadab, the son of Recab, had commanded them not to drink wine, build houses, sow seed, or plant vineyards. They told Jeremiah that they had always been obedient to their forefather's wishes. It was only when Nebuchadnezzar had invaded the land that they chose to come to the region of Jerusalem for protection.

After the Recabites had given Jeremiah their answer, the word of the Lord came again to him. God told Jeremiah to go to the people of Judah and tell them that they needed to learn a lesson from the Recabites. He pointed the Judeans to the faithfulness of the Recabites to their forefather's wishes. In contrast, God's people would not listen to their Father, the Lord God. God had spoken repeatedly to them through his prophets, but they refused to listen. God challenged them to turn from their foreign gods, but they would not. Jonadab's descendants were more faithful to their human forefather than God's people were to their God.

Because of the unfaithfulness of his people to his wishes, the Lord was going to bring a great disaster on the people of Jerusalem. As for the Recabites, God would reward their faithfulness. They would never lack a descendant to serve the Lord. God would always have someone in their family to worship him.

Sometimes even the heart of the believer can be divided. The obedience of the Recabites is a challenge to us to strive to walk in absolute obedience to God. Are we willing to lay everything down to be obedient to him today?

For Consideration:

- Have you committed yourself to being completely faithful to the Lord? What are your areas of weakness?

- Have you been guilty of compromise in your walk with the Lord? Explain.

- Is there any way that unbelievers put us to shame in terms of their devotion to and excitement in what they believe?

For Prayer:

- Ask the Lord to show you if there is any way you have been compromising in your faith.

- Ask the Lord to give you a heart that is dedicated entirely to him.

42

Jeremiah's Scroll

Read Jeremiah 36

I n chapter 36 the Lord asked Jeremiah to get a scroll and to write down the words he had given him for Israel, Judah, and the other nations. Writing these prophecies down would preserve them for the generations to come. Jeremiah was to begin with the very first message he had received in the days of Josiah. This is one of the reasons why we have his book today.

In verse 3 we discover that the Lord's desire for his people was that they would read Jeremiah's words and repent when they saw the terrible things that he had planned for them in judgment of their sin. It was the will of the Lord to forgive their sin and heal them as a people. Jeremiah's written word would be used of God to bring this repentance and forgiveness.

In obedience to the command of the Lord, Jeremiah sent for Baruch, who was a secretary. As Jeremiah dictated, Baruch wrote down the words of the prophecies the Lord had given to Jeremiah. When he finished dictating, Jeremiah asked Baruch to go to the temple on the next day of fasting and read the words of the scroll to the people who had gathered from all over Judah to worship. It should be noted that at this point, Jeremiah was restricted (for reasons unexplained in the text) and could not go to the temple of the Lord. But his scroll could go where he could not. Baruch not only served as a secretary to Jeremiah but he also read the prophecies to the people in Jeremiah's absence. His ministry was vital.

Notice in verse 7 that when Jeremiah sent Baruch, it was his desire that Judah, on hearing this word, would repent. He wanted to see his people restored to the Lord. He believed that the written word could, by God's grace, bring his people to the point of repentance and restoration.

Baruch did what Jeremiah asked him to do. He went to the temple and read the words of the scroll to those who had gathered for worship from all over Judah. An individual by the name of Micaiah heard the words that Baruch read in the temple that day (verse 11). He was touched by what he heard and went to the secretary's room in the royal palace to meet with the officials who were there. He told the officials everything that Baruch had read. The officials then sent Jehudi to find Baruch and ask him to bring the scroll to them so they could hear the words (verse 14).

When Baruch arrived, he was asked to sit down and read the contents of the scroll. As the officials listened, they were troubled and decided to take the scroll to the king so that he could hear it. It is quite amazing to see what the Lord was doing here with Jeremiah's written word. While Jeremiah could not go the temple himself, God took his word to the temple through Baruch.

In verse 17 the officials asked Baruch how he had received these words. Baruch told them that Jeremiah had dictated the prophecies to him. When the officials heard this, they recommend that Baruch and Jeremiah hide and not tell anyone where they were (verse 19). While they felt that they needed to take these words to the king, they could not guarantee that he would respond favorably to what he heard. They suggested that Baruch and Jeremiah hide, in case the king's response was unfavorable.

The officials took the scroll and placed it in the room of Elishama the secretary for safekeeping. They then went to the king to tell him about the scroll and the words it contained.

When the king heard their report, he sent Jehudi to get the scroll and read it aloud to him and the officials. As the king listened, he sat by a fire. When Jehudi had read three or four columns of the scroll, the king cut those columns with a knife and threw them into the fire. As the officials watched, Jeremiah's scroll was destroyed in the fire.

The king and his attendants showed no fear as the scroll was burned (verse 24). The king's heart should have been broken by the sin of his people. The words of the scroll should have brought him to the awareness that he and his people were in serious trouble. The king and his attendants, however, were unmoved. They showed no remorse over the condition of the land. Their hearts were hard. By burning the scroll, they openly showed their defiance of God and his holy word.

Notice in verse 25 that the officials who had brought the scroll to the king had pleaded with him not to burn it; however, the king had refused their counsel. Instead, he ordered Jerahmeel to find Baruch and Jeremiah and arrest them. Verse 26 tells us, however, that the Lord had hidden them. The God who called Jeremiah to write the scroll and Baruch to read it also protected them when they obeyed. What an encouragement this is for us. When God calls, he also protects. We can act in boldness to do what the Lord calls us to do.

After the burning of the scroll, the word of the Lord came again to Jeremiah. God asked him to take another scroll and rewrite all the words he had written on the first scroll that Jehoiakim had burned (verse 28). He was also to speak a very particular word to king Jehoiakim.

Jehoiakim had not liked what Jeremiah prophesied in the scroll about Babylon coming to destroy the land, and he had refused to accept this word from the Lord. Jeremiah was to tell unfaithful Jehoiakim that he would have no one to sit on the throne in his place. His body would be thrown out and exposed to the heat by day and the frost by night. God would punish him, his children, and his attendants for their wickedness. God would bring on them the disaster he had pronounced through Jeremiah. In chapter 22 Jeremiah had told Jehoiakim that he would have the burial of a donkey—dragged away and thrown outside the city (22:18–19).

Jehoiakim had his chance. He had held the word of the Lord in his hands and had thrown it into a fire. That was the last opportunity he had for repentance. The judgment of God fell on him that day. He had rejected the Lord and his word for the last time. There is a lesson here for us as well. We should never turn our backs on what the Lord is saying to us.

From verse 32 we understand that Jeremiah took another scroll and Baruch again wrote down the words of Jeremiah. Not only were all the words of the first scroll recorded in the second, but many other words were also written that day. This scroll contained even more than the first scroll. Jehoiakim believed he was hindering the word of God by burning it, but God cannot be limited. The replacement scroll was even more detailed than the first. God's word will advance regardless of what people do to it. History has shown us that people have often tried to destroy the word of God, but they have never been able to do so. God's word cannot be destroyed (see Isaiah 40:8).

For Consideration:

• Consider how the king and his officials tried to hinder Jeremiah. What do we learn here about God's protection and guidance? How does this encourage us to minister with boldness?

• What encouragement do you receive from the fact that the Lord's cause advanced here despite the efforts of the king and his officials to hinder it?

• What personal obstacles have you been facing in your life and ministry? Is God able to overcome those obstacles and advance his kingdom?

For Prayer:

• Thank the Lord for the word he has given us. Thank him that he preserves that word no matter what people may try to do to it.

• Thank him that he protects his servants.

- Do you know of someone who has been resisting the word of the Lord like Jehoiakim? Take a moment to pray for this individual.

43

Jeremiah and Zedekiah

Read Jeremiah 37

Chapter 37 tells us something of the relationship that existed between Jeremiah the prophet and Zedekiah the king. This chapter speaks of a time before Jeremiah was put in prison. At this particular time, the Babylonian army had encamped around the city of Jerusalem.

Zedekiah had been made king of Judah by Nebuchadnezzar, who controlled this part of the world. Zedekiah ruled in place of the rightful king, Jehoiachin, who had rebelled against Nebuchadnezzar. Zedekiah proved to be wicked and did evil in the sight of the Lord. Verse 2 tells us that neither he nor his attendants paid any attention to the words of the Lord or to Jeremiah the prophet.

While Zedekiah was not interested in the word of the Lord, verse 3 tells us that he sent Jehucal and Zephaniah the priest to Jeremiah, asking the prophet to pray for them. Why would Zedekiah send this request to Jeremiah when he refused to listen to him at other times? Obviously, the context has something to do with this.

Verses 4 and 5 give us an idea of the historical context of

this particular prophecy. Jeremiah had not yet been put in prison, and he was free to move among the people. The army of Pharaoh had marched out of Egypt to help Zedekiah fight the Babylonians. When the Babylonians heard this, they abandoned their siege of Jerusalem in order to war against Egypt. Zedekiah's hopes were raised that Jerusalem would be saved from Babylon by an alliance with Egypt. Could it be that this was the answer that they were looking for? Would Babylon be defeated by the Egyptians and cease being a threat to Judah? It was in this context that Zedekiah asked Jeremiah to pray. Did the king want God to bless the Egyptians so that they could defeat Babylon?

The word of the Lord came to Jeremiah at this time with a message for Zedekiah. Pharaoh's army, which had marched out in support of Judah, would be defeated and return to Egypt. The Babylonians would return to Jerusalem and would be successful in capturing the city and burning it to the ground (verse 8).

Zedekiah had put his hope of security in the king of Egypt instead of in the Lord. God told him that he was deceiving himself by trusting in Egypt. Jeremiah told Zedekiah that the Babylonian capture of Jerusalem was so sure that even if the Babylonian army was defeated, the Lord would use the wounded and battered soldiers to burn down the city. Nothing would stop the purpose and plan of Almighty God.

Zedekiah failed to see that his problem was not Babylon but his own sin. He felt that if he could get rid of Babylon, then everything would be fine. But it was his rebellion and sin against God that was the real cause of Jerusalem's destruction. Zedekiah could not save himself from judgment. He could not fight God with weapons of war. No matter what happened to the enemy, God would still bring his judgment.

After the Babylonian army had withdrawn to meet the Egyptians, Jeremiah started to leave the city to go to his property in Benjamin (verse 12). Jeremiah knew that the Babylonians were going to return very shortly to Jerusalem. They would conquer the city and burn it down. Could it be that Jeremiah was simply moving to a place that was safer than the city of Jerusalem?

Jeremiah did not get very far. Verse 13 tells us that when he reached the Benjamin Gate, the captain of the guard recognized him, accused him of deserting to the Babylonians, and placed him under arrest. Jeremiah was brought before the city officials.

The officials were angry with Jeremiah. Obviously, the messages of judgment that Jeremiah had been speaking did not help matters. Jeremiah was beaten and imprisoned in a house that had been made into a prison. Jeremiah's quarters left much to be desired, and he feared for his life (see verse 20). He was locked in a vaulted cell in a dungeon and left there for a long time (verse 16).

There are times when we wonder about the purposes of God in our lives. Why was Jeremiah imprisoned? Why was he placed in such horrible surroundings? Why did the one person who was faithful to God have to suffer so terribly at the hands of the unbelievers? These are questions that we cannot easily answer. God knows what he is doing, and he has a purpose and plan in everything he does.

In verse 17 Zedekiah again sent for Jeremiah when he was in the dungeon and brought him to the palace to speak to him. Could it be that this was the reason for the confinement? Did the Lord want to speak to Zedekiah? Was Jeremiah confined for the sake of Zedekiah? Notice that Zedekiah spoke privately to Jeremiah. He asked him if there was a word from the Lord for him. Jeremiah told him that the Lord was going to hand him over to the king of Babylon.

While Jeremiah was in the presence of Zedekiah, he asked the king why he was put in prison. He also asked the king where the prophets were who had prophesied that Babylon would not attack Jerusalem. These prophets had been proven false because Babylon had already attacked. If Jeremiah's prophecy was true, then why was he in prison?

Before leaving the king's presence, Jeremiah made a request. He pleaded with the king not to send him back to the dungeon in the house of Jonathan. Jeremiah was afraid that if he returned to the dungeon, he would die. Zedekiah granted Jeremiah's request and put him in the courtyard instead. In an act of kindness, he also ordered that Jeremiah be fed with bread each day, as long as the supply lasted during the siege.

There are many lessons to learn in this chapter of Jeremiah.

We see that we cannot escape from God's judgment. We see how God is able to use even wounded soldiers to accomplish his purposes. What an encouragement this should be to us. We are often like those wounded soldiers, but God can use us because he does not need our strength.

We also see in this chapter how God offered yet another opportunity for Zedekiah to repent. This opportunity was costly for Jeremiah. He languished in the terrible conditions of a dungeon cell. Would you be willing to face this in order to reach out in Jesus' name to those who need to hear?

Notice in this chapter, as well, how the Lord protected Jeremiah by giving him favor in the eyes of Zedekiah so that he was fed and protected in the courtyard. In all this we see the hand of a sovereign God working out his gracious will in all the difficulties and trials that came Jeremiah's way.

For Consideration:

- Have you been trying to escape something that God has been leading you to do? Explain.

- Would you willingly surrender to the difficulties Jeremiah went through to speak the word of God to those who need to hear?

- What do we learn here about the sovereignty of God in the things that come our way?

- What particular struggles are you facing right now? Is God able to use these in your life?

For Prayer:

- Thank the Lord that he is in control of the situations that come our way and that he will use every situation to accomplish his purposes through us.

- Thank the Lord for the people he places in our path to remind us of the word of God and his purposes for our life.

- Thank the Lord that, no matter what comes our way, he is there to protect and guide us, even as he was for Jeremiah.

44

Cast into a Cistern

Read Jeremiah 38

J eremiah's life as a prophet was not easy. We have seen how
his own hometown rejected his prophecies and wanted to
kill him. He had even been imprisoned for what he spoke. At
one point he was put in shackles and publicly humiliated because
he dared to speak out against the evil of the land. Here again in
this chapter, we see something of the struggle of the prophet in his
ministry to wicked Judah.

Jeremiah's problems increased when four important men
heard what he had been telling the people. Shephatiah, Gedaliah,
Jehucal, and Pashhur were upset that Jeremiah had been telling
the people that whoever stayed in the city of Jerusalem would
die by the sword, famine, and plague, but whoever surrendered
to the Babylonians would live. These leaders did not approve of
Jeremiah discouraging the people defending the city by saying
that all was lost. They wanted Jeremiah to be put to death for
treason against his own people.

From a human point of view, we can understand what these
officials were saying. Jeremiah's words would have been a
discouragement to those who were trying to defend their land. We

need to understand, however, that it was not the will of the Lord that his people keep their land. God reserves the right to strip us of the blessings he gives us. What was important here was the will and purpose of God. The people of Judah had forgotten that they lived in the Promised Land by privilege, not by right. They had rebelled against God who had given them all they had, and they were suffering his righteous judgment.

The four officials brought their concern to King Zedekiah who put Jeremiah into their hands to do as they pleased. The officials took the prophet to an old, empty cistern and lowered him into this pit with ropes (verse 6). Jeremiah sank down into the mud at the bottom of the cistern. We can only imagine how difficult this was for the man of God. We must admire his commitment to speak the truth of God and suffer the consequences.

An Ethiopian by the name of Ebed-Melech came to Jeremiah's rescue. Ebed-Melech was a servant in the royal palace, and he spoke to the king about what these men had done to Jeremiah. He warned the king that Jeremiah would surely die in the cistern if left there (verse 9). Zedekiah ordered that he take thirty men and lift Jeremiah out of the muddy pit. It is unclear why Ebed-Melech required thirty men. It may be that the king anticipated some opposition to the rescue.

Ebed-Melech brought some articles of clothing from the treasury and let them down by rope to Jeremiah. He instructed Jeremiah to put this material under his arms for padding. Ebed-Melech was very concerned for Jeremiah and his comfort. When the officials let Jeremiah down into the cistern, there was no mention of rags to protect his arms. This action on the part of Ebed-Melech was noticed by God and recorded for all generations to see. God is not blind to the small things we do for his servants.

Jeremiah was lifted up out of the cistern and brought to the courtyard (verse 13). Although he was still confined in prison, his life was out of immediate danger and extreme discomfort. God had rescued him from the hands of his enemy. Notice here as well that God would bless Ebed-Melech for what he had done. Later, God promised to rescue him when Babylon broke into the city (see 39:16–18).

After these events Zedekiah again called for Jeremiah to be

brought to the temple. There the king asked Jeremiah to be honest with him and not hide anything from him that the Lord said. Zedekiah had many opportunities to hear the word of the Lord through Jeremiah. While he often called for Jeremiah, the king was not ready to repent and turn to the Lord.

Zedekiah swore a secret oath to Jeremiah that he would not kill him or hand him over to those who were seeking his life. There was a soft spot in his heart for Jeremiah, but Zedekiah did not have the courage to defend God's prophet or be publicly associated with him. He met with Jeremiah in secret and made private promises to him. When the officials had earlier come to him about Jeremiah's messages, he had handed the prophet over to their wishes. The king seems to have been greatly influenced by people. His heart was divided. He wanted to hear Jeremiah but did not have the courage to stand up for what was right. He was concerned about what others were saying. We have all met people like this.

Jeremiah told Zedekiah that by surrendering to the king of Babylon, his life would be spared and the city would not be burned (verse 17). God provided a way for him to save his life, the lives of his family members, and the city of Jerusalem.

Zedekiah shared openly his fears with Jeremiah. He told the prophet that he was afraid of the Jews who had already been taken into captivity. He was afraid that if he surrendered to Babylon, the Jews would mistreat him. Surely they would have felt that he should have done more to defend their city. He felt responsible to hold on to the city. He saw himself as the last hope for his people. By surrendering, he would have to answer to the Jews, and Zedekiah was afraid of their reaction. It was this fear of what others would say and do that kept him from obeying God and surrendering to Babylon.

Zedekiah had a false sense of responsibility. He believed that he needed to stand firm and hold on when God was asking him to let go. There have been times in my ministry and life when I have tried to hold on when God was asking me to surrender. In Zedekiah's case, he had heard the will of God for him through Jeremiah but did not want to give up. He saw surrender as failure, whereas, in reality, it was God's will.

Jeremiah told Zedekiah that he would not be handed over to the

Jews. If he obeyed the Lord, things would go well for him and his family. If Zedekiah refused to surrender, God's wrath would be on him. The women of the palace would mockingly remember him as the king who was misled and overcome by his closest friends and counselors. In his moment of trial, he would be deserted by those he considered his friends.

In verse 22 Jeremiah told King Zedekiah that the women would say that his feet were sunk in the mud. This reminds us of what Jeremiah had just been through in the cistern. This is a picture of despair and hopelessness. This is what would happen to Zedekiah. The difference between Jeremiah and Zedekiah was that in the case of Zedekiah, there would be no one to rescue him. He, his wives, and his children would be captured, and his friends would desert him.

Zedekiah listened to what Jeremiah told him. He asked that Jeremiah keep their conversation secret on pain of death. Obviously, this was a reflection of Zedekiah's fears. He was terrified that the Jews would find out that he had been speaking with Jeremiah. He threatened to kill Jeremiah if he ever revealed the nature of their conversation. He told the prophet that if the officials asked him about this conversation, he was to tell them that he had been pleading with the king not to send him back to the house of Jonathan where he had been imprisoned.

The officials did find out that Zedekiah had been speaking with Jeremiah. When questioned about his time with the king, Jeremiah simply told them what the king told him to say. Jeremiah remained in the courtyard prison until the city of Jerusalem was captured.

Probably what is most striking here is the character of Zedekiah and his fears. Here was a man who did not have moral courage. He was governed by his fears. He refused to trust the Lord. By contrast, Jeremiah faced his fears and trials boldly. He confidently spoke the word the Lord gave him. While Jeremiah suffered much, God's hand of protection was on him; whereas, Zedekiah would perish. Obedience to God is always the safest place to be.

For Consideration:

- What does this chapter teach us about the small things we do for others? Consider the example of Ebed-Melech.

- Why do you suppose God allowed Jeremiah to be put in the cistern? Consider the impact it had on Ebed-Melech. Consider also how Jeremiah used this illustration to communicate to King Zedekiah that his feet too would be stuck in the mud, but there would be no one to deliver him.

- What do we learn about the character of Zedekiah? Have you ever met people like Zedekiah?

For Prayer:

- Thank the Lord for the way he sends his servants to encourage us in our time of need.

- Zedekiah was afraid to surrender to the will of the Lord. Ask the Lord to give you the courage to be able to surrender everything to him.

- Ask the Lord to set you free from the fear of what people think.

- Ask God to give you the wisdom to know when he is asking you to persevere and when he is asking you to surrender.

45

Jerusalem Conquered

Read Jeremiah 39

For a long time the prophet Jeremiah had been prophesying that the Babylonians would capture the city of Jerusalem. He had been persecuted for these prophecies. The test of a true prophet was that what he said actually happened (see Deuteronomy 18:21–22). In this chapter we see how the city of Jerusalem was taken in fulfillment of the prophecies of Jeremiah.

In the ninth year and tenth month of the reign of Judah's King Zedekiah, Nebuchadnezzar of Babylon laid siege to Jerusalem, Judah's capital city. It was not, however, until the eleventh year and fourth month of Zedekiah that the city wall was finally broken through. This meant that the city was under siege for eighteen months.

When the army did break through the city wall, Nebuchadnezzar and his officials entered Jerusalem and took seats in the Middle Gate. This action symbolized that they were now the official leaders of the nation. When Zedekiah and his soldiers saw the enemy in the city, they attempted an escape.

Notice in verse 4 how they attempted this escape. They waited until it was dark, left by way of the king's gate between the walls, and headed out to the desert region of the Arabah. It is important for us to understand here that Jeremiah had often told Zedekiah that if he surrendered to the king of Babylon, all would go well. If he refused to surrender, however, he, his family, and the city would suffer the severe judgment of God.

Despite the word of the Lord to him through Jeremiah the prophet, Zedekiah did not trust the Lord. He chose to take matters into his own hands and attempt an escape. Like the prophet Jonah, long before him, he felt that somehow he could run from the Lord.

Zedekiah's attempted escape was futile. The Babylonians pursued and captured him. Zedekiah was taken to Nebuchadnezzar where his sentence was pronounced. Just as Jeremiah had prophesied, Zedekiah saw the king of Babylon face to face (32:4).

Zedekiah's sons, the nobles, and officials were slaughtered in his sight (verse 6). Then Zedekiah's eyes were blinded, and he was put in shackles and exiled to Babylon. He was humiliated as a king and allowed to live to further suffer this humiliation.

As Jeremiah had prophesied, Babylon set fire to the royal palace and the houses in the city. The wall surrounding Jerusalem was then broken down, leaving the capital uninhabitable. Finally, there were only the charred remains of a city placed under the judgment of God.

Nebuzaradan, the commander of the Babylonian imperial guard, took the people of Jerusalem into exile. All that remained in the land were the poor who owned nothing. To these individuals the commander of the imperial guard gave vineyards and fields. The Israelites living in the northern kingdom would eventually intermarry with foreign settlers from Assyria and Babylon. They would become a hated race of people known as the Samaritans.

Nebuchadnezzar gave particular orders that his men not harm Jeremiah. They were to look after him and do whatever Jeremiah asked (verse 12). It is quite incredible to see the protection of the Lord here. Obviously, Nebuchadnezzar had heard about the prophecies of Jeremiah predicting that Nebuchadnezzar would capture Jerusalem. Jeremiah had called for a total surrender to the king of Babylon and had even been put in prison for his "pro-

Babylon" stand. Therefore, Nebuchadnezzar did not see Jeremiah as an enemy.

In obedience to the orders of their king, Nebuzaradan and the other officials had Jeremiah taken out of prison. He was handed over to a man by the name of Gedaliah, who was appointed by Nebuchadnezzar to rule over the captured land of Judah (see 2 Kings 25:22). By handing Jeremiah over to Gedaliah, the officials were, in reality, telling Gedaliah that he was to care for the prophet. Jeremiah was to be protected by order of the king of Babylon.

The section from verses 15 to 18 is a word that Jeremiah received for Ebed-Melech, the Ethiopian who had rescued him from the cistern in chapter 38. Jeremiah received this word while he had been confined in prison. God asked Jeremiah to tell Ebed-Melech that he was going to fulfill his word against the city of Jerusalem. Disaster was going to befall the city. In that day, however, God would rescue Ebed-Melech. He would not be handed over to those he feared because he had trusted in the Lord when he helped Jeremiah. God is not blind to what is done to his servants, and he rewards those who minister to them.

We see in this chapter the futility of trying to flee from the Lord. Zedekiah futilely tried to escape the judgment of the Lord, but he could not. Men like Jeremiah and Ebed-Melech who surrendered to the purpose of God were rewarded for their obedience. God protected those who were faithful to him. God was true to his word and true to those who trusted him.

For Consideration:

• What does this passage teach us about trying to escape the judgment of God?

• Have you ever been guilty of ignoring the will and purpose of God? What does the example of Zedekiah teach us about the danger of doing so?

• God shows us here in this passage that there is a blessing for those who are faithful to him and his word. Are there any areas of your life where you have a hard time trusting the Lord?

For Prayer:

- Thank the Lord that he rewards those who are faithful to him.

- Do you know someone who is resisting the Lord and his word? Take a moment to pray that the Lord would open the eyes of this person before it is too late.

- Ask the Lord to give you grace to obey like Jeremiah and Ebed-Melech, even when it costs you something personally.

46

Governor Gedaliah

Read Jeremiah 40:1–41:3

As chapter 40 begins, Jeremiah was discovered among the captives who were being led off in chains into Babylon. Nebuzaradan discovered him among this group and had him released from his chains in the region of Ramah.

The commander reminded Jeremiah that the Lord his God had decreed that this disaster would come on the city of Jerusalem. Everything had happened exactly as the Lord his God had said it would. Notice in verse 3 that the commander even knew why this disaster had happened to the people of God—it was because the people had sinned against their God and refused to obey him.

The words of Jeremiah the prophet were known even among the Babylonians. Babylon was more willing to accept the word of God than were God's own people. For years the people of Judah had rejected his prophecies; whereas, here in this Babylonian military commander, Jeremiah found someone who agreed with what he had been saying all along.

Nebuzaradan freed Jeremiah from his chains and told him that he would care for him if he wanted to go to Babylon (verse 4). However, if he wanted to go back to his homeland, he was free to do that as well. The commander gave Jeremiah freedom to go wherever he wanted.

Before Jeremiah indicated his intent, the commander told him to go back to his people. He told him in particular to go to Gedaliah, the governor, and live with him. While he recommended that Jeremiah return to Gedaliah, he still gave him freedom to go where he pleased. Notice in verse 5 that he provided the prophet with provisions for his return trip. He even gave him a present, although we are not told what it was. These verses reveal that God gave Jeremiah favor with the enemy.

Jeremiah returned to his homeland to live with Gedaliah, the governor. Those who remained in the land were, for the most part, poor and unskilled people. They were disorganized and helpless.

Verse 7 tells us that some Judean army officers and scattered soldiers who had escaped capture went to visit Gedaliah at Mizpah. This city was the center for Babylon's provisional government in Judah. There Gedaliah told these men that they were not to be afraid of Babylon. Instead, he encouraged them to settle down in the land and serve the king of Babylon. He promised that if they did this, all would go well for them. We are left wondering how much Gedaliah was being influenced by the words of Jeremiah. This was what Jeremiah had been preaching to the people for many years.

In verse 10 Gedaliah told his people that he would represent them before the Babylonians in Mizpah. He encouraged the remnant to plant their fields and harvest their crops. He challenged them to make the most of their situation and to surrender to the will of the Lord. Gedaliah knew that rebellion would get them nowhere. He was also aware of the prophecies of Jeremiah. It was his responsibility to help the remaining Judeans to rebuild a life for themselves among the ruins.

The Judeans who had fled to neighboring countries such as Moab, Ammon, and Edom heard that Nebuchadnezzar had placed Gedaliah over those who remained in the land. They too decided to return to Judah and live there. Verse 12 tells us that they harvested an abundance of wine and summer fruit. The blessing of God was obviously on them as they lived in obedience to his purposes for them. There among the ruins, God's blessing fell on the obedient remnant.

In verse 13 Johanan came to Gedaliah at Mizpah to tell him that Baalis, the king of the Ammonites, had asked a man by the name of Ishmael to kill Gedaliah. Johanan offered to get rid of this threat by killing Ishmael. Gedaliah refused to believe Johanan's report.

In time, however, Ishmael came to see Gedaliah at Mizpah. As they were eating together, Ishmael struck Gedaliah with the sword, killing him. Ishmael also killed a number of Judeans and some Babylonian soldiers as well, probably those at the banquet.

While we are not specifically told why Ishmael killed Gedaliah, we can assume that he was not in favor of this willingness to surrender to the Babylonians. Ishmael did not accept Gedaliah as the leader of Judah. He had a different idea as to how things needed to work in Judah. He was unwilling to submit to the purposes of God.

For Consideration:

• What does this passage teach us about making the most of the situations God places us in?

• Have there been times in your life when you were unwilling to surrender to the will and purpose of the Lord? Have you ever taken matters into your own hands, like Ishmael?

• What do we see here concerning the hand of the Lord in Jeremiah's life? How does this encourage you to stand firm in the call of the Lord in your life?

For Prayer:

• Ask the Lord to give you the grace to accept his purpose for your life and to make the most of it.

• Thank the Lord for how he looks after those who love and faithfully serve him.

• Ask the Lord to forgive you for the times when you have rebelled against his purpose.

47

Fear in the Camp

Read Jeremiah 41:4–42:22

I n the last meditation, we saw how Ishmael had killed the governor, Gedaliah, and slaughtered some Judeans and Babylonian soldiers in Mizpah. As you can imagine, this caused confusion and fear, as it was an extreme violation of Babylonian domination. Nebuchadnezzar would not stand idly by but would certainly punish this behavior. The people who remained in the land were afraid. Chapters 41 and 42 give us an idea as to what happened in the days that followed the assassination of Gedaliah.

In verse 4 we discover that Ishmael's wrath did not stop with the assassination of Gedaliah and those near him. The day after the assassination, before anyone really knew what had happened, a group of eighty men were on their way to Jerusalem to offer grain offerings and incense. They had shaved their beards, torn their clothes, and cut themselves. The practice of cutting was a pagan practice. These men were not aware of the assassination of Gedaliah. They were aware, however, that Nebuchadnezzar had broken through the city wall and conquered Jerusalem. They also knew that God's people had been taken into exile to the land of Babylon. It is quite likely that they were coming in mourning over what had happened in the land. The fact that they had cut themselves indicates that they were not true believers following the laws of Moses. They were, however, concerned about their land.

When Ishmael heard about the arrival of this group of men, he went out to meet them. Notice here that he pretended to be crying. He offered to take them to see Gedaliah. What these individuals did not know was that Gedaliah was dead and that Ishmael was going to take them to their death as well.

Ishmael took them into the city and had them slaughtered. He then threw their bodies into a cistern. Ten of these men, however, told Ishmael that they had a stash of wheat, barley, oil, and honey hidden in a field. Ishmael decided to let them live so he could get this food. This shows us the condition of the land at the time: food was in short supply.

Why did Ishmael kill the men who had come to worship? It was not without reason that he asked them if they wanted to come with him to meet Gedaliah. Could it be that he saw them as supporters of Gedaliah and his cause? Ishmael wanted to rid the land of Gedaliah and all his supporters.

Verse 9 reminds us that the cistern where Ishmael threw the bodies of these men had been built by King Asa who had been attempting to fortify the city against the invasion of King Baasha of Israel. This story relates to a time of civil war among the people of God.

Having killed the men who had come to present their offerings, Ishmael then made prisoners of the rest of the inhabitants of Mizpah (verse 10). He set out to take them to the Ammonites. Some believe that his intent was to sell them as slaves. At this time there was tremendous confusion in the land. The people had just gone through terrible tragedy when Nebuchadnezzar came and conquered the land. Then Ishmael added to their trouble. These were difficult days for the people of God.

Johanan came to the rescue of these people (verse 11). Johanan was the one who had originally warned Gedaliah of the plot of Ishmael. When Johanan heard what had happened in Mizpah, he took all his fighting men and went to confront Ishmael. The two forces met in Gibeon. The captured people were happy to see

Johanan and immediately fled to his side. In the battle that ensued, Ishmael and eight of his men escaped and fled to the Ammonites. Johanan understood the new difficulties involved in living in Mizpah (verses 16–18). Ishmael had invited the wrath of Babylon on the area. It was not certain what Nebuchadnezzar would do when he learned that Gedaliah and some Babylonian soldiers had been killed. Johanan also knew that Baalis, the king of Ammon, was behind the assassination of Gedaliah (40:14) and that Ishmael had fled to Ammon. In the mind of Johanan, the survivors were not safe at Mizpah. They needed protection from Ishmael, Ammon, and Babylon. Egypt seemed to be the only safe place around, so he decided to lead these people to Egypt where they hoped they could live in peace.

In chapter 42 the people with Johanan decided to seek the will of the Lord for them in this matter of taking refuge in Egypt. They approached Jeremiah and asked him to inquire of the Lord about whether they should go to Egypt. They wanted the blessing of the Lord on their journey.

Jeremiah agreed to pray for them. He told them that he would return and tell them everything the Lord told him. The people told Jeremiah that they would do everything the Lord told them, even if it was not what they wanted to hear.

It was not until ten days later that the word of the Lord came to Jeremiah. During this time the prophet had to wait on the Lord to hear what he would say. God speaks when he wants to speak. Many times we do not have the patience we need to wait on the Lord. How many times have we simply lost patience with God's timing and did things the best we knew how, instead of waiting for his clear direction and guidance?

When the word of the Lord came to Jeremiah, he called the people together to tell them what the Lord had said. God said that they were to stay in Judah, the land he had given to their ancestors, and he would build them up (42:11). Jeremiah told them that the Lord was grieved because of the disaster that he had brought on them. They were not to be afraid of the king of Babylon because the Lord promised to protect them. God promised to show compassion on them and restore them in the Promised Land. Jeremiah warned them, however, that if they chose to disobey the word of the Lord and go to the land of Egypt, then the sword they feared would overtake them. The famine they dreaded would follow them into Egypt. Jeremiah told them that if they were determined to go to Egypt, they would die by the sword, famine, and plague. Not one of those who went to Egypt would survive. Just as God's anger had been poured out on Jerusalem because of its disobedience, so it would be poured out on those who went into Egypt in disobedience to his will. They would never see their homeland again.

Jeremiah knew that the people would refuse to listen to the word of the Lord. He reminded them of their promise to do whatever the Lord told them to do. When Jeremiah returned with a word that conflicted with their own plans for deliverance, however, the people broke their promise and chose to disobey the command of the Lord. By their rebellion they sealed their fate. Their journey would be cursed because they did not trust the Lord to protect them in the Promised Land. Just as God could sovereignly protect an obedient remnant in Judah, he could also sovereignly judge a disobedient remnant in Egypt.

The story of the return of God's people to Egypt is tragic. We can understand the reasoning of the people here. They had suffered tremendously and needed protection. Babylon had killed or exiled their loved ones and left them with nothing. Ishmael had added to their misery by his slaughter and attempt to force them to live in Ammon. The uncertainty of what lay ahead of them was an additional stress. Babylon would certainly come against them and perhaps Ammon also. All this was too much to bear. They did not want to live in insecurity any longer, so they took matters into their own hands and did the best they knew how. They fled to Egypt for comfort and security, instead of fleeing to their compassionate and almighty Lord.

What would you have done in this situation? Many times we become so overwhelmed that we no longer trust the Lord. Pain can tempt us to turn our backs on God and seek refuge in harmful places. We can become like this remnant who returned to Egypt, the land of their former bondage.

All too many people, like this remnant in Judah, give up under the pressure. How many times has the Lord tested our faithfulness to him though suffering and trials? What would it take for you to fall and turn from the Lord? How much pressure or how many trials would it take for you to turn your back on him? If we are honest with ourselves, this is indeed a very scary question. Only by God's grace can we overcome. May God give us the grace to trust in him today.

For Consideration:

- Have you ever found yourself in a situation similar to God's people in this section of Scripture?

- What is the source of your strength? What will get you through the trials and temptations in life?

- How many times have you taken matters into your own hands and not waited for the revelation of God's will and purpose?

For Prayer:

- There are those who listen to God when things are going their way but turn their backs on him when he asks them to do something they do not like. Ask the Lord to give you grace to be faithful in all things and at all times, even when it is not what you want.

- Ask the Lord to give you the patience to wait on him and his will. Ask him to give you the patience not to move until you know his leading and direction.

- Is there an area of your life right now where you are not in the will of the Lord? Ask the Lord to give you his strength for obedience in this area.

48

In the Land of Egypt

Read Jeremiah 43–44

J eremiah had just announced the word of the Lord to the remnant with Johanan. The Lord had told them not to seek refuge in the land of Egypt. Instead, they were to remain in the land of Judah and rebuild the land that the Lord their God had given them. Azariah refused to believe that what Jeremiah had spoken was from the Lord. In verse 2 he accused Jeremiah of lying and said that Baruch had convinced Jeremiah to mislead the people so that they would be captured by the Babylonians.

Why did Azariah accuse Jeremiah of listening to Baruch, Jeremiah's secretary? Perhaps it was because Baruch was the person who read the prophecies of Jeremiah in public when the prophet was restrained in prison (see 36:6). Perhaps, the people had seen more of Baruch than they had seen of Jeremiah.

As the word of the Lord did not please Johanan and the people with him, they decided to disregard the Lord's command. Johanan and his officers led them into Egypt, where they settled in the city of Tahpanhes. Notice in verse 6 that Jeremiah and Baruch were included with those who went to Egypt. It is hard to say whether

Jeremiah went to Egypt of his own free will or whether he was taken by force.

In Egypt the word of the Lord again came to Jeremiah. God told Jeremiah to gather some large stones and bury them in the brick pavement at the entrance of Pharaoh's palace in Tahpanhes. He was then to prophesy that the Lord was going to send Nebuchadnezzar, king of Babylon, into Egypt. Nebuchadnezzar would spread out his royal canopy above these stones. He would attack Egypt and bring death to all who were destined to die, captivity to all who were destined to captivity, and the sword to all who were destined for the sword. God's rebellious remnant could not flee from the wrath and judgment of God. No matter where they were, they would not escape. They would find no security in Egypt.

Jeremiah told the refugees that this would happen to them when Nebuchadnezzar came to Egypt. He prophesied in verse 12 that the Babylonian king would set fire to the temples of the gods in Egypt and take their gods to Babylon. Jeremiah compared Nebuchadnezzar to a shepherd who wrapped his coat around himself and left. This is what Nebuchadnezzar would do to Egypt. The conquest of Egypt would be as simple as putting on a coat and leaving. Nebuchadnezzar would come to Egypt, wrap Egypt around him, and leave unharmed. Egypt would be demolished and its temples burned to the ground. God's people would experience all over again the terrible tragedy they had experienced in the land of Judah.

Chapter 44 records that the word of the Lord came a second time to Jeremiah when he was in Egypt. Through Jeremiah the Lord reminded his people of the great disaster they had seen in Jerusalem. This had happened to them because of their sin. They had provoked the Lord to anger by worshiping other gods. The Lord reminded his people of how he had spoken repeatedly to them through his servants the prophets, calling them to turn from their evil, but they had refused to listen to the Lord. They did not turn from their idolatry but continued to burn incense to other gods. Because of this, the anger of the Lord had come on them. Their towns were reduced to ruins, and Jerusalem lay in a pile of rubble.

God asked the people why they would bring a similar disaster on themselves in Egypt by continuing to practice idolatry (44:7–8). After surviving God's judgment in Judah, they were pursuing it in Egypt by the same sins. They were risking cutting Judah off from the land of the living and leaving themselves without posterity. God asked them why they burned incense to the gods of Egypt. Would not the same judgment fall on them in Egypt as in Judah? Did they really think that the Lord did not see what they were doing in Egypt? By not learning their lesson, they brought the wrath of God on themselves again. They would destroy themselves by repeating past sins.

God promised to destroy those who were so determined to take asylum in Egypt (44:11–14). God's judgment would come to Egypt by the sword and the famine. This idolatrous remnant would become an object of scorn and reproach to the nations around them. God promised to judge them just as he had judged Jerusalem. Only a few fugitives would ever return to Judah. Only those who submitted to the judgment of God and humbled themselves would survive and return to the land God had promised to their ancestors.

How important it is for us to submit to what the Lord wants to do in us. There are times when we want to run away from his discipline, which is for our good. Instead of humbly submitting to what God is doing, we seek an easy way out. In so doing, we miss the blessings God wants to bring into our lives through these trials. Those who refuse the discipline of the Lord will suffer his further judgment. May God teach us to trust what he is doing.

When the people heard the words of the Lord through Jeremiah, they told the prophet clearly that they would not repent (44:16). They told him that they would continue to burn incense to the Queen of Heaven and offer drink offerings to her. Their ancestors had done this in Judah, and they were going to continue doing it themselves so that they would have plenty of food and prosperity. They clearly told Jeremiah that they believed that ever since they had stopped burning incense to the Queen of Heaven, things had gone badly for them. They believed that judgment had come on them because they had not been worshiping the Queen of Heaven.

The women told Jeremiah that their husbands knew what they were doing and had not stopped them (44:19). In so doing, the husbands condoned the actions of their wives. The wives justified their idolatry on the basis that their husbands had allowed them to offer these sacrifices. It did not matter to these women what the Lord said. All that mattered was what their husbands said (or in this case, what they did not say).

How blind we can become in our rebellion. When we want to practice sin, we can find our own justification for it. Satan will do his best to turn our eyes from the clear teaching of the Word of God. He will point us to others who are doing what we are doing. These other sinners may even be our spiritual leaders. We must not be deceived—the Word of God alone is our guide.

Notice in this chapter how hardened these people had become to the things of God. They did not want to hear what the prophet had to say. Their act of rebellion in leaving Judah had made them more stubborn against the things of God. The more they rebelled, the harder they became. They openly practiced their idolatry and openly refused to listen to the Lord. They wanted nothing to do with him. We can only imagine the hurt in the heart of God and his servant Jeremiah upon hearing these statements.

Jeremiah reminded the people that the Lord saw and remembered the incense that was offered in the streets of Jerusalem to their foreign gods (44:21). It was when he could no longer endure their wickedness that the Lord had cursed their land and made it desolate. It was because they had refused to follow his laws that the Lord had judged them so severely. The people were blind to what was happening. The enemy had twisted their understanding, and they believed his lies.

Jeremiah told the people to go ahead and offer their sacrifices to the Queen of Heaven (44:25). But God would not listen to their cries anymore. They could sacrifice to the Queen of Heaven, but, in so doing, they rejected the God of Judah. They could not serve God and the Queen of Heaven. From that day forth, they were the enemies of God. His wrath was on them, and they would perish in their sin. Very few would escape his wrath to tell the story of what happened in Egypt. The world would see who was right. The word spoken through the prophet Jeremiah would be proven true.

God gave them a sign that he would punish them for their evil (44:29–30). He told them Pharaoh Hophra would be handed over to his enemies as Zedekiah had been handed over to Nebuchadnezzar. When this happened they would know that the word of God was true.

We see here the struggle between truth and falsehood. The enemy was very busy deceiving God's people. They believed his lies and their hearts were hardened. They turned their backs on the Lord their God, and brought his judgment on themselves.

These people had a decision to make, and they chose to rebel against God and worship the Queen of Heaven. God allowed them to make that decision but withdrew his presence and his grace from their lives. If you can hear the Lord today, do not harden your heart. Submit to his leading and discipline before you can no longer hear him.

For Consideration:

• Why is it so hard for us to accept the discipline of the Lord?

• What has the Lord been saying to you through your trials?

• What stands between you and the purposes of the Lord today?

• Have you ever had a moment in your life when you willingly chose to disobey the Lord? What was the result?

For Prayer:

• Ask the Lord to give you ears to hear him in your trials.

• Ask him to forgive you for the times you turned your back on him and his will for your life.

• Thank him for his mercy. Thank him that he still calls out to you today. Thank him that he has not turned his back on you.

49

A Brief Word to Baruch

Read Jeremiah 45

C hapter 45 is the shortest chapter in the book of Jeremiah.
Here Jeremiah spoke particularly to Baruch. It may be
helpful to say a few words about Baruch. Baruch had
been a faithful secretary for Jeremiah, writing down the words
the prophet dictated to him. Not only did Baruch write down the
words of the prophet Jeremiah but he also read them to the people.
Jeremiah was not always able to get to the people to speak to
them. For a period of his life, Jeremiah was restricted in prison.
During this time Baruch took the writings of the prophet and read
them to the people. He was also entrusted with the deed to a piece
of property that Jeremiah had purchased while in prison. Baruch
was a vital part of the ministry of Jeremiah, and the prophet owed
much to him.

Baruch's ministry was not always easy. In chapter 36 we read
that Baruch and Jeremiah had to hide from King Jehoiakim after
the king learned of the contents of Jeremiah's prophecies (36:19,
36). In chapter 43 we read that Baruch was accused of being a
Babylonian sympathizer (43:3).

Verse 1 tells us that the word of the Lord came to Jeremiah

for Baruch. This particular word came after Baruch had finished writing the words of Jeremiah on a scroll in the fourth year of Jehoiakim. This was before Nebuchadnezzar destroyed the city of Jerusalem. (We have noted before that the book of Jeremiah is not always in chronological order.)

In verse 3 we see that Baruch was feeling worn out, and he could not find any rest. His heart was heavy, and he groaned under the load. He felt as if the Lord was adding sorrow to his pain. We are not told particularly here why Baruch was feeling this. Part of the struggle may have been with the message he had just written down. Jeremiah's message was one of doom and destruction for the city of Jerusalem. Baruch's heart was heavy and burdened.

The Lord knew exactly what Baruch was feeling. He was not alone in his suffering. God knew the pain of his heart, and this alone would have been an encouragement to Baruch. Just to realize that the Lord understood what he was going through would have been a blessing.

Jeremiah reminded Baruch that, despite what he was feeling, the purposes of the Lord would be accomplished. God would overthrow what he was going to overthrow and uproot what he had destined to be uprooted. These were days of terror and evil in the land. God was going to judge his people because of their sin.

Verse 5 is the key to this chapter. Here God asked Baruch why he should seek good things for himself when the whole nation was going to be destroyed. Obviously, Baruch was concerned about his own pain. His pain, however, was nothing compared to the suffering God's people would face in the coming months. Baruch's complaining was like a soldier in the heat of battle whining about a stubbed toe when all around him his friends were being killed by enemy arrows.

How easy it is for us to see only our own pain. Soldiers who go to war understand that they will have to put aside their comfort and be willing to suffer. Athletes preparing for competition realize that they will have to discipline themselves to win. Workers must be willing to forsake the comforts of their bed to prepare for work. The Lord Jesus asked the disciples to leave their nets to follow him. Jesus himself suffered when he laid down his life. Jesus clearly taught us that the servant would not be above the master:

"Remember the words I spoke to you: 'No servant is greater than his master.' If they persecuted me, they will persecute you also. If they obeyed my teaching, they will obey yours also. They will treat you this way because of my name, for they do not know the One who sent me" (John 15:20–21).

Baruch was complaining about missing out on great personal achievements for himself while the people of God were heading straight to an earthly and eternal judgment. Baruch's fixation with his own suffering was unhealthy. His grumbling was a sin. Through Jeremiah the Lord challenged him to lift up his eyes and realize that he was not the only one suffering in the world. Compared to the suffering Judah would face, his personal trial was very mild indeed.

God also encouraged Baruch in this chapter. In verse 5 God promised him that while he would have to learn to face suffering, he would be protected. Wherever he went, he would escape with his life. God would not take the suffering away, but he would protect Baruch in the suffering.

One of the greatest sins of God's people as they wandered through the wilderness was the sin of complaining. In 1 Corinthians 10:10–11 we read: "And do not grumble, as some of them did— and were killed by the destroying angel. These things happened to them as examples and were written down as warnings for us, on whom the fulfillment of the ages has come."

Because of their grumbling spirit, the Lord sent a destroying angel to devour his people in the wilderness. This chapter challenges us to learn to be content with those things the Lord has given us. It challenges us to trust in the Lord and what he is doing. How easy it is for us to fall into the trap of thinking only of our pain and suffering. Baruch's suffering would not be taken from him, but God's hand would be on him in that suffering. If Baruch watched closely, he would have much cause to rejoice at what God was doing.

For Consideration:

• Have you ever found yourself preoccupied with your own suffering and pain?

- Could it be that one of the tactics of the enemy is to focus our attention on our pain and suffering? What happens when we focus too much on ourselves?

- Take a moment to consider what God has given you. Let the reality of the presence of God fill you and cause your heart to rejoice.

For Prayer:

- Thank the Lord that he promises to be with us in our pain and suffering.

- Ask the Lord to enable you to see his hand in your pain.

- Ask him to give you grace to know his joy in the midst of your pain and suffering.

50

A Word to Egypt

Read Jeremiah 46

With this chapter we begin a section of the prophecy of Jeremiah in which he spoke to the nations. To this point, he had spoken to the people of God. In chapters 46–51 God selected specific neighboring nations and spoke of their judgment (see 25:15–26). Here in chapter 46 we read two prophecies given by Jeremiah to the land of Egypt.

The first prophecy dealt with a particular battle at Carchemish by the Euphrates River (verses 1–12). This battle would take place between Pharaoh Neco and King Nebuchadnezzar in the fourth year of King Jehoiakim of Judah. It was in Carchemish that these two great forces would meet, and Nebuchadnezzar would defeat the Egyptian army.

Jeremiah spoke here about what would happen to Egypt on that day. Egypt was called to prepare its shields to go out to battle. They were to harness their horses and take up their positions for battle. They were to have their armor on in preparation for the attack. Their spears were to be polished. As they stood ready for battle, the Lord asked them what they saw.

In verse 5 we are given a picture of the battle that would take place. There was terror on all sides. Soldiers were retreating, and powerful warriors were defeated. They fled so quickly that they did not even take the time to look back. Their only objective was to escape with their lives. The fastest among them could not escape fast enough. The strongest among them failed. They stumbled together, and no one escaped. Notice here that all this happened in the north by the River Euphrates. This is where Carchemish was located.

The scene that Jeremiah described here was one of helplessness and defeat. There was nothing Egypt could do. Her defeat was certain because her enemy was too powerful. Notice in verse 7 how Egypt felt about herself. She told herself that she would rise and cover the earth like the Nile River, destroying the cities and people in her way. She boasted of her strength and power. What could stop her? Stopping her was like trying to stop the Nile River in its swelling. Egypt was an arrogant and powerful nation. At one point in her history, she was unrivalled on the earth; but her time was ending.

God called Egypt and her allies to charge into battle (verse 9). Notice that the nations of Cush, Put, and Lydia were fighting beside Egypt. They were a force to be feared. Indeed, like the swelling Nile, they intended to destroy everything in their way.

What they did not understand was that this day belonged to the Lord as a day of his vengeance against them. This would be the day of their defeat. The sword of the Lord would devour them until it was satisfied. God would take vengeance on his foes. There in the region of Carchemish, God would offer up Egypt as a great sacrifice. As proud and as powerful as she was, she was no match for Almighty God. Ultimately, the battle does not belong to the strong but to whomever the Lord himself determines will win. Everything is in his hands.

In verse 11 God called Egypt to go up to Gilead and get balm. Gilead was known for its balm used to soothe and heal wounds. Notice here, however, that this balm would be applied to her wounds in vain. The best balm in the world would not bring healing to these Egyptians. God had withdrawn his healing presence from them. They were under his judgment.

The nations would hear of Egypt's defeat. The cries of her

warriors would fill the earth. One warrior after another would stumble and fall. Their end had come. How long will God plead with our nations? How long will he plead with us? When will he withdraw his presence?

Jeremiah warned the Egyptians here that they were accountable to the God of Israel and Judah. He reminded them that the patience of God had a limit. They would have to face his judgment. As powerful as they were, they would be stripped of everything and stand before the God of Israel and Judah to be judged.

From verse 13 to the end of the chapter, Jeremiah announced a second prophecy to the people of Egypt. This prophecy related to the coming of Babylon to conquer Egypt at a later point. Babylon would defeat Egypt at Carchemish, but they would also invade the land of Egypt at a later time. We have already seen how God told Jeremiah that Nebuchadnezzar would set up his throne in the land of Egypt (43:10). Jeremiah continued with this same theme.

This prophecy was to be announced in Egypt and proclaimed in the prominent cities of Migdol, Memphis, and Tahpanhes (see 43:7). The warriors in these cities were to take their positions and prepare for battle. The sword of the Lord's wrath was coming to devour. These powerful warriors would be laid low because the Lord himself would push them down. In verse 16 Jeremiah painted a picture of these mighty warriors falling over each other in their attempt to escape. The Egyptian army was comprised of many different nations and peoples who allied with Egypt. In the day of God's vengeance, these allies would abandon their post when they saw that Egypt would fall. They would turn their backs on the Pharaoh of Egypt, claiming that he was only a loud noise. The Pharaoh had boasted of his great power and ability, but his words did not match his strength. These individuals had flocked to Pharaoh for his protection. Israel was one of those nations who had put her confidence in Pharaoh. But these nations would be disappointed. Ultimately, all who put their confidence in human strength, and not in the Lord God, will be disappointed.

Through Jeremiah the Lord warned Egypt that someone would come who was like Tabor and Carmel, which are high mountains in Israel (verse 18). The day was coming when a great king (Nebuchadnezzar) would come and defeat Egypt. The people of Egypt were told to pack their belongings for exile. The great city of Memphis would be laid waste and be without inhabitants.

Egypt was compared to a beautiful heifer (verse 20). While that heifer grazed in the prosperity of the land, a gadfly was coming. That stinging fly would bite and kill the heifer. Egypt's warriors were compared to well-fed calves that would flee in the day of battle. The fatted calf was one that lived in pampered conditions, ready to be killed.

Like a fleeing serpent, Egypt would hiss in retreat (verse 22). The enemy would pursue her with axes. They would chop down her trees and forests to make weapons. They would come at her as a plague of locusts whose number could not be counted.

Egypt would be put to shame and handed over to the people of the north (the Babylonians). The God of Israel was going to bring punishment on Amon the god of Thebes, on Pharaoh, and on all who relied on Egypt for help. They would all be handed over to Nebuchadnezzar.

Notice in verse 26 that God promised that the day was coming when Egypt would again be inhabited. The judgment of God would last only for a certain time, after which God would restore a measure of blessing to Egypt. In his judgment God would still be merciful to the nation of Egypt.

This prophecy about Egypt related also to Israel (verses 27–28). Israel, as a nation, had turned her back on God and sought the protection of Egypt. With the defeat of Egypt would also come the defeat of the people of God who were under Egypt's protection. God reminded his people, however, that he would not forget them forever. Though they had disobeyed him and trusted in Egypt, he would still restore them as a people in his time. He would bring them back from the land of their exile and build them up as a nation again. He promised that one day they would live in peace and no one would make them afraid.

Fear sent the people of God to Egypt. They feared the nation of Babylon. They were unable to trust in the Lord their God and chose to run to the open arms of Egypt. God understood their fear. While he did not condone their behavior, he promised to set them free from their fear.

In verse 28 he told Israel not to be afraid. He reminded his people that he was with them. Though there would be chaos and devastation all around them, God promised to care for them. While they would be disciplined, it would be in justice. He would punish them for their sin, but he would not forsake them. He challenged them in the midst of this coming devastation to trust him and his promises to them.

God did not promise his people freedom from suffering. He did challenge them, however, to trust him and not be afraid. Can you trust God in your trial? Can you believe that he will do what is right? Don't fear what God is doing in your life. Surrender to him, and let him accomplish his perfect will in you.

For Consideration:

• What do we learn here about putting our confidence in people? What other things do people put their confidence in today?

• What does this chapter teach us about putting our confidence in God?

• What do we learn here about God's mercy in judgment?

• Do you have a hard time surrendering to the discipline of the Lord in your life? How has God been disciplining and training you recently?

For Prayer:

• Thank the Lord that we can trust him and his purposes.

• Ask him to help you to put your confidence in him alone.

• Thank the Lord that he does care enough for us that he takes the time to discipline and train us to be closer to him.

51

A Word to the Philistines

Read Jeremiah 47

Having spoken to the Egyptians in chapter 46, Jeremiah next prophesied to the Philistines. Notice here in verse 1 that this prophetic word came before Pharaoh had attacked Gaza, one of the principle Philistine cities. From this reference, it might be easy to assume that the fulfillment of the prophecy of Jeremiah would be found in this attack of Pharaoh. Jeremiah's prophecy, however, related more to a particular Babylonian attack. The attack of Egypt on Gaza was only a prelude to an even greater devastation that would occur.

The prophecy regarding the Philistines began with a prophetic picture of waters rising in the north. Those waters would become an overflowing torrent onto the land of the Philistines. Everything would be covered by these waters. The towns and their inhabitants would cry out because of the terror of these overflowing waters.

What did this torrent of water represent? Verse 3 seems to answer this for us. Jeremiah spoke about the sound of galloping horses and the rumbling of enemy chariots. The sound of this approaching army would so terrify the people that fathers would not even turn to help their children because they would be paralyzed with fear. They would know that nothing could stop this advancing army coming on them like a raging torrent of water. The fathers' hands would hang limp and helpless at their sides. It is important to note here that this army would come from the north. This was very likely the same army (Babylon) that Jeremiah spoke about when he prophesied of Judah's destruction. On his military campaign, Nebuchadnezzar conquered not only Judah but also many of the surrounding nations as well.

Jeremiah prophesied that the day of God's judgment had come for the nation of Philistia. They had been living comfortably without any real thought of judgment, but that day would come.

There is a day of judgment coming for us as well. Like the Philistines, many people are living their lives with no thought of that day. Jesus described what it would be like at his Second Coming: "For in the days before the flood, people were eating and drinking, marrying and giving in marriage, up to the day Noah entered the ark; and they knew nothing about what would happen until the flood came and took them all away. That is how it will be at the coming of the Son of Man" (Matthew 24:38–39).

How we need to be ready for this day. We do not know when that day of accounting will be for us. We must live each day with the understanding that we will one day have to give an account of our lives to our God.

Notice in verse 4 that all Philistines would be destroyed and cut off. No survivor would be left to run to the neighboring towns of Tyre and Sidon. Notice in verse 5 the response of the people of Philistia to this judgment. The inhabitants of Gaza would shave their heads in mourning. The citizens of Ashkelon would be silenced, and the remnant on the plains would cut themselves in a pagan symbol of mourning. They would all groan under the judgment of God.

In verse 6 the people of Philistia were pictured asking how long the sword of the Lord would punish them. They begged the Lord to return his sword to its resting place. They cried out for his judgment to stop. You can feel their pain in these words. They could not endure any longer.

While their anguish was understandable, Jeremiah asked them a question in verse 7. How could the Lord's sword of judgment rest when it had been commanded to attack? There is no power on earth that can stop what God commands. That sword could not be sheathed until it had accomplished everything the Lord had ordered. The people could do nothing to reverse the Lord's plan. Their end had truly come.

This prophecy is a challenge to us today. The sword of God's judgment will once again be unsheathed against all who turn their backs on the Lord. When the Lord commands it to fall, there will be nothing to stop it. It is easy for people to live each day putting the future day of judgment out of their thoughts. As it was for Philistia, the sword of God's judgment will one day be unsheathed again. May God convict us of this truth and help us to focus our lives on the Lord and his work on earth.

For Consideration:

• What does this chapter teach us about the judgment of God?

• Are there any areas of your life where you are not living in obedience to the Lord? What are they?

• Is the Lord righteous in his punishment of sin? What must we do to be prepared for that judgment?

For Prayer:

• Ask the Lord to search your heart and show you any areas of your life that are not right with him today.

• Do you know someone who is living in rebellion against God today? Take a moment to ask the Lord to open the eyes of this person to the reality of the judgment to come.

• If you are a believer today, thank God that through the Lord Jesus Christ you have been spared from the sword of his judgment.

52

A Word to Moab

Read Jeremiah 48

H ere in chapter 48 Jeremiah spoke the word of the Lord to the people of Moab. He spoke to the individual cites of the nation and prophesied the judgment of God against them. The Moabites were the descendants of Lot, and they were often the enemy of Israel (see Genesis 19:37; Numbers 22).

Jeremiah began by addressing the city of Nebo. Deuteronomy 34:1 tells us that Moses went up to a mountain in the region of Nebo to view the Promised Land before he died. Jeremiah prophesied that this region would be ruined. The city of Kiriathaim would be captured and disgraced. Their stronghold would be captured and shattered.

The country of Moab would no longer be praised. The enemy would capture Heshbon and make plans for the downfall of the nation. The city of Madmen, another important Moabite town, would be put to silence as the sword pursued the inhabitants.

From the city of Horonaim, cries of despair would be heard from those experiencing great destruction and havoc. Moab would be broken. Her little ones would cry in anguish and despair. All the way from Luhith to the region of Horonaim, people would flee from the approaching army, weeping with anguish as they went. In verse 6 Moab is compared to a bush in the desert. This expression is hard to understand. Could it be that this is a description of Moab under the judgment of God? Even as the wilderness is barren and unproductive, so this would be her future. Her people would be as rare as bushes living in a barren and unproductive wilderness.

Notice in verse 7 how they had been trusting in their deeds and riches. Because of this they would be taken captive. Chemosh, their chief god, would be taken captive with them into exile, along with the pagan priests and officials. It was a common practice in ancient times for the idols of conquered nations to be taken and then displayed in the triumphal procession on the return from battle in order to show the superiority of the conqueror's gods over those of the conquered (see Isaiah 46:1–2).

It is important to note here that one of the reasons for the captivity of Moab was that they had put their confidence in their own deeds and riches. What a challenge this is for us in our materialistic culture. How easy it is to depend on our own wisdom and strength. In times of prosperity, it is easy for us to forget that everything belongs to the Lord, and without him we would have nothing. Our confidence needs to be in the Lord and him alone. It is sometimes not until we lose what we have that we realize how utterly dependent we are on God for everything. Pride is not only the sin of the unbeliever; it is also the sin of the believer.

In verse 8 Jeremiah told the Moabites that the destroyer would destroy every town in their country. Not a single town would escape his judgment. The valley and the plateau would be destroyed. God's judgment would be complete. The call went out to put salt on the land of Moab so that nothing would again grow in her soil. This would leave her desolate with no one to live in her.

God pronounced a curse on those who were not diligent in doing the work of the Lord, which was a work of judgment (verse 10). God had called the destroyer to bring its power against the land of Moab. If those executing this task took pity on Moab, they themselves would be cursed. They were not to keep their sword from bloodshed. They were to swing it with vengeance and execute God's plan.

A Word to Moab ● 245

Moab had lived in peace from her youth (verse 11). She had never been disturbed, like wine left in its flask without being moved. Wine that is left in this way keeps its flavor and strength. The best wine is left undisturbed. Moving it from one flask to another will destroy its flavor and weaken it. Moab had remained undisturbed. The days were coming, however, when the Lord would send the enemy to pour her out and smash her flasks. Moab, like so many people, had become settled and complacent. Moab had been trusting in her riches and deeds for national security. She felt strong and powerful, as if nothing could harm her. God needed to bring her to an awareness of who she really was in his sight. Many of us need to be brought to this point as well.

When God poured out Moab like wine, she would be ashamed of her ways. In particular, she would be ashamed of her god Chemosh (verse 13). She would be ashamed like the house of Israel was ashamed in Bethel. It was in Bethel that the Israelites had set up a golden calf to worship (see 1 Kings 12:27–33). Like Israel, Moab would come to understand the futility of trusting in any other god than the Lord God of Israel.

Notice in verse 14 the pride of Moab in her warriors. These men claimed to be mighty men, valiant in battle, but they were no match for the God of Israel. Moab put her trust in military force, but it would prove to be futile—Moab would be destroyed. Her towns would be invaded, and her finest young men would be slaughtered. A call went out for Moab's neighbors to mourn for her. All who knew her fame were called to cry out. Her mighty scepter would be broken.

God called the city of Dibon, on the Arnon River, to humble herself and sit on parched ground (verse 18). Parched ground is that which is emptied of the blessing of God. This would be the destiny of these people. Dibon would be destroyed, and she would sit in thirst.

The people who lived along the Arnon River in the nation of Ammon were called to stand by the road and watch the people of Moab fleeing from the heat of battle. Aroer was called to witness this great public judgment of God. It was the intention of the Lord that observers would see his judgment and learn from Moab the horrible consequences of human pride.

Verses 21 to 24 list the names of the towns that would come under the judgment of God. God's judgment would be very specific. Hearing their towns named would have made this prophecy more real to the people. Sometimes it is so easy to see things in a general sense that we fail to realize the seriousness of what God is saying.

Moab's horn would be cut off (verse 25). As an animal's defense, the horn was a symbol of strength. With her military power destroyed, Moab would be humbled and left defenseless. Notice that not only was her horn cut off but her arm was also broken. A warrior with no weapon and a broken arm is helpless against the enemy.

Moab would be forced to drink the cup of God's wrath (verse 26). She would become sick and wallow in her vomit. She would become an object of ridicule and scorn. This is very different from what she was before the judgment of God. She had been living quietly, trusting in her accumulated riches. She trusted in her human efforts and her military force. She was confident and proud as a nation but would become like a drunk, crawling in vomit.

In verse 27 Jeremiah reminded Moab that she had mocked and scorned the people of Israel in their time of distress. The Moabites felt that they were far removed from such judgment; however, they would experience the same thing. As they had mocked Israel, they would be mocked by other nations.

The people of Moab were called to abandon their towns and flee to the rocks and caves of the mountains. Obviously, the enemy would destroy these towns and cities and render them unsafe places to live. The inhabitants would escape to the mountains and caves.

Moab's pride was described as being very great in verse 29. God was very much aware of this pride. As a nation, Moab had become insolent and boasted in her accomplishments. Nothing Moab boasted about, however, could save her from God's judgment.

Notice in verse 31 that the Lord wailed over Moab. He moaned for the men of Kir Hareseth. He wept for them as the defeated city of Jazer had wept at its defeat (see Numbers 21:32). The fruit vines of Sibmah had spread out as far as the sea. This was evidence of

Moab's great wine and fruit trade. The destroyer, however, would fall on the ripened fruit.

Joy and gladness would be removed from the orchards and fields of Moab. The Lord would stop the flow of wine in the presses. No one would tread the grapes anymore. There would be no more shouts because of the abundant harvest. The only shouting that would be heard in the land would be the shouting of despair and grief from cities across all of Moab (verse 34). The waters of Nimrim, known for its well-watered pastures, would be dried up. The blessing of God would leave the land.

The judgment of God would also fall on those who had been offering pagan sacrifices on the high places. God would judge those who had been burning incense to their gods. This nation was to be held accountable to the one true God of Israel. Moab would be judged because, in her pride, she had rejected him.

All nations are accountable to God. All will one day bow the knee to him. They will one day surrender to him as their Lord, whether willingly or by force. How important it is for us to share the message of salvation with the nations.

God took no delight in judging the people of Moab. Notice in verse 36 that his heart lamented for them. Their accumulated wealth and riches were gone. They were left stripped and barren.

In this prophecy the people of Moab could be seen in mourning (verse 37). Their heads were shaved and their beards cut off in a symbol of anguish. Their hands were cut, and they wore sackcloth over their waists as they grieved for their condition. Throughout the land, on the rooftops and in the public squares, there was nothing but mourning. God had broken the nation of Moab like a jar that no one wanted. Those around her were horrified at what they saw.

A great eagle was swooping down with its wings spread out over Moab (verse 40). This bird of prey was swooping down to devour. Kerioth would be captured. The hearts of the bravest of warriors would melt like the heart of a woman in labor. Moab would be destroyed as a nation because she had dared to defy the Lord in her pride.

Moab's future was very bleak—terror, the pit, and a snare awaited the people. Those who escaped the terror would fall into a pit. Whoever climbed out of the pit would be caught in the snare. No one would escape God's judgment.

A great fire of judgment had gone out from Heshbon (verse 45). The fugitives stood helpless before it. A blaze came from Sihon (an ancient king of the region, see Numbers 21:21–26) to burn the foreheads of the Moabites and the skulls of the noisy boasters. Moab's glory would be removed as when someone's hair is burned off with fire. Her boasting and pride caused her death.

The worshipers of Chemosh would be destroyed. Moab's sons and daughters would be taken into exile. The once-glorious and proud nation would be destroyed and left barren and empty. This prophecy was fulfilled when Nebuchadnezzar returned to the region in 581 BC to stop a rebellion in Moab and Ammon.

Jeremiah prophesied in verses 47, however, that the day was coming when the Lord would again restore Moab's fortune. God would not hold onto his anger forever. Even in his judgment, he would show mercy and compassion.

We see here in this chapter that the great sin of the people of Moab was pride. They were like wine that had never been moved. They had not been disturbed, and as a result had become proud and arrogant. They trusted in themselves, their wealth, and their military. They felt no need for God. There are times when we too fall into this same sin. There are times when the Lord needs to pour us out and break our pride so that we realize our need of him.

For Consideration:

• What evidence of pride do you see in your own life?

• Have you ever experienced the Lord "pouring you out"? What lessons did you learn from this?

• What does this chapter teach us about pride and how God feels about it?

For Prayer:

- Ask the Lord to search you, to root out any pride and self-reliance.

- Ask the Lord to pour you out so that you can be more useful to him and his kingdom.

- Ask the Lord to build the fruit of humility into your life.

- Ask him to forgive you for your pride.

53

A Word to Ammon and Edom

Read Jeremiah 49:1–22

I n chapter 49 Jeremiah the prophet spoke to a number of nations. God's word was not just for Israel, but for all nations. These nations had seen God work in the lives of his people. They had seen his power and his might. They knew the God of Israel to be a powerful and holy God, yet they did not come to him. They would be held accountable before the God of Israel for this.

Ammon (verses 1–6)

In his prophecy concerning the nation of Ammon (see Genesis 19:38), Jeremiah began by asking why the Ammonite god Molech lived in Israel (in the territory of the tribe of Gad). When the Assyrians captured the northern kingdom of Israel in 722 BC and deported these ten tribes into exile, the Ammonites seized the territory of the tribe of Gad. There in the land that God had given to his people, the neighboring Ammonites set up their god Molech. Not only did the Ammonites take Israel's land but they also insulted and mocked the people of God in their time of trial. We read about this in Zephaniah 2:8: "I have heard the insults of

Moab and the taunts of the Ammonites, who insulted my people and made threats against their land."

God saw what had happened to his people and the land he had given them. While they were in exile because of their sin, God was going to watch over their land. He was concerned about what was being said about his people.

The day was coming when the sound of the battle cry would be heard in Rabbah, the capital city of Ammon (verse 2). This region would become a mound of ruins. Its villages would be set on fire. Israel would one day drive out those who had driven her from her land.

The city of Heshbon was called to wail; Ai was destroyed; Rabbah was to cry out, put on sackcloth, and mourn. Inside the walls of the city, Jeremiah foresaw people running frantically from place to place. Their god Molech would be taken into exile. Their officials would be led off and could not help them. The people would be left defenseless before the anger of the Lord God of Israel.

The people of Ammon had boasted in their fruitful valleys and had trusted in their riches. They believed that they were safe, and no one would attack them. They lived in false security and felt confident in themselves. But God would judge this nation. He would bring terror on the Ammonites. Their neighbors would turn against them. They would be driven away as a people, and no one would come to their rescue.

Notice in verse 6 that while God would severely judge the Ammonites, he promised that, in time, he would restore their fortunes. His anger would not be forever. In his anger, he would remember mercy.

We see here how the Ammonites had taken advantage of God's people in their time of weakness and had mocked them. It is true that the people of God were being judged at this time because of their evil, but, even in this, God expected the Ammonites to respect the Israelites as his children.

I am reminded of how David respected King Saul. Even when Saul was not living as he should have lived, David refused to speak evil of the man God had chosen to be king over Israel. I believe that the Lord blessed David and his ministry because of this. We are challenged here in these verses to examine our own attitudes and actions toward others, even those who are under the discipline of God.

Edom (verses 7–22)

The next nation in this section of prophecy is the nation of Edom. These people were the descendants of Esau. Once again, Jeremiah began with a question to the Edomites: "Is there no longer wisdom in Teman?" Teman was a city in Edom known for its wisdom. The prophet foresaw a time when Edom's wisdom would be gone. The once-great nation of Edom would flee to deep caves to hide. A great disaster was coming to this nation, and their human wisdom could not stop it.

Jeremiah told the Edomites in verse 9 that if grape pickers had come to them, they would have left a few grapes on the vine. This was a reference to one of the Old Testament laws. Anyone picking grapes was to leave some on the vine for the poor and needy (Leviticus 19:10). Those who would come to harvest Edom in judgment, however, would strip the nation bare, leaving nothing. Even a thief would only take what he considered to be of value, but the judgment of God would be complete. God would uncover the hiding places and search out every corner for judgment. All that would remain would be the orphans and widows. God would care for the helpless, but everyone else would be taken away.

Jeremiah reminded the Edomites in verse 12 that if those who did not deserve to drink the cup of God's wrath had to drink it, then Edom should not be surprised if she had to drink it as well. This seems to be a reference to the children of Israel. As God's only covenant nation, Israel should have obeyed God and avoided judgment. If God punished his own people for their rebellion, what should rebellious Edom expect when she had no relationship with God? Edom was not to think that she could escape the wrath of God.

The region of Bozrah, Edom's capital city, would become a ruin and an object of horror forever (verse 13). An envoy would be sent to the nations to assemble against Edom and attack it (verse 14). God was going to make Edom small and despised. At one point in her history, she had inspired terror in others. Geographically,

Edom was located in a mountainous region surrounded by cliffs, making it extremely difficult for an enemy to attack. Edom was compared to an eagle that builds its nest in the heights where no one can reach it. Although Edom felt secure, God would bring her down.

Jeremiah told Edom that she would become an object of horror (verse 17). The people that passed by would be appalled and would mock her because of her defeat. Edom was compared to Sodom and Gomorrah, which were overthrown in the days of Abraham and Lot (Genesis 19:24). Edom would be destroyed, and no one would live in this region again.

Edom would be chased from its land in an instant (verse 19). As powerful and as secure as she felt, she would be brought down quickly, like the prey of a hungry lion. Who can stand against God? What leader or king can challenge Almighty God?

God's judgment of Edom would come. The young of her flock would be dragged away and her pasture would be destroyed (verse 20). When Edom fell, the earth would tremble, and the terror of what happened would spread all the way to the Red Sea. A great eagle would swoop down on Edom, spreading its wings to destroy the nation. On that day the hearts of Edom's great warriors would melt like that of a woman in labor. They would cry out in terror, knowing that their time had come.

When Jeremiah announced this prophecy, Edom felt secure in herself and that no one could harm her. Her confidence was in her military strength, geographical location, and wisdom. She felt that she had everything under control. Edom would be more surprised than anyone to see her end come.

How confident we become in ourselves. Jeremiah challenges us here in his prophecy to the Edomites not to put our confidence in our human strength and wisdom. Who can challenge the Almighty? Who can stand against his purposes? Though we make our nest high in the rocky cliffs where no one can touch us, God can bring us down. What we need to understand is nothing in this life will last forever. One day we will have to leave it all behind and stand before the God of Israel. How important it is to be right with God. Nothing can be hidden from him, and we cannot stand against him. Our only hope is to surrender to the sovereign and loving God of the universe who stands ready to forgive all who call on his name.

For Consideration:

- Ammon would be judged because of its attitude toward the people of God. Have you ever wrestled with your attitude toward one of God's children?

- What does this section teach us about our attitudes toward God's children, even when they are not living in his will?

- What does Jeremiah's prophecy to Edom teach us about our own temptation to trust in human resources? Can you see anything of yourself in this prophecy to Edom?

For Prayer:

- Ask the Lord to give you a proper attitude toward his children. Ask him to forgive you for any wrong attitudes.

- Ask the Lord to help you to understand how frail you really are. Ask him to teach you to rely not on yourself but on him alone.

54

A Word to Damascus, Kedar, Hazor, and Elam

Read Jeremiah 49:23–39

Jeremiah continued with his prophetic messages to the nations. In the second part of chapter 49, he addressed another four nations. We will consider these nations individually.

Damascus (verses 23–27)

The first people Jeremiah addressed in this section were the inhabitants of the city of Damascus, the capital of Syria. Jeremiah tells us what would happen in neighboring cities when they heard of the defeat of Damascus: Hamath and Arpad would be dismayed and disheartened. They would become troubled like a restless sea. Damascus would become feeble. She would be stricken with panic and flee. Pain and anguish would grip her like a woman in labor.

In verse 25 a question was asked: "Why has the city of renown not been abandoned?" Jeremiah was asking why such a great and glorious city could not have been abandoned by the enemy and left in its beauty. Why did this city of renown have to be destroyed, seeing that it brought delight to so many people?

Despite the glory and honor of Damascus, her young men

would fall in the streets, her soldiers would be silenced, and the city would be burned. The fortress of her great king Ben-Hadad would be destroyed.

The renown city of Damascus was a delight to many. She was beautiful to behold and wonderful to visit, but she was not right with her maker. Outwardly, everything seemed to be perfect; but God does not look at the outward appearance. God looks at the heart, and her heart was not right with the Holy One of Israel.

Kedar and Hazor (verses 28–33)

Jeremiah spoke next to the people of Kedar and Hazor. God called for the nation of Babylon to attack these people. The people of Kedar, descendants of Ishmael (Genesis 25:13) were nomadic. Mostly, they lived in tents and took care of sheep. Verse 29 tells us that their tents and their sheep would be taken from them and their camels and goods carried off. They would be forced to leave their nomadic lifestyle. Everything would be taken from them. Those who saw what happened to Kedar would shout in terror.

The people were told to flee quickly to the deep caves because Nebuchadnezzar had plotted against them. He was approaching quickly, so no time could be wasted in seeking an escape.

A call went out to Nebuchadnezzar to attack a nation at ease. This nation, being nomadic, did not live in cities with protective walls but in open fields in tents, with no protection from the enemy. These people would be an easy target for Nebuchadnezzar, who would take their camels and their herds and scatter the people to the wind. Disaster would come on them from all sides.

The region of Hazor would be desolate. Jackals would roam freely where the people used to live (verse 33). Their land would no longer be suitable for grazing sheep but become barren and desolate.

The people of Kedar and Hazor did not have the reputation of Damascus. They were, for the most part, unnoticed people living quietly by themselves. These people, however, had no relationship with the Lord. While they were unnoticed by others, God noticed them. No one escapes his watchful eye. Every nation is accountable before God, from the insignificant nomadic tribesman to the inhabitants of the great city of Damascus.

Elam (verses 34–39)

Jeremiah prophesied finally to the people of Elam. This particular prophecy was spoken concerning Elam early in the reign of Zedekiah, the final king of Judah.

God reminded Elam that he would break her bow. The bow was a symbol of her military power. According to Isaiah 22:6, the Elamites were skilled archers. God spoke to the area of their greatest pride. In destroying their bow, he would humble them as a people. He would shatter the very thing they depended on.

God would then bring against Elam the four quarters of heaven. The four winds of his judgment would be sent to scatter them as a people to every nation. Disaster would fall on the Elamites, and God would pursue them with the sword until they were destroyed. God would set up his throne in Elam, like a conquering king. He would bring all her officials before that throne and slaughter them. No one would be able to contest his reign.

Notice, however, in verse 39 that in time the Lord would once again restore the fortunes of the people of Elam. When the time was right, he would return to them and restore their blessing.

Elam's confidence was in her military skill. Her archers were famed for their accuracy. Her confidence was not in God but in human strength. We dare not trust in our own abilities. Our confidence must be entirely in God and his enabling. What is your bow today? Maybe that bow is your spiritual gift or your natural abilities. The fact of the matter is that if we do not recognize our absolute dependence on God and not our gifts, we could be in the same situation as the Elamites. We dare not trust our gifts, our wisdom, or our strength. Our complete and total confidence must be in the Lord God alone.

We see here that the judgment of God fell on the nations that were not right with him. No one escaped that judgment. From the least to the greatest, all had to give an account before God. As human beings, we are often deceived. We look at the outward appearance, but God looks at the heart. We may look good to others. We may be tremendously gifted and with those gifts fool many. But God will never be deceived because he sees our hearts.

For Consideration:

- What outward signs do we look for to prove that someone is right with God? Are these legitimate indications?

- Is it possible to trust in the gifts of God and not in God himself? Explain.

- What is the challenge of this chapter in regard to evangelism?

- Is it possible to be deceived into thinking that everything is all right between God and us when, in reality, we are very wrong? In what were these nations putting their confidence?

For Prayer:

- Ask the Lord to search your heart to see if you are right with him.

- Ask the Lord to cleanse you so that you will be a person of integrity.

- Ask the Lord to move through his church and purge out the hypocrisy that often reigns in our midst.

55

A First Word to Babylon

Read Jeremiah 50:1–16

In the last few chapters, the prophet Jeremiah had been speaking to the nations. The final nation on his list was the nation of Babylon. This was the nation that had caused so much trouble for the people of God and the surrounding nations. God had much to say to Babylon in the next two chapters.

This prophetic word was to go out to the nations (verse 2). A great banner was to be symbolically lifted so that the nations could see. Babylon was going to be captured. Her gods Bel and Marduk would be put to shame and filled with terror. They who had inspired terror in others would become terrified themselves.

Jeremiah prophesied that Babylon's defeat would come from a nation to the north. That nation would attack and devastate her land. Both men and animals would flee in the day of her attack. Historically, the defeat of the Babylonians would come in 539 BC through the Medes and the Persians under the leadership of Cyrus and Darius.

In the day that Babylon would be laid waste, Israel would see a great revival (verse 5). In those days the people of Israel and Judah would seek the Lord with tears. They would ask for the way to Zion and set their faces to returning to their homeland. As a people, they would again bind themselves to the Lord in an everlasting covenant that would not be forgotten, unlike the first covenant.

Part of the covenant spoken of here related to the promise that God had made to their ancestors to give them the land of Israel. Notice, however, that the focus of these verses is not so much the restoration of the land God promised to their ancestors but rather a returning to the Lord their God. The people of Israel would come in tears, seeking their God. Although there was a certain spiritual renewal among God's people when they returned from the Babylonian exile, that renewal did not last very long. It seems more likely that the day is coming when the world will see an even greater spiritual renewal of Israel.

Jeremiah compared the Israelites to lost sheep (verse 6). Their spiritual and political leaders had led them astray. This resulted in them being scattered and roaming dangerously in the mountains, forgetting what it was like to live in peace. They were devoured by their enemies. Their enemies felt that they had a right to afflict them because they had turned their backs on the Lord their God. The Lord placed the blame squarely on the shoulders of Israel's leaders. God's sheep had perished because they were not cared for by their spiritual shepherds. This shows us the importance of good spiritual guidance. As a shepherd of God's people, I see the responsibility I have before God to care for the sheep he has placed under my care.

Babylon had devoured God's people and felt no guilt in doing so. She saw herself as the instrument of God to bring judgment on his sinful and rebellious people. Jeremiah challenged this attitude. We should take no delight in exercising the discipline of the Lord. We should do it with the utmost humility, realizing that we too could fall. Babylon was the instrument of God's judgment, but she carried out this judgment with a proud and boastful heart. How careful we ought to be so we don't fall into the same trap.

A warning would ring out in Babylon. The inhabitants were told to flee to the mountains like goats (verse 8). They were to hide because the Lord was going to stir up an alliance of nations from the north that would oppose Babylon. These warriors from the north would be skilled in battle and would not return from their attack empty handed. God would give them victory over Babylon. The great Babylon would be plundered. And those who plundered her would have their fill (verse 10).

Babylon had rejoiced greatly in destroying other nations. When she pillaged God's people, she was like a heifer threshing the grain. One of the ways grain was separated from the stalks in ancient times was to have oxen tread the grain. The Bible clearly tells us that when an ox was used to thresh the grain, it was not to be muzzled but permitted to eat the grain as it worked (Deuteronomy 25:4). For the ox this was a very pleasant task. The ox could eat all it wanted when treading the grain. Babylon was compared to the ox treading the grain. She was excited to be able to crush God's people and benefit from their possessions.

The Babylonians were like neighing stallions ready to break out in their excitement. The picture here is one of the great delights they had in defeating God's people. Babylon's heart delighted in executing God's judgment; whereas, God's heart was broken. It grieves him to discipline his children. God takes no delight in wrath and judgment. Those of us who exercise his discipline must always do so with his sorrowful heart.

Babylon's mother would become ashamed of her (verse 12). She who had been the greatest of all the nations would be reduced to nothing. She would become the least of all the nations. Her land would be uninhabited and desolate. She would become an example of God's severe judgment. The nations would be horrified.

The enemy would be called to take a position against Babylon (verse 14). The archers were commanded to draw their bow and shoot their arrows. They were not to spare their arrows but to shoot without mercy because Babylon was being judged by the Lord for her crimes. A cry would be heard from every side of Babylon. She would be surrounded by the enemy and forced to surrender. With her towers fallen and her walls broken, she would be left defenseless. This was the day of the Lord's vengeance. It would be done to her as she had done to others.

The sower and the reaper would be cut off from Babylon, and she would not enjoy the fruit of the harvest. She who harvested nations would not even be able to harvest her own gardens. The time would come for God to harvest Babylon. The nations she had sown into her empire through military campaigns would be released to their own lands. Babylon would no longer be able to hold them. God would proclaim release to the captives of Babylon.

Babylon would have to answer the Lord God of Israel for how she had treated his people. It was with great arrogance that she had conquered the people of God. She had delighted in the demise of God's people, and she would pay the price. God would hold Babylon accountable for her actions and take his righteous vengeance on her.

For Consideration:

* What does this passage teach us about the heart of God in how he disciplines his people?

* Have you ever found yourself callously judging others? How does this attitude differ from God's judgment?

For Prayer:

* Ask the Lord to give you his heart for others who are wandering from the truth.

* Ask the Lord to forgive you for the times you have been callous and judgmental of others and have not had your heart broken for their condition.

56

God's Vigorous Defense of His People

Read Jeremiah 50:17–46

In these verses Jeremiah continued his prophecy concerning Babylon. He had spoken in verses 11–16 of the reason for her judgment. God would bring his vengeance on Babylon for her treatment of his people. Jeremiah reminded Babylon that Israel had been scattered (verse 17). Lions had chased her away from her land. The first lion was the nation of Assyria that had captured and deported the northern kingdom in 722 BC. Then Babylon had captured the southern kingdom in 586 BC, and the crushing of Israel was complete.

Although the Lord had called these nations against Israel to discipline his people for their sin, these nations had been too cruel in their oppression of his people (see Isaiah 10:5–19). The Lord saw what had happened to Israel at the hands of the Assyrians and the Babylonians, and he would punish these nations for their evil. God promised to restore the people of Israel to the Promised Land. God's flock would once again graze on the mountain of Carmel and in the rich pastures of Bashan (verse 19). There in her own land, Israel would have peace and be satisfied with the abundance of God's provision.

It is true that Israel had been guilty before her Lord and was being punished for her crime. The day was coming, however, when her sins would be forgiven. In those days a search would be made for the guilt of Israel, but there would be none. All her sin and guilt would be forgiven and removed (see 31:34). This is the amazing thing about the forgiveness of the Lord. When he forgives, he forgets. The sins that you have been forgiven for today will never again be brought against you. God will remember them no more. Our friends and loved ones may remember them, but God will never hold them against us again. Israel's crime would be erased from the books.

Some commentators see in verses 19–20 a reference to a future time when national Israel will dwell in the Promised Land in safety, prosperity, and salvation. These conditions were not completely fulfilled after the return of the exiles from Babylon.

In verse 21 a call went up to attack the Babylonian areas of Merathaim and Pekod. Their judgment had come. The enemy was to kill and destroy all those in these regions. In verse 22 Jeremiah spoke of the noise of battle that raged in the land. Babylon, who had been the hammer of the whole earth, would be broken. Babylon had broken many nations to pieces, and her time of destruction would come.

God would set a trap for Babylon. She would be caught in that trap because she had opposed the Lord God of Israel. She would be held accountable for her actions. The Lord would open his arsenal and bring out his weapons against Babylon (verse 25). As a sovereign God, no one would be able to oppose him.

God called the nations to come out against Babylon. They would cut her down, thresh her, and pile her up in heaps like grain. She would be destroyed as a nation with no remnant left. Even her young bulls would be led to the slaughter.

Jeremiah heard the sound of the fugitives and refugees fleeing from Babylon to Zion. These people rejoiced as the hand of the Lord was set against their oppressor. God had taken vengeance on Babylon for what she did to his temple in Jerusalem.

Jeremiah foresaw the enemy archers being summoned to come up against Babylon (verse 29). They were not to let anyone escape who tried to flee. Babylon was to be repaid for her evil deeds.

God's Vigorous Defense of His People ● 265

What she had done to others would be done to her. Because she had dared to defy the Lord God of Israel, her young men would fall in the streets. Her soldiers would be silenced in the day of the Lord's judgment. As powerful as she was, there was nothing she could do against the power of the Lord.

God set himself against Babylon because of her pride. She is described in verse 31 as being arrogant. The arrogant would fall and stumble. There would be no help for her on her day of judgment. She would be left alone and defenseless. She would fall, and no one would help her up. Her towns would be burned.

In her pride Babylon never imagined that this would ever happen. She felt secure and confident. She was more surprised than anyone to find out that all she had accumulated would be taken from her in an instant.

God's people had been oppressed and held captive (verse 33). What these oppressors did not realize was that Israel's Redeemer was strong. This Redeemer would vigorously defend the cause of his people. God is passionate about his people. Jesus reminds in Matthew 25:40 that what we do to the least of his children, we do to him. His connection with his children is very strong. He is with them in their pain. Jeremiah prophesied that God would vigorously defend his children. What an encouragement this is to us today. The Lord himself will come to our defense. He has our interests at heart.

The Lord would bring a sword against Babylon because of what she had done to his people (verse 35). Babylon's officials and her wise men would fall by the sword of his judgment. Her false prophets and soldiers would also fall prey to that sword. They would be filled with terror on the day of the Lord's wrath. Babylon's horses and chariots would be slain. All the foreigners associated with her in her evil deeds would suffer the same judgment. Her treasures would be plundered. A great drought would dry up her waters as the blessing of God was taken from the land. As a nation that loved false gods, Babylon would go mad with terror on that great day of judgment from the one true God.

The once-glorious nation would become a desert (verse 39). The hyena would roam its streets, and the desert owl would live there. The land would remain desolate and would never again be inhabited. Babylon would never again be the nation she once was. God would overthrow her as he overthrew the land of Sodom and Gomorrah.

A great army was coming from the north. This great force of many kings was being stirred up from the ends of the earth. The Medes and the Persians and the nations associated with them seem to have been the alliance that Jeremiah is referring to here. This alliance of nations was armed with bows and spears. They were a cruel force that would not show mercy on Babylon. They would come like the sound of a roaring sea, riding on their warhorses. They would come in battle formation ready to attack.

The Babylonian king, hearing reports of this advancing army, would despair. His hands would hang limp at his side. Anguish would grip him like the pains of a woman in labor. There was nothing he could do to defend his empire.

God would come against Babylon like a hungry lion (verse 44). Babylon would be chased from its land in an instant. There would be no real battle here. Babylon would fall quickly. She was no match for the Lord God. What had taken her years to accumulate would be taken away in a moment. Babylon could do nothing against God's judgment. She could not stand against him or challenge what he was doing. She was helpless before the all-powerful God of Israel, who vigorously defended his people.

Babylon was called to hear what God had planned against her (verse 45). She would be dragged away and destroyed. At the sound of her defeat, the earth would tremble. Other nations would be given cause to reflect on their own destinies. The defeat of this great nation gives us cause to reflect as well.

Babylon fell because of pride. She had delighted in her conquest of God's people. She failed to realize that the God of Israel vigorously defends his people. We will never understand why God would so love and defend us, but this passage is a real encouragement to us in our times of trial and oppression. God will defend us in his time. He does not sit idly by as others oppress and offend his people. In his time he will judge righteously.

For Consideration:

- What does this passage teach us about God's relationship with his people?

- What is the challenge of this passage concerning our treatment of God's children?

- Babylon would lose everything she had accumulated over the years. What does this passage teach us about how frail we really are as human beings?

- What is your particular struggle as a child of God today? What encouragement do you receive from this passage? Will God come to your defense?

For Prayer:

- Ask the Lord to help you to treat his children with respect and dignity.

- Ask him to forgive you for the times when you wrongly treated one of his children.

- Ask him to remind you of how frail and dependent you are on him for everything.

- Thank him that he is able to defend you against anything the enemy can throw at you today.

57

Babylon's Incurable Wound

Read Jeremiah 51:1–12

The judgment of Babylon continues here in chapter 51. The Babylonians had done much damage to the people of God and their land. They had taken great delight in devastating the land of Judah. God was not blind to what they had done to his people, and their time of judgment would come.

Chapter 51 begins with an announcement that the Lord was stirring up the spirit of a destroyer against Babylon and the people of Leb Kamai. The phrase *Leb Kamai* literally means "in the midst of those who rise up against me." It is generally agreed that Leb Kamai refers to Babylon, the land that had risen up against God.

Notice that the Lord told Babylon that he would stir up the spirit of a destroyer. There was something taking place in the spiritual realm here. God was stirring up the forces of evil to unleash their power on the nation of Babylon. It is unclear how this actually took place. The Lord, by withdrawing his protective presence, enabled the power of the enemy to be unleashed on Babylon. That destroyer would come in the form of foreigners who would invade Babylon and devastate her land. The enemy would surround her and oppose her on every side.

In verse 3 the Babylonian archer was told that it was futile to string his bow. Any resistance was futile. It would not help Babylon to put on her armor because she could not possibly prevail against the Lord. Babylon's strong young men would not be spared but devastated in the day of God's judgment. They would fall fatally wounded in the streets. This would happen to them because the Lord God of Israel and Judah had not forsaken his people. Even though the land of Israel and Judah was full of guilt and even though they deserved to be punished, God would not forsake them because they were his children. How thankful we need to be that even in judgment the Lord remembers those who belong to him.

A call went out to the inhabitants of Babylon, perhaps to God's people living there, to flee for their lives. The destroyer was coming. He would devastate the land because it was the time of the Lord's vengeance. He was going to repay Babylon for what she had done to his people. If the people in Babylon did not flee, they would be caught up in this great judgment of God.

At one point in her history, Babylon was like a gold cup in the hands of the Lord. She was his instrument to make the earth drink of his wrath. She accomplished his purposes on the earth. However, she would fall and be broken. How many servants of God have fallen like Babylon? In our days we have seen great servants of God fall. Many of these servants were mightily used of God to accomplish his purposes on the earth. At a given point in time, however, they fell. Their ministry or their testimony was broken, and those who trusted them were devastated. Like Babylon, their pride was their downfall. The fall of Babylon challenges us to consider how frail we are and how easily we too could fall.

In verse 8 Jeremiah told the people what their response to the fall of Babylon should be. He called them to wail for her and grieve her downfall. They were not to rejoice or see in this a means of advancing themselves. They were not to look on in pride. Instead, they were to grieve deeply in their hearts. A servant had fallen. This was cause for sorrow and grief.

Notice secondly in verse 8 that Jeremiah challenged the people to get balm for Babylon's pain. Their grieving and weeping was to lead to action. God's people were to seek to be a means of healing for this fallen servant. They were to offer their balm to bring relief.

God still challenges his people to be instruments in the healing of fallen servants. For us, this balm can come in many forms. Certainly, it comes in the form of prayer for others. It may also come in the form of encouraging and edifying words or actions to build up those who are wounded. How easy it is to become critical of those who fall. We might avoid them like a plague or not want to be associated with them. God challenges us to be instruments of healing and reconciliation.

Jeremiah told his listeners in verse 9 that, in the case of Babylon, there would not be healing. Not everyone will be healed. Verse 8 challenges us to be instruments of healing, but verse 9 reminds us that in the real world, not everyone will be healed and restored to a right relationship with God. Babylon's wounds were too advanced, and her judgment was sealed.

The Lord was going to vindicate his people by judging Babylon (verse 10). They were to proclaim this in Zion. God had done wonderful things for his people. He had taken up their defense, and this was cause for rejoicing. God was raising up the kings of the Medes to be his instruments of justice against Babylon. Arrows were being sharpened. The Medes were to take up their shields and prepare for the battle. God was going to revenge the desecration of his temple by the Babylonians. He would come in power and judge those who had hurt his people and destroyed his temple. The capture of Babylon by the Medes in 539 BC was a fulfillment of this part of the prophecy (see Daniel 5:30–31).

The enemy's banner was going to be raised to announce its presence (verse 12). That banner was going to approach the walls of Babylon. A call would go forth to reinforce the guard on the wall in preparation for the attack that was coming. The Lord would not fail to carry out his purposes against Babylon.

There are several important challenges here in this prophecy. Babylon is described as a golden cup in the hands of the Lord to exercise his judgment on the earth. She was blessed and empowered to be that instrument of judgment. As important as she was, however, she fell into disgrace. Her pride and arrogance brought her downfall. God's people were to feel the pain of that fall. They were to be instruments of healing for her. While Babylon's wound was incurable, not everyone's is. There will be some who will be restored. May God grant that we would be balm for the wounded, bringing healing and restoration.

For Consideration:

- Consider Babylon, the golden cup in God's hands. What does this passage teach us about our frailty and pride?

- Have you met any fallen servants of God? What caused their falls?

- What is the challenge of this passage to us about being healers? Are there individuals the Lord would have you to minister to today?

For Prayer:

- Thank the Lord that in his judgment he remembers mercy and compassion.

- Ask the Lord to help you to be an instrument of healing for his people.

- Take a moment to pray for one of God's children who has fallen away from him.

- Ask the Lord to protect you from pride and keep you faithful to him.

58

The Prosperity of
the Wicked

Jeremiah 51:13–40

God told the Babylonians in this section that though they had lived by many waters and were rich in treasures, their time of judgment had come. They would soon be cut off. God was going to punish them for their sin. In verse 14 the Lord promised that he would fill Babylon with invaders as numerous as a swarm of locusts, and this enemy would joyfully triumph.

Ultimately, there was nothing that the Babylonians could do about this. The Lord God was leading this attack against them. What could they do against him, the Creator and Sovereign of the universe? He made the earth by his power (verse 15). His great wisdom founded the world and stretched out the heavens. When he thunders, the heavens roar. He makes the clouds rise. He sends lightning and brings the wind out of his storehouses. As powerful as Babylon was, she and her false gods were no match for the Lord God of Israel.

The Babylonians were senseless creatures (verse 17). Their goldsmiths made idols that had no power. These false gods were worthless objects of mockery. They would perish in Babylon's day of judgment.

The descendants of Jacob, although humbled by the Babylonians, had a superior God. Israel would inherit the Lord and his blessings; whereas, Babylon would inherit destruction. The God of Israel is superior to all other gods. He is the Maker of all things. He made Israel and loves her as his own. His people are his inheritance. As powerful and as mighty as he is, God is also very personal and loving. He desires a deep personal relationship with his people. He delights to call them his inheritance.

Probably referring to the Medes, the Lord referred to an unnamed entity as his war club (verse 20). With this club the Lord would shatter nations, people, and animals. With his weapon, God determined to judge Babylon for her evil (verse 24). God was going to repay her for her crimes, particularly for the evil she had done in Zion.

God was against Babylon. He promised here through Jeremiah to stretch out his own hand against the one who had been destroying the whole earth. He would roll Babylon off a cliff and make her like a burned out mountain. When you roll something off a cliff, you expect that it will be smashed to pieces and never seen again. As a burned out mountain, Babylon would be stripped of all her blessing and fruitfulness and left with nothing. Notice in verse 26 that the Lord told the people of Babylon that no rock would be taken from them to form a new construction. Their influence would be destroyed from the earth. Never again would anyone build on their principles and culture. Because Babylon was not completely destroyed when the Medes conquered her in 539 BC, many commentators believe these verses refer to a future destruction in the end times (see Revelation 18).

A banner was to be lifted up in the land, announcing the presence of the enemy (verse 27). A trumpet would sound calling the nations to prepare for battle. They were to go up against Babylon. They were to send their warhorses like swarms of locusts to attack Babylon. The kingdom of the Medes was going to be raised up against Babylon. The whole land would tremble when the Lord unleashed his judgment against her.

Babylon's warriors, as powerful as they were, would stop fighting (verse 30). Instead of pushing boldly forward, they would hide in their stronghold. They would be afraid. Their strength would end. Their towns would be set on fire and their gates broken down. They would be left defenseless against the attack of the enemy.

Jeremiah described one messenger after another coming to the king of Babylon to announce that city after city had been conquered and destroyed or that another river crossing had been seized. They announced to the king that yet another marsh had been set on fire and that his soldiers were terrified. You can feel the despair that must have risen up in the heart of the king of Babylon as these messengers came one after another to announce doom.

The Lord compared Babylon to a threshing floor (verse 33). As stocks of grain lie on a threshing floor, Babylon would be cut down and trampled by the Lord in judgment. The time of harvest would come for this powerful nation.

In verse 34 Israel spoke out to God about what Babylon had done to her. The people of God told him that Nebuchadnezzar had devoured them and thrown them into confusion. The land God had given to his people was like an empty jar. They reminded God that Babylon had swallowed them like a serpent and filled his stomach with the blessing God had given them and their ancestors.

Notice in verse 35 how God's people cried out to him concerning the violence that had been done to them. They cried out to the Lord to hold the Babylonians responsible. They asked that their blood be on the Babylonians and that God would judge Babylon guilty of crimes against his people.

God heard the cry of his oppressed people. Through his servant Jeremiah, he reminded them that he would defend their cause and avenge their blood. God would not turn his back on them.

Babylon would be called to account for her crimes against Israel. Verse 13 stated that Babylon lived by many waters. Here in verse 36 God told Babylon that he would dry up her seas and springs. She would become like a pile of rubbish. The wild jackals would wander through her streets. Her land would become desolate with no one living in it.

The people of Babylon had their moment of greatness. They had roared like lions. A great feast had been set before them, and they had eaten their fill. They had shouted with laughter as they feasted on the flesh of the nations. But they would go to sleep and never wake up. They would be led as lambs to the slaughter. One moment they would be rejoicing, and the next moment they would be dead. Their end would come suddenly.

We see in this section that the God of Israel is a very personal God who defends the cause of his people. When they cried out to him, he heard their cry and came to their defense. Babylon had her moment of greatness but that would end. Jeremiah reminds us here of how quickly Babylon would lose everything she had accumulated by her cruelty.

The Psalmist too learned that God does judge evil. Asaph, wrestling with the prosperity of the wicked, wrote: "This is what the wicked are like—always carefree, they increase in wealth. Surely in vain have I kept my heart pure; in vain have I washed my hands in innocence. All day long I have been plagued; I have been punished every morning. If I had said, 'I will speak thus,' I would have betrayed your children. When I tried to understand all this, it was oppressive to me till I entered the sanctuary of God; then I understood their final destiny. Surely you place them on slippery ground; you cast them down to ruin" (Psalm 73:12–18).

Asaph understood what Jeremiah was saying here. Those who abandon God may prosper for a moment, but they are on slippery paths. Jeremiah tells us that Babylon would sleep and not wake up. In an instant all their greatness would be destroyed.

God's eternal judgment will come. We should never envy the prosperity of the wicked. Instead, we should look beyond their momentary prosperity to their final judgment. The gospel writer Mark put it this way: "What good is it for a man to gain the whole world, yet forfeit his soul?" (Mark 8:36).

For Consideration:

• What does this passage teach us about God's concern for his people?

• What do we learn here about the prosperity of the wicked?

• Have you ever found yourself envying the prosperity of the wicked? What is the challenge here in this passage for you?

For Prayer:

- Thank the Lord that he is concerned about what you are going through right now.

- Ask him to allow you to see things from his perspective.

- Do you know someone who has not yet understood the final judgment? Take a moment to pray that the Lord would open this person's eyes to the reality of that judgment.

59

Remember Jerusalem

Read Jeremiah 51:41–64

erse 41 begins with a warning to Sheshach. Many
commentators believe that this was another name for
Babylon, derived from the name Shach, which was one
of Babylon's false gods. Some believe that an annual festival
in honor of Shach was being observed the very night the nation
of Babylon was captured by the Medes. Although Sheshach
(Babylon) had been the boast of the whole earth, she would be
seized. Other nations would look on in horror at the downfall of
this great and powerful empire.

The sea would rise up with its roaring waves and cover
Babylon (verse 42). Quite likely, the sea referred to here was
the multitude of invaders who would come pouring down from
the north to overwhelm her. In that day, Babylon's towns would
become so desolate that no one would live or travel there.

In verse 44 Jeremiah referred to another of Babylon's gods,
Bel, being punished. He would be forced to spew out what he had
swallowed. Babylon had swallowed many nations. Israel was one
of those nations. God was going to release all the captive nations
from the grasp of Babylon. Her influence would disappear, and

the other nations would no longer stream toward her. Babylon's wall would fall.

Before bringing his judgment against Babylon, however, a call went out to those who were captive in her. "Come out of her, my people!" cried the Lord (verse 45). The captives were told to run for their lives because the fierce anger of the Lord was going to fall. All who remained in her would be destroyed. God was preparing his people to return home after their exile in Babylon.

The day would come when rumors would circulate concerning an approaching enemy (verse 46). These rumors would be of violence. They would speak of rulers rising up against rulers. God told his people not to be afraid when they heard these rumors, for he was accomplishing his purposes. Jeremiah challenged his people in this section to place their confidence in the Lord God when these events began to unfold.

Similarly, the events of the end times are in the hands of the Lord. When we see them unfolding, we should not despair. Instead, we should be encouraged because God will be about to unfold his final plan.

How easy it is for us to lose heart when trials and struggles come our way. To lose heart is to lose our focus on a sovereign God. It is to forget that he is working out his purposes for this world. God has never surrendered the control of this world to people. He remains in control. No one can take that from him. The events of your life are in his hands. He will use all your situations to accomplish his purpose. You can trust him.

In verse 47 he reminded his people that the day would come when he would punish the idols of Babylon and leave the nation under their protection in complete disgrace. On that day of judgment, the other nations would shout for joy. They would rejoice when they saw the destroyer coming from the north to attack their oppressor. Babylon's defeat would mean that the demands of justice were satisfied (see Revelation 18:20).

In verses 49–53 Jeremiah spoke to God's people in exile in Babylon. This great empire would fall because of what she had done to God's people (verse 49). She had slain many in Israel and in other lands. The Israelites still alive in Babylon should leave quickly for their distant homeland, remembering the Lord and

Jerusalem. Why were they to remember Jerusalem? Could it have been because of what the Babylonians had done to Jerusalem? Was God calling them to remember Jerusalem so that they would be reminded of their sin that had caused their exile? Could it be that they were to remember Jerusalem as a symbol of hope? It was in Jerusalem that the blessing of God would again fall as the Lord cared for his people and exercised justice in the earth.

God's people had been disgraced and insulted because foreigners had entered their land and defiled the temple (verse 51). The days were coming, however, when God would punish those who had so disgraced his people. Israel's enemies would groan. Even if Babylon reached the sky and fortified all her strongholds, she would be no match for God. In verse 53 God again assured Israel that he would destroy Babylon.

The sound of a battle cry would come from Babylon. Through the land a cry of great destruction would be heard. The Lord would silence Babylon. He would send waves of enemies against her like great waters pounding her shore. Under these attacks Babylon's warriors would be captured and their bows broken. God would repay her in full for the crimes against his people. Her officials and wise men as well as her mighty warriors would fall to sleep and never wake again.

The Lord Almighty declared that Babylon's thick wall would be broken down and her high gates set on fire. The notes in the NIV Study Bible tell us that the wall surrounding the city was a double wall. The outer wall was 12 feet think, and the inner wall was 21 feet thick. These walls were separated by a dry moat, 23 feet wide (NIV Study Bible, Grand Rapids, Zondervan, 2004). The leveling of these walls would be a major undertaking. Babylon felt secure behind these walls, but God was going to destroy them. Babylonians would labor in vain to try to defend their city.

This prophecy concerning Babylon was written on a scroll and given to a Judean military officer by the name of Seraiah who was taken to Babylon with King Zedekiah. Seraiah was told to read these words aloud to the people when he arrived in Babylon. Jeremiah told him that after he had read the words of the scroll to the people, he was to publicly declare: "O Lord, you have said you will destroy this place" (verse 62).

After Seraiah had publicly declared the destruction of Babylon, he was to take the scroll, tie a stone to it, and throw it into the Euphrates River, declaring that even as this scroll sank to the bottom of the river, so Babylon would sink and rise no more as a nation.

God had not forsaken his people. The day would come when God would defend their cause and defeat their foe. Until that time they were to remember Jerusalem and the promises God made concerning that city. The Israelites were not to lose heart because God would come to them in his time.

For Consideration:

* What encouragement is there in this passage for those who are going through trials today?

* "To lose heart is to lose sight of God." Do you agree with this statement? Explain.

* What comfort do you take in the fact that God is sovereign and in control of all the events of life?

* What obstacles do you have to face in this life? What do we learn from this passage about the Lord being able to break down the strongest barriers?

For Prayer:

* Thank the Lord for his sovereign control of life.

* Are you facing a difficult trial in your life today? Thank the Lord for his great promises to you.

* Ask the Lord to help you to keep your focus on him in your trial.

* Thank him that no obstacle is too big for him.

60

The Conquest of Jerusalem

Read Jeremiah 52

T he prophecy of Jeremiah ends in chapter 51. The final chapter of this book is historical in nature and tells us the story of how Jerusalem fell. Much of the material is similar to that recorded in 2 Kings 24–25. Jeremiah had told his people that Jerusalem would fall and that they would be taken captive to Babylon. Here in this last chapter, we see how this actually happened. This validates the prophecy that Jeremiah spoke.

The chapter begins with the reign of Zedekiah, the last king of Judah. He was twenty-one when he became king and reigned in Jerusalem for eleven years. As a king, Zedekiah did evil in the eyes of the Lord, just like his predecessor, Jehoiakim. It was because of this evil that the Lord God determined to punish the people of Jerusalem and to "thrust them from his presence" (verse 3). He did this by delivering them into the hands of the Babylonians. Notice here that sin can *thrust* us from the presence of the Lord. While the Lord does not abandon his people, sin and rebellion against God can take from us his blessing and his evident presence.

Zedekiah rebelled against the king of Babylon. He chose not to listen to the Lord's counsel through Jeremiah and submit to the discipline of the Lord for his own good and the good of Judah. Because of this, the army of Nebuchadnezzar marched against the city of Jerusalem. They camped outside the city and built siege ramps against it. From verses 4 and 5, we understand that Babylon maintained their siege of the city for about a year and a half. Near the end of the siege of Jerusalem, the famine in the city was severe.

The Babylonians broke through the city wall (verse 7). Even though the city was surrounded, Zedekiah's army attempted to flee at night through a gate between two walls. They left the city and headed toward the desert region of the Arabah. They were pursued by the Babylonians and overtaken in the plains of Jericho. Zedekiah was captured and taken to Nebuchadnezzar. The king of Babylon slaughtered Zedekiah's sons and officials in his presence. Zedekiah was blinded before being led in chains to Babylon, where he was a prisoner until the day of his death.

In the nineteenth year of Nebuchadnezzar, the commander of the imperial guard, a man by the name of Nebuzaradan, came to Jerusalem. He set fire to the temple, the royal palace, and all the houses in Jerusalem. He burned down every important building and also broke down the city walls. He carried into exile a number of the poorest people and artisans. Included among those exiles were those who had voluntarily surrendered to Babylon. He left behind some of the poorest people to work the vineyards and the fields.

Verses 17–23 record the looting of the temple before its destruction. The Babylonians broke up the bronze pillars, the movable stands, and the basin that were used in the temple worship. They took these objects of bronze back to Babylon with them. They also carried back with them all the temple utensils made of bronze, silver, and gold.

Verse 21 tells us that the bronze pillars were twenty-seven feet high and eighteen feet in circumference. These pillars were hollow in the middle and were the thickness of four fingers. The capital on top of the pillars was about seven and a half feet high and decorated with pomegranates of bronze all around. All together there were ninety-six pomegranates on the sides of the capital. There was also another one hundred bronze pomegranates on the top of the capital. This shows us the incredible artwork that went into the construction of these pillars. They were very costly indeed. These, however, were stripped down and taken to Babylon. The temple of the Lord was completely destroyed.

Among the prisoners who were taken that day were Seraiah (the chief priest), Zephaniah (the priest next in rank), and three of the doorkeepers (verse 24). Nebuzaradan also took the officer in charge of the fighting men, seven royal advisers, a chief secretary, and sixty of his men. All these individuals were taken to King Nebuchadnezzar, who had them executed.

The exile to Babylon came in various stages. In the seventh year of Nebuchadnezzar (597 BC), 3,023 Jews were exiled. In the eighteenth year of Nebuchadnezzar's reign (586 BC), another 832 were taken from Jerusalem to Babylon. In his twenty-third year of reign (581 BC), 745 more were exiled. In total about 4600 were taken into exile. This number may include only males or only males from Jerusalem, as it differs from others accounts (see 2 Kings 14 and 16). Many other Judeans perished in the fight to defend the city.

In the thirty-seventh year of the exile of King Jehoiachin of Judah, Evil-Merodach, son of Nebuchadnezzar, became king of Babylon (verse 31). He released Jehoiachin from prison and treated him with great honor, even more than the other kings who were in Babylon. Jehoiachin was able to put aside his prison clothes and eat at the king's table for the rest of his life.

There are a couple of things that need to be mentioned here regarding Jehoiachin. In 2 Kings 24:12 we learn that Jehoiachin had surrendered to the king of Babylon as Jeremiah had told him. He was one of the few kings who was willing to surrender to the discipline of God. Zedekiah, for example, tried to escape when Jerusalem was captured. Jeremiah had promised that things would go well for those who willingly surrendered to Babylon. We see here the fulfillment of that promise. Because Jehoiachin willingly surrendered to Babylon and submitted to the discipline of the Lord, he was honored by God in the end.

Similarly, we should not run from what the Lord wants to do in our lives. We should ask the Lord for the grace to surrender to his ways and let him teach us what we need to learn through his righteous discipline.

Some Jewish historians say that when Nebuchadnezzar was punished by God with mental illness and sent to live among the wild animals, his son Evil-Merodach took his place. This story is recorded in Daniel 4:33. It appears that Evil-Merodach celebrated and profited from his father's illness. When Nebuchadnezzar was restored to power, he had his son thrown into prison for his misconduct. In prison he met Jehoiachin and befriended him. If this is true, it would explain why Evil-Merodach, when he became king, elevated Jehoiachin and fed him at his table until the day he died. This can be seen as a picture of the restoration of Judah from exile.

God's ways are very strange at times. He orchestrates circumstances in life to work out his perfect purpose. He honors those who honor him. This chapter reminds us that the word of the Lord is true. God will fulfill all his plans and purposes. The judgment Jeremiah spoke about came to pass. Everything happened exactly as Jeremiah had prophesied, down to the smallest detail.

Jeremiah had faithfully proclaimed the judgment of Judah and other nations through difficulty and persecution. He watched as God fulfilled the word he had given him to speak. The book of Jeremiah reminds us of the consequences of not taking God's word seriously. May God raise up in our day men and women who will take God at his word and live obediently in its holy light.

For Consideration:

• What does this chapter teach us about the truth of the word of the Lord?

• What do we learn here about how God honors those who honor him?

• Consider for a moment what God's people lost because of their disobedience to him? What personal warning do you take from this?

• What have we lost because or our disobedience to the word of God?

For Prayer:

- Thank the Lord that his word is true.

- Thank him for how he is able to work out all situations for his glory and our good.

- Thank him that he honors those who honor him. Ask him to show you anything in your life that does not honor him.

Lamentations

61

Self-Made Yokes

Read Lamentations 1

The book of Lamentations is a song of woe concerning the condition of the land of Judah that God had judged. God's people had been sent into exile and lost everything. Jeremiah the prophet expressed his grief in this book. It should be noticed that the book is set out in a poetical fashion. Each verse of the first four chapters begins with a letter of the Hebrew alphabet, although this is not visible in the English translation. One purpose of this book is to memorialize the faithfulness of God in punishing his covenant people for forsaking their relationship with him. The book also speaks of God's compassion in chapter 3 and his consolation in chapter 5.

Jeremiah began by speaking about the city of Jerusalem. This city was once full of people, but it had become deserted and empty. He compared the city to a widow, once great among the nations but now deprived of her husband. She grieved and mourned for her loss. The one who was once a queen among the provinces had become a slave. She once ruled, but now she was being ruled and dominated. Tears ran down her cheeks, and there was no one to comfort her. Her lovers had abandoned her, and her friends had betrayed her and become her enemies.

Judah had been afflicted and sentenced to harsh labor (verse 3). Instead of being relieved from her trials, she was sentenced to even more punishment and sent into exile. She found no rest from her worries and was overtaken by her enemies.

The roads of Jerusalem were abandoned. They mourned because no one used them anymore to go to the great feasts. The gateways of the city too were desolate. The priest and the maidens grieved and groaned in bitter anguish. All was desolate and abandoned.

Judah's enemies had become her masters (verse 5). They took over her land. While the people of God were being dominated, her enemies lived at ease in the land. The Lord afflicted Jerusalem because of her many sins. Her children were sent into exile and held captive.

As Jeremiah looked at the scene before him, he saw that all the splendor of Jerusalem's glorious past had departed. Her princes were like deer that could find no pasture. In their weakness they fled from their enemies because they had no more strength to fight or defend themselves.

As she wandered in her affliction, Jerusalem was conscious of her glorious past and the wonderful treasures she used to have (verse 7). She had fallen into enemy hands, and there was no one to help her. Instead of looking up to her in respect and admiration, her enemies laughed at her destruction.

Jerusalem had sinned greatly against the Lord her God. She was in a wretched state because of her judgment. Those who used to honor her began to despise her because of her ruined condition. The Lord stripped her of glory, and she groaned in her shame and humiliation.

Jerusalem's filthiness was part of her and clung to her skirts (verse 9). She was being punished by the Lord for continuing in sin without regard for its consequences. The fact that this filthiness clung to her symbolized that it was part of her very nature. She did not repent and return to the Lord and his ways. Instead, she continued to live her sinful lifestyle, unconcerned about where it was leading. Jerusalem's fall was described here by Jeremiah as being "astounding."

There are many people like this in our day. They know that they are living in sin. They know that they are wrong, but they are unconcerned. They really do not think beyond the present. They live for the pleasures of the moment and do not seriously consider their accountability before the Lord.

Jerusalem's enemies took all her treasures. The pagans entered her temple and desecrated it. Before the capture of Jerusalem, Gentiles were forbidden the privilege of entering the Lord's temple (see Nehemiah 13:1–3). The sins of God's people had stripped them of God's presence and left them without protection from the enemy. The Lord then gave the enemy free access to the temple and its treasures because they had become worthless to him. His own people had already desecrated the holy places.

How important it is for us to deal with our sin. We cannot allow sin to continue in our personal lives or in our churches. If we do not confess and repent of our sin, it will strip us of the Lord's blessing and power. The Lord may turn us over to the enemy for discipline (see Romans 1:18–32; 1 Corinthians 5:1–5).

Notice how powerless God's people had become. They groaned as they searched for bread (verse 11). They bartered the treasures that remained simply to have enough food to stay alive. Jerusalem cried out to the Lord to consider her plight.

"Is it nothing to you?" Jerusalem asked those who passed by unconcerned about her devastated condition (verse 12). "Is any suffering like my suffering?" God had truly inflicted his people with tremendous suffering. He was angry at what their sin had done to them and their relationship with him. He sent the fire of his holy judgment from on high into the city's very bones. He spread his net and brought his people down. He left them desolate and faint.

Jeremiah compared the sins of his people to a great yoke (verse 14). God took the sins of his people and wove them together into a yoke. He then put this yoke on their necks, as oxen are yoked. The yoke sapped them of their strength and left them under the control of others. The amazing thing here was that the yoke was made from their own sins.

We ourselves are responsible for the yoke of sins we wear. We see again that it is our sins that render us powerless before the enemy and strip us of our blessing. The yoke we wear is really of our own making. Sin brings its own bondage.

The Lord rendered powerless all Jerusalem's warriors and sent an enemy against them. His nation was defenseless. Her young men were crushed. Jerusalem was trampled in the winepress of God's judgment as the enemy prevailed. The city wept with tears overflowing from her eyes. No one came to comfort her in grief. Her children were desolate, abandoned, and powerless before her enemies.

Jerusalem cried for help in this time of distress, but no one came to her aid. It was in the purposes of God that her neighbors would become her foes. They would turn their backs on her as an unclean thing.

Speaking for Jerusalem, Jeremiah confessed the reason for Judah's condition. The Lord her God was righteous and holy, and she had rebelled against him, turning her back against his covenantal commands. Judah was experiencing the covenantal consequences of disobedience (see Deuteronomy 28). Her young men and maidens had gone into exile. They were stripped of the blessings of God. They called out to their allies, but they had betrayed them. They turned to their priests and elders, but they had perished in the city as they searched for food. God's people were left truly alone with no help.

God's people were in distress, and their hearts were disturbed. Outside in the streets, the sword was continuing to kill their children and friends. Inside their homes, people were dying of hunger.

Jerusalem's enemies heard her groaning and distress but did not come to her aid. Instead, they rejoiced at her fall. In her distress, Jerusalem cried out to God to defend her and render judgment among the nations that mocked her (verses 21–22). These nations too had turned their backs on God.

It is hard to read this passage of Scripture without feeling the pain of God's people. They had been defeated and abandoned as he had forewarned. God had woven a yoke of bondage out of their sins that had sapped them of their spiritual strength and vitality, leaving them powerless before their enemies.

It is hard not to think here about the spiritual condition of

God's people in our own day. How many believers are living in the same defeat as God's people in Jeremiah's day? There are believers who do not seem to have any power over sin and the devil. They are a very unhappy people who are tormented. They are bound by a yoke that they themselves have woven out of the material of their wicked deeds.

The fact of the matter is that we do not have to leave that yoke on our necks. We do not have to continue to live under the oppression of the yoke of sin. The Lord Jesus came to set us free from the bondage and slavery of our wickedness. By God's grace we can cast off that yoke right now. We can be set free from the oppression and powerlessness that seems to be our lot under the bondage of sin. Confess your sin right now and be reconciled to God. Take off that yoke, and let his blessing fill you again.

For Consideration:

- What is the connection here between sin and powerlessness in the Christian life?

- What evidence do you see of a yoke of sin in our day?

- Should we be grieving over the condition of the church in our day? Explain.

For Prayer:

- Is there evidence of a yoke of bondage in your life? Ask the Lord to set you free from this yoke.

- Do you know of someone who is caught in bondage today? Take a moment to pray that the Lord would set this person free. Ask the Lord to show you how you can minister to this individual in a time of need.

- Take a moment to pray that the Lord would move in the life of your church and restore power and blessing.

62

The Lives of the Children

Read Lamentations 2

J eremiah's lament continues here in chapter 2. He began by speaking about the anger of the Lord toward his people. "How the Lord has covered the Daughter of Zion with the cloud of his anger!" God's children were covered with the darkness of his wrath. God had cast down their beauty from the heights of glory to the depths of agony. They had known the richness of the blessing and presence of God, but all that had been taken from them. God had thrown their blessings away from them. They, who had been the footstool of God's throne, were seen as unworthy (see 1 Chronicles 28:2). They were left wondering whether God had even remembered them.

In his anger the Lord had swallowed up the houses of Jacob his people (verse 2). They had been destroyed as the enemy came in and burned their capital city to the ground. The fortified cities of Judah were destroyed, and her kingdom and rulers were brought to dishonor. Verse 3 tells us that in his anger, the Lord cut off every horn in Israel. The horn symbolized power because an animal uses its horns for defense. The Lord had broken the power of Israel. Her strong and influential men were humbled. God withdrew his right hand of protection as the enemy approached, leaving Judah defenseless. The enemy invaded like a raging fire and consumed everything.

God had become an enemy to his children. He strung his bow and shot his arrow, killing all who were at one time pleasing in his eyes. In his wrath he poured out his anger on the Daughter of Zion, his own child. He swallowed up all her palaces and destroyed her strongholds. He gave her great cause to mourn.

In verses 6–11 tragedy is seen coming to all parts of life in Judah. Once a prosperous garden, Judah had been laid waste (verse 6). Her place of meeting with the Lord, the temple itself, was destroyed. The appointed feasts and Sabbaths were forgotten. There was no longer any cause for rejoicing in the land. The Lord rejected her kings and priests and the altar where the sacrifices were made for sin. God would no longer accept his people's sacrifices and praise. They had turned their backs on him for the last time. Now he turned from them.

The palaces of the land were handed over to the enemy. These enemies raised a shout of victory in the house of the Lord as on a feast day. There was certain boldness here in the hearts of the enemy. They went into the temple of the Lord and proclaimed victory for their evil cause. There was no fear in their hearts as they stepped into the Lord's house.

The Lord had determined to tear down the city walls of Jerusalem (verse 9). He would not withhold his hand from judgment. He would stretch out his measuring line to measure what would be destroyed.

Jerusalem's gates had sunk into the ground. Her bars were broken down and destroyed. Her king and her princes were sent into exile. The Mosaic law could no longer be practiced because the temple was destroyed. The Lord no longer sent visions to the prophets. The Lord ceased to speak to his people. They had refused to listen, so he refused to speak.

We see in this passage a real decline in spirituality as God became distant. The people no longer lived according to the laws of God, and the Lord no longer moved among them in power. The prophets no longer heard messages from the Lord. The sin of God's people had driven God from among them.

The elders of the land sat in silence on the ground (verse 10). They were humbled and had nothing to say. They sprinkled dust on their heads and wore sackcloth as a sign of mourning. The young women of Jerusalem bowed their heads in shame and grief.

As Jeremiah looked at the scene before him, his eyes filled up with tears. He was in torment as he thought of what had happened to his people. His heart was broken because his people were devastated. Jerusalem's children fainted in the streets from weakness. Children cried out to their mothers, asking for bread and wine, but there was none. The children died slowly in their mothers' arms.

Jeremiah looked at these scenes, and his heart was broken. "What can I say to you . . . that I may comfort you?" he asked Jerusalem. What can you say to a people who have lost everything? Jerusalem's wound was very deep. Who could heal that wound? Was it even possible for her wound to be healed?

In verse 14 Jeremiah reminded his people of one of the reasons for their fall. He told them that the visions of their prophets were false and worthless and did not expose their sin. Instead, their prophets had lied and kept the people from repentance. This provoked the sure judgment of God.

We see here the importance of prophecy. The role of the prophet was to warn God's people of their unrighteousness toward God and their injustice toward others. The true prophet was to reveal the heart of God in an attempt to bring his people back in line with the clear teaching of the Scripture. When God's people wandered from the holy path, they were dangerously exposed to their enemies.

I have often asked myself why I write these devotional commentaries. This passage encourages me to persevere. I am reminded here that the Word of God is essential if we are to be healthy and whole as believers in this world. The words of the prophets of old are essential if we are to see our sins exposed and fend off the enemy.

Because the prophets had failed to teach and warn God's people, they fell into rebellion against God and his word. The result was the judgment of God. The Lord brought an enemy against his people. The once-glorious city was humbled and put to shame. Her enemies swallowed her up and rejoiced at her fall (verse 16).

The Lord had often warned his people of the judgment to come, but they refused to listen. Because of this God overthrew them without pity and let their enemy gloat over them. He empowered the enemy against them (verse 17).

God's people cried out in their pain, and the Lord let them weep. Their tears flowed day and night, like rivers. They had no relief from their grief.

Jeremiah called on God's people to cry out to him throughout the night watches (verse 19). Jeremiah called them to lift up their hands to the Lord in their pain. They were to plead with him for the lives of their children, who were dying from hunger in the streets. Their rebellion against God not only affected them but their children as well. The children were perishing because of the sins of their parents. Jeremiah asked them to consider the impact that their rebellion was having on their children. The situation in Jerusalem was so desperate that some people resorted to eating their own children to survive (verse 20).

Notice in verse 20 that the prophets and priests were killed in the house of God. There was no respect for the house of the Lord or his servants. Both young and old were perishing in the streets by the sword. The Lord had slain them in his anger. He had turned from them because of their sin. In that day of judgment, the Lord summoned against them terrors on all sides (verse 22). No one escaped his wrath.

Notice in this chapter the decline of spirituality in the land. People had turned their backs on God and rejected the clear words of the true prophets. The people did what was right in their own eyes. Their false prophets did not warn them of the coming judgment on their sin, and they continued to live in deception. This resulted in the Lord withdrawing his presence from them, leaving them unprotected. Their sin caused them to wither away spiritually as a people. The Lord came and destroyed his own nation. The children were affected as well. The children starved in the arms of their mothers, and parents ate their own children to survive.

Jeremiah called his people to awaken to the reality of what

was happening in their land. He challenged them to lift up their hands to God in prayer for the condition of their nation. In verse 19 he called them to weep and cry out to the Lord for the lives of their children, who were perishing in the streets.

For Consideration:

- To what extent has the enemy come in and conquered God's people today?

- What kind of faith are we passing on to our children?

- To what extent does our disobedience affect others?

- What does this passage teach us about the role of the prophet or the preacher of God's Word in our day?

For Prayer:

- Take a moment to pray that God would enable you to pass on a real faith to your children and to those of the next generation.

- Do you see a lack of spiritual power in the church today? Ask the Lord to restore his power and presence to his church.

- Take a moment to pray for those who preach the Word of the Lord today. Ask that God would enable them to boldly speak his truth.

- Take a moment to pray for those who suffer in your community.

63

It Is Good to Wait Quietly

Read Lamentations 3:1–27

Here in this section of the book of Lamentations, the prophet Jeremiah spoke very personally about his experience of the discipline of the Lord. Jeremiah was not a bystander in all the things that had been happening in Jerusalem. He experienced all that God's people experienced in their capture, exile, and discipline. The pain and agony of God's judgment fell on him as well. Jeremiah described his experience of God's discipline in this section and how he dealt with it.

Jeremiah began by saying that he knew what it was like to suffer under the discipline of God's rod. He knew what it was like to be afflicted. There were times when the prophet felt like the Lord had driven him away and made him walk in the darkness of his judgment instead of the light of his blessing. It was a place of confusion and chaos for Jeremiah. In verse 3 Jeremiah tells us that he felt at times that the Lord's hand was being turned against him. Circumstance after circumstance in his life seemed to confirm that, for some reason, the hand of the Lord and his blessing were no longer on him as they had been.

Physically, the discipline of the Lord was taking its toll on the prophet (verse 4). His skin and his flesh were growing old, and his bones were broken. In other words, the stress of this discipline had affected him physically. He was growing old before his time. Jeremiah felt that God had besieged and surrounded him with bitterness and hardship (verse 5). He lived in darkness, like the dead. No matter what Jeremiah did, he could not seem to escape from this darkness. He felt imprisoned in his despair and found no relief through prayer. It was as if God did not want to hear from him (verse 8).

Jeremiah felt as if God was blocking him at every turn with immoveable stones (verse 9). He could not move to ease his pain. There was no longer any evidence of the blessing of God on the path he walked. God had made his paths crooked and difficult and filled with pain.

In verse 10 Jeremiah compared God to a hungry lion or bear lying in wait for him on the path. When Jeremiah passed by, God jumped out like a hungry bear, dragged him from the path, and tore him apart. God then left him alone in that ravaged condition.

God drew his bow and made the prophet the target for his arrows (verse 12). Jeremiah became the laughingstock of his people. They even made up mocking songs about him. The prophet was the target of the insults of the people he sought to help.

According to Jeremiah, God filled him with bitter food and drink (verse 15). All his experiences were harsh. Instead of bread, the Lord had given him stones to eat, and this had broken his teeth (verse 16). Jeremiah felt trampled into the dust.

"I have been deprived of peace," said Jeremiah (verse 17). He had forgotten what prosperity felt like. All his glory as a child of God was gone. He had hoped for great things from the Lord, but he was greatly disappointed. He found no more hope in the Lord his God. God had removed his blessing and his presence.

The affliction, the wandering in the dark, and the bitterness were his daily experiences (verse 19). Jeremiah could not escape these things. They seemed to absorb his thoughts. Very likely, he found it difficult to sleep at night. His heart and his soul were downcast within him. He was discouraged and depressed, and he could not shake it. These were very difficult days for the prophet.

Have you ever been in Jeremiah's situation? What do you

do when you find yourself discouraged? We see in the next few verses just what Jeremiah did and where he turned his focus.

In all of his pain and difficulty, Jeremiah was reminded that the Lord is a God of tremendous love and compassion (verse 22). It was only because of God's great love and compassion that Jeremiah was not consumed. He knew that the compassion of the Lord never failed but was renewed every day to his people. Like the manna God provided fresh each morning to the Israelites, so his mercies were fresh and new each day. If there was one thing that Jeremiah could count on, it was the faithfulness of God.

In the prophet's sorrow, the faithfulness of God was his comfort. He knew that he could rely on God no matter what came his way. He knew that God would always be faithful to his word and his people. Everything God did came out of that faithfulness. Never would he let his people down. He would always care for them and love them. While people often fail, God would never fail.

It is true that there were many times when Jeremiah was left in the dark, uncertain about what was happening, but God would never forget him. It would be easier for loving parents to forget their child than for God to forget his child. No matter how dark things got, Jeremiah staked his life on this faithfulness of God. He would wait for the Lord to reveal his purpose and come to rescue him.

I remember as a little child a time when I was waiting for my parents to pick me up at a meeting. They were late in coming, but I knew that no matter what happened, they would show up. The only way they would not show up was if they had forgotten that I existed, and that I knew was impossible. I knew that if I remained where I was, they would leave no stone unturned to find me. I was confident in this. Jeremiah, like a little child, had this same confidence. He knew that God would not forget him. All he could do was to wait in silence until the Lord arrived. God was his portion. He belonged to God, and God belonged to him. God would not abandon him. Jeremiah would wait for the Lord (verse 24).

Jeremiah was also reminded that the Lord is good to those who hope in him and seek him (verse 25). He would not abandon his people. He would come to them in love and compassion. The time was coming when Jeremiah knew that the door would open, and the Lord would come rushing through with arms wide open to greet him and enfold him to his breast. He would again experience the wonderful love and fellowship of God. Everything would be restored. All he could do for the moment, however, was to wait in confident hope and bear the yoke God had called him to bear.

Notice how Jeremiah tells us here that it is good for us to bear the yoke (verse 27). God does not put us through difficulties for nothing. There is a purpose for everything we go through. God is working out his purposes and plan in our lives. Jeremiah challenges us to bear the yoke and trust in the faithfulness of God. In doing this we will not be disappointed.

For Consideration:

• How important is it for us to understand the truth of God's faithfulness in our struggles?

• What does this passage teach us about suffering in our lives? Have you ever experienced how good it is to bear the yoke of God's discipline? Explain.

• What comfort do you take from this passage in your particular trial? What promise is there for you in this chapter?

For Prayer:

• Thank the Lord for his faithfulness.

• Ask the Lord to forgive you for the times you doubted his faithfulness and believed that somehow he had forgotten you.

• Ask him to remind you of his faithfulness in your present struggle. Ask him to give you grace to put your trust and hope in him.

• Take a moment to pray for a fellow believer who is facing a struggle right now. Ask God to give this person hope.

64

The Justice of God

Read Lamentations 3:28–66

Having described to us what he was feeling as he experienced the discipline of the Lord, Jeremiah then turned his attention to the character of God. It would be easy for us to assume that because of all his suffering, Jeremiah felt that God was unjust. He reminded his readers, however, that the Lord God was a God of tremendous justice. He could not be accused of sin in this discipline. Let's take a moment to examine what Jeremiah tells us about the justice of God in the suffering that was taking place in Judah.

Jeremiah began by challenging his readers to sit alone in silence. Notice the reason for sitting in silence: God had laid a burden or yoke on them (see verse 27). There was something very important for them to understand here. The Lord God is a sovereign God who had caused these things to happen to them. He had a purpose in all that he did. To fight against what God was doing in this judgment was to fight against God himself. Jeremiah knew that God would work out his purpose through all the trials he went through. He challenged the people of Judah to not run from what the Lord was doing in their lives but rather to wait on him and let him accomplish his perfect will.

It is never easy to accept the discipline of the Lord. Jeremiah challenged his people to bury their faces in the dust and place their hope in the Lord (verse 29). He challenged them to offer their cheeks to the one who wanted to strike them. God's people were to recognize and bear their disgrace with humility and patience.

Some see here in this picture of offering the cheek to the one who would slap it, a reference to what the Lord Jesus would do for us. It is uncertain if this is the intent here, but the picture is still important. The Lord Jesus left us this example to follow. He allowed his cheek to be slapped. He willingly surrendered to the attack of the enemy for us. He challenged us to turn the other cheek when we are insulted or beaten (Matthew 5:39; 26:67).

The only way we can bear humiliation with patience is to believe that the Lord is the one who is in control of all the events and circumstances of life. As a sovereign God, he will work out his purposes for our good and his glory. No matter what people may do to us, we know that God is greater and able to turn even the worst situation into something good.

Our suffering may be for a time, but there is one thing certain. The Lord is faithful and will not cast off his children forever. He may, for a moment, allow us to pass through tremendous grief; but in his time, he will be compassionate toward us. He will renew his expression of unfailing love toward us. He will not abandon us forever. The day was coming when the Lord would return to his people. We need to be confident in this as well. We live in hope and confidence in a loving God.

In verse 33 Jeremiah reminded the people that the Lord does not willingly bring affliction or grief to his children. There are times when he allows things to happen to us, but he does not take delight in allowing us to suffer. It grieves his heart to see us in our affliction. Jeremiah reminded his people in verses 34–36 that the Lord saw when they were mistreated. He knew when their rights were denied and when they were deprived of justice. These things did not escape his notice.

Nothing can happen without the Lord's decree (verse 37). It is not just the good things that we need to accept from the Lord but also the bad. Jeremiah reminded his people in verse 38 that both calamities and good things come from the Lord. There are times when the Lord blesses, and there are times when he disciplines. Both are for our good. We are more than willing to accept the blessings but not so willing to accept the discipline. Jeremiah calls us to accept both. When the Lord chooses to discipline us for our sin, what right do we have to complain? Is he not doing what is right? All the terrible things that had happened in Jerusalem were because of Judah's sin and evil. God's people were being corrected and disciplined because of their evil ways. God was just in what he was doing. God's people had no right to complain. Like a guilty child, they could only accept their discipline and learn their lesson. In all this, God was just.

Jeremiah called his people to examine their ways (verses 40–42). The Lord was disciplining them for a purpose. Through this discipline, he was calling them to return to him. Jeremiah petitioned his people to lift up their hands in prayer, confess their sin and rebellion, and beg him to forgive them.

In order to bring them back to himself, the Lord had to exercise a very stern discipline. He had to cover them with his anger (verse 43). He chased after them and slew them without pity. Like a parent sending a child to a room, God separated himself from his people. He covered himself with a cloud and hid from them. For a period of time, he would not listen to their prayers. He allowed them to fall and become the scum of the earth (verse 45). Their enemies spoke out against them boldly. They suffered terror, pitfalls, ruin, and destruction. These things were not easy, but discipline was never intended to be easy. God's people were being destroyed. His heart grieved for them (see Isaiah 63:9).

Until the time that the Lord came to bring relief from discipline, tears flowed unceasingly from the eyes of Jeremiah (verse 49). He continued to plead with God and to wait on him. While his heart was deeply grieved for what has happening around him, Jeremiah continued to wait on the Lord in tears. He had confidence that the Lord would come to them in his time. He modeled for the people of Judah what they should do during their time of punishment.

Jeremiah's enemies hunted him without cause as those who hunted birds for sport (verse 52). Jeremiah's enemies threw stones at him, seeking to get him to fall into a pit. They wanted to end his life. There were times when they came very close to killing him, and he thought he was going to die.

In those times, however, Jeremiah called out to the Lord his God. Right there in that pit, he lifted up his voice to God (verse 55). God heard him and rescued him. Could it be that Jeremiah was recalling the time when he was thrown into the cistern? At that time the Lord did come to rescue him. He was pulled out of that cistern and his life spared. Jeremiah recalled how the Lord had answered him in the past. He had every confidence that the Lord would answer him in the future.

In Jeremiah's time of trouble, the Lord came to his rescue. He did not close his ears to Jeremiah's request. The Lord took up Jeremiah's cause. He told him not to fear (verse 57). The Lord did see the wrong that had been done to him and his people and upheld their cause.

Jeremiah took great comfort in what the Lord had done for him in the past. It was true that Jeremiah did not see the answer to his current problem. For the moment the Lord's face was hidden, and Jeremiah's prayers did not seem to be answered. Jeremiah knew, however, that his requests were not ignored. God's timing was not the same as his. When the time was right, God would move and come to his aid again. Until that time he could only trust that God was in control and that he would do what was right. It is not always easy to wait on the Lord. We can only wait on him if we trust him. Jeremiah saw no reason to doubt the purposes and plan of God.

Jeremiah knew that God heard the insults of his enemies. He knew that God knew all about their plots against him (verse 61). What they whispered in secret God heard in the open. God had listened to their mocking songs about his child Jeremiah. Jeremiah did not need to explain to God what was happening. God already knew.

How many times do our prayers reflect a lack of understanding of God and his character? How often have we sought to explain to God our circumstances, as if he did not know? How often have we sought to convince God that he ought to help us, as if we felt that he needed to be convinced? What do your prayers reflect about what you think of God? Is he a God who needs to be convinced to help us? The God Jeremiah knew was already aware of his child's pain and did not need to be convinced to help him. Would you as a loving parent need a lot of convincing to help your child in a difficult situation? Neither does God.

Confident that the Lord knew what was happening to him, Jeremiah called on the Lord to exercise his justice on the earth. He asked God to pay back his enemies for their evil (verse 64). He petitioned God to put a veil over their hearts so that their hearts would be plunged into darkness. He asked that the curse they inflicted on others be brought back to them. He asked God to pursue his enemies and destroy them. He placed his full confidence in the Lord God and waited for him to act.

For Consideration:

- What does this chapter teach us about God's control over the trials and suffering in our lives?

- Why is it so hard to wait on the Lord in our struggles?

- What do your prayers reveal about what you think of God?

- What has the Lord accomplished in you through struggles and trials in life?

For Prayer:

- Thank the Lord that he is in control of the events of your life.

- What struggle are you going through today? Take a moment to thank the Lord that he knows all about it.

- Ask the Lord to give you patience to wait on him in your time of trial. Thank him that in time he will come to your aid.

65

Your Punishment Will End

Read Lamentations 4

Jerusalem was a city that had been richly blessed by God. Its temple, once full of gold and precious gems, had been looted and broken to pieces. Jeremiah compared the precious people of God to the demolished temple. The city, the temple, and the inhabitants of Jerusalem were smashed and scattered on the streets like bits of worthless pottery.

In verse 3 Jeremiah compared his people to wild animals. Even jackals nursed and cared for their young, but God's people were not like this. Instead, like the ostrich, they abandoned their young. Job spoke about the ostrich in Job 39:14–17: "She lays her eggs on the ground and lets them warm in the sand, unmindful that a foot may crush them, that some wild animal may trample them. She treats her young harshly, as if they were not hers; she cares not that her labor was in vain, for God did not endow her with wisdom or give her a share of good sense."

In what way did God's people abandon their young? Part of the answer can be found in what God's people were going through at that time. The enemy had come in and stripped them of everything they had. The land faced a severe famine, and children had nothing to eat. We saw in chapter 2 that the young ones were perishing in their mothers' arms because there was no food. It should be remembered that this was the result of the sins of the parents who had turned their backs on the Lord their God and brought his judgment. They had abandoned their children partly because there was nothing to feed them but also because they had turned their back on God and left them with no spiritual heritage to follow. The tongues of the infants stuck to the roofs of their mouths because of thirst. The parents had nothing to offer them to drink. Children sat begging for bread, but no one gave them any. They were dying of hunger and thirst because their parents were unable to provide for their basic needs.

This had not always been the case. There was a time in the lives of these people when they had eaten the delicacies of the land (verse 5). They had rejoiced in the wonderful blessing of God and had eaten until they were satisfied. They had once been dressed in the purple of royalty, but now they lay in ash heaps.

Could this be said of many believers today? There are those who once lived close to the Lord and knew what it was like to feast on the riches of his Word and his Spirit. But they wandered from him and, like the people described here, now lie in the spiritual ash heap.

God did not hesitate to punish his people for their sin. Their punishment was compared to the punishment of Sodom and Gomorrah that God overthrew in the days of Abraham (verse 6). In an instant their great city Jerusalem was destroyed because of its rebellion against God. Judah's princes, who were brighter than snow and whiter than milk, with healthy bodies whose appearance were red like rubies and sapphires, had become blacker than soot in starvation (verse 8). They were no longer recognized in the city. Their skin was shriveled on their bones. Their skin was as dry as a stick. The comparison here is striking. They once had so much, but now they had so little. Everything was lost. They withered away, and their children suffered with them.

Those who were killed by the sword were far better off than those who lived to face the famine. Those who remained suffered tremendously with hunger. They wasted away from lack of food. The famine was so severe in the land that even compassionate women cooked and ate their very own children to survive (verse 10).

The Lord did not hold back his anger. Verse 11 tells us that he had kindled a fire against Zion and consumed her foundations. Nothing was left when the fierce anger of the Lord was unleashed on the land.

The kings of the earth could not believe that enemies could ever enter the city of Jerusalem and conquer it (verse 12). Such was the reputation of the people of God, who had once been a strong and undefeated people. They were once victorious over all their enemies when the Lord God was with them. He had blessed them with riches and power. Their enemies respected them and their God (see Joshua 2:8–11).

Judah was judged by God because of the sin of her prophets and priests who had shed the blood of the righteous. Justice had been removed from the land. The priests of Jeremiah's day did not listen to the cause of the innocent. They refused to care for the helpless and favored those who ignored the word of God. In the case of Jeremiah, they had sought to kill him. They did not want to hear the word he spoke to them. They cast him in prison for challenging them in their evil ways.

Notice the result of this evil in the land. The people groped through the streets like the blind (verse 14). They were defiled with the blood of the righteous. They were considered as unclean as lepers, and no one would help them as they fled before the enemy. They were detested. The Lord had scattered his people, and he no longer watched over them. The priests and the elders were treated like common people. The Lord did not favor them because of their position (verse 16). The people sought for help, but there was none. Their eyes grew weary watching for allies. But not a nation in the world could come to their aid. They were helpless under the discipline of the Lord.

God's people were hunted every step of the way as they tried to hide (verse 18). They could no longer walk safely in the streets. Their days were ending. Those who pursued them were as swift as eagles. They chased them over the mountains and lay in wait for them in the deserts. There was nowhere they could flee for safety.

The Lord's anointed were caught in a trap (verse 20). They thought that they would be safe under the shadow of the Lord even though they were surrounded by foreign nations. That confidence was in vain. It is not that they could not trust the Lord—the Lord was completely worthy of their trust and confidence. The problem was that they had turned their backs on God and still expected him to come to their aid.

The day was coming when the enemies of Israel would also know the reality of God's judgment (verse 21). The land of Edom, for example, would drink of the cup of the Lord's judgment. She would be stripped naked. She had mocked and rejoiced at the defeat of the Lord's people, but her time was coming.

When the children of Israel were in exile, they cried out to the Lord in agony and expressed their grief over how Edom had treated them. Listen to their cry in Psalm 137:7: "Remember, O LORD, what the Edomites did on the day Jerusalem fell. 'Tear it down,' they cried, 'tear it down to its foundations!'"

Jeremiah reminded Judah that the day was coming when her punishment would end (verse 22). God would not prolong her exile. He would come to her aid and expose the evil that had been done to her. God had not forgotten his people. They were to take comfort in the fact that he was going to return to them.

We see in this section how powerless the people of God had become. Their sins had destroyed them and left them helpless before their enemies. Children suffered because of the sins of the parents. They lost everything in their rebellion and sinfulness. They paid a very high price for their rebellion. But God would not abandon them forever. He would return to them when they had learned the lessons he needed them to learn. His discipline was harsh, but it was for a purpose.

For Consideration:

• Notice how Jeremiah described here the defeat of the people of God and the astonishment of the nations. Do we experience the same astonishment when we see the church living in powerlessness?

- Consider the effects of sin in the lives of God's people. What does this section teach us about the devastating consequences of sin?

- What comfort do you take from the fact that the Lord's discipline lasts only for a certain period of time?

For Prayer:

- Have you been experiencing the discipline of the Lord? Ask the Lord to teach you what you need to learn in this discipline.

- Thank the Lord that he has never forgotten you in your trial.

- Ask the Lord to reveal to you anything that blocks his power and victory in your life and the life of your church.

66

Remember Us

Read Lamentations 5

I n this final chapter, the prophet Jeremiah called on the Lord to remember his people in their time of suffering and trial.

He began in verse 1 by asking the Lord to remember what had happened to them as a people. He reminded the Lord of the shame and disgrace they had endured. Their inheritance had been stripped from them and handed over to foreigners. They had become orphans and widows because of the oppression of the enemy.

Their land was once a prosperous land. Now they had to buy their water from their enemy (verse 4). They cut wood for their fire at a price. It is unclear how this actually worked itself out. Could it be that they were taxed for everything they used? We know that the enemy had imposed a heavy tax on the people who remained in Judah. The simple blessings they had taken for granted now cost them dearly.

As a people, they were growing weary and tired of running from their enemies (verse 5). They had been oppressed. Their enemies were always nipping at their heels, making their lives miserable. In order to survive, they had to submit to Egypt and

Assyria. They could no longer support themselves. They had to depend on others.

These things had happened to them because of the sins of their ancestors (verse 7). Their ancestors had turned their backs on God, and they were now bearing the punishment. While they were not innocent in this matter, they were suffering because of the sins of their ancestors. Our sins never affect us alone but also touch many people in our circle of influence. No one's sin is isolated. How important it is for us to deal with the sins the Lord reveals to us.

Notice the result of sin in the land (verse 8). Tyrants ruled over them. They had to risk their lives to get enough food to eat. The sword of the enemy was all around them. They were starving and full of fever. Their women and the virgins of the land had been ravished by the enemies. Their princes had been hung by their hands, and their elders were shown no respect. Their young men were forced to toil at heavy millstones, and their young boys staggered under the load of wood they were forced to carry.

The city was left barren and abandoned (verse 15). The elders had been taken from the land. The music stopped as joy was completely stripped from them. Their dancing was turned to mourning.

They were a royal people, but the crown had fallen from their head. All this had happened because they had sinned against the Lord their God. Now their hearts grew faint with grief and sorrow. Their eyes were dim. The land of God's people was desolate. Jackals prowled over the land that had once been busy and prosperous.

Despite all these terrible things, Jeremiah reminded his people in verse 19 that the Lord reigned forever, and his throne endured from generation to generation. Things were falling apart in the land, but Jeremiah was not shaken in his faith in a sovereign God. This was his hope.

If God were not in control of life, we would be without hope. No matter what happens in life, we have a God who is in charge. He will work out the details of our life for good. We can be confident in this.

While Jeremiah was confident in the fact that God was in control of all things, he did not understand his purpose. He wondered why the Lord had left them for so long in their suffering and pain. We will certainly not understand the ways of God. There are times when he will stretch us in our faith and patience. There will be times in our lives where we wonder if we can even endure the burden he causes us to bear. There have been different times in my life when I have been stretched by the Lord in such a way. I would have been defeated had I not believed that the Lord was a sovereign God who was in control of all the events of life.

God's ways are often beyond our ability to understand. This is where Jeremiah was at this point. He did not understand what God was doing. He felt the weight of the trial. He wondered why the Lord was leaving him for so long under the burden of this weight. In all of it, however, he trusted that the Lord was still in control and in his time would return to him.

In verse 21 Jeremiah asked the Lord to restore his people to himself. He asked him to renew them as he had done in the past. Jeremiah asked the Lord: "Restore us to yourself . . . unless you have utterly rejected us and are angry with us beyond measure."

We need to understand here that the prophet did not actually believe that the Lord had rejected them forever. He was asking the Lord, who promised never to abandon them, to be faithful to his promise. He was, in reality, saying: Lord, unless you have chosen to break your promise and reject us forever, I am asking you to prove that you are a God of truth and restore us as you have promised. He called God to be faithful to his character and his word.

In this final chapter, Jeremiah thrust himself on God. He did not understand his ways. The burden he felt was very heavy. In all of this, however, Jeremiah chose to take God at his word and trust in his sovereign care. He called God to remember him and his people.

There are times when this is all we can do. There are times when all we can do is wait on the Lord and trust his working.

For Consideration:

- Have you ever found yourself in the situation that Jeremiah was in here in this chapter, when you simply did not understand what God was doing and felt helpless under his discipline? What advice does Jeremiah have to give us here?

- How did Jeremiah deal with the pain he was experiencing in this chapter? What comfort did he have?

- Is there any reason to doubt that the Lord will be faithful to his word?

For Prayer:

- Thank the Lord that while we do not always understand what he is doing, we can trust that he always does what is right.

- Ask the Lord to give you patience to wait on him in your moment of trial.